THE BIG BROTHER BOOK OF LISTS

THE BIG BROTHER BOOK OF LISTS

Robert Ellis Smith, Deborah Caulfield,
David Crook and Michael Gershman

Cartoons by Bill Mauldin and Paul Conrad

PRICE/STERN/SLOAN
Publishers, Inc., Los Angeles
1984

Cartoons by Paul Conrad © 1973, 1975, 1976, 1980, 1981, 1983, Los Angeles Times, Reprinted with permission.

Cartoons by Bill Mauldin © 1949, 1950, 1961, 1966. Used by permission of Bill Mauldin and Will-jo Associates, Inc.

Copyright© 1984 by Michael Gershman
Published by Price/Stern/Sloan Publishers, Inc.
410 North La Cienega Boulevard, Los Angeles, California 90048

ISBN: 0-8431-0849-5

CONTENTS

PREFACE

"To understand the breakdown of the American constitutional system and the emergence of a '1984' society, we must recognize the radical impact of the Cold War. [It] encouraged a strong elite-dominated government... the gradual acceptance of the need for secrecy and uncritical deference to national security claims. Internal security bureaucrats became increasingly insulated from external accountability... By the 1970's, the intelligence bureaucrats—J. Edgar Hoover of the FBI, Henry Kissinger of the NSC, or Richard Helms of the CIA—had become independent powers, effectively establishing national policy, even at times independent of the occupant of the oval office."

ATHAN THEOHARIS, *Spying on Americans*

ACKNOWLEDGEMENTS

This book could not have existed without the pioneering work of a number of dedicated investigative reporters who have made the invisible government of the United States more visible to the citizens it is supposed to serve.

Chief among these is David Wise, whose work alone and with Thomas B. Ross (see bibliography), was central to this book. John D. Marks's work alone and with Victor Marchetti deserves similar acknowledgement as do the herculean efforts of Thomas Powers, Jim Hougan, Frank Donner, Athan Theoharis, David Garrow, Jules Archer and James Bamford. No citation such as this can adequately repay these men for braving psychological, financial and physical pressures to tell American citizens what their government was too afraid, too appalled or too ashamed to tell them. The authors hope this book can serve as a brief introduction, and that interested readers will go on to explore their works in full.

Similarly, Victor Navasky's investigation of the Red Scare in Hollywood, David Caute's careful examination of McCarthyism, Jay Robert Nash's debunking of FBI myth and William Manchester's thoughtful history of America since the New Deal deserve special mention.

Great thanks must be paid to John Seeley, who joined this project late, but not too late to make a significant, and much appreciated, contribution. His prodigious input gave the sections on media, mind control and McCarthyism a clarity and focus previously lacking.

We would also be remiss in not mentioning the help provided by the Community Access Library Line in Montebello, California. Individuals who contributed to or reviewed the manuscript include Kathy Blundo, Dr. Carl Jensen, Suzy Kalter, Dr. William Lutz, Bill McCall, Kathleen McCarthy, Richard Mahler, Joyce Pinney, Thea Rahmani, Marvin Schlossman and B. Lynne Zika.

Finally, the authors owe an enormous debt of gratitude to Lawrence Dietz, our editor. In helping us define what was and what wasn't Big Brotherish, he transformed an inchoate mass of material into a manuscript, and that manuscript into a book.

INTRODUCTION

While researching this book, we were asked repeatedly by friends and acquaintances, "How close *are* we to 1984 as it was envisioned by George Orwell?" The lists, notes, quotes, and anecdotes in this book make it frighteningly clear that over the past 36 years (*1984* was written in 1948) we have come perilously close to the world that Orwell described.

To bring this material into focus, to show that what we included were not isolated oddities of history, we picked a random date and bought a stack of American newspapers to see how many appropriate news items we could find to illustrate "Big Brotherism." The date we picked was June 22, 1983 (only 192 days from the beginning of calendar 1984).

On that day, the Detroit *Free Press* reported, "CIA Director William Casey is the fourth Reagan administration official [to be sent a letter from Rep. Donald Albosta (D-Mich.), asking] how the 1980 Reagan campaign obtained White House briefing materials prepared for then-President Carter."

Another item in the same paper noted, "Now we have the Federal Emergency Management Agency, better known as FEMA, a bureaucracy with a mandate... to convince the American public that nuclear war, although nasty and far from fun, is survivable... when the bomb is screeching downward and we are running for our lives, FEMA wants us to take a few minutes to fill out change-of-address forms before we evacuate."

The paper also quoted former CIA Director William Colby as saying his current anti-nuclear activities were "a logical extension of what I was doing in the intelligence business. At the CIA it became obvious to me that the real function of intelligence is not to win battles but to help with the peace, to avoid the kind of destabilizing surprises that can occur."

Don Shoemaker noted in the Miami *Herald* that President Reagan's Executive Order 12356 required "perhaps as many as 100,000 government employees who have access to use classified information to sign a 'nondisclosure' agreement as a condition to access to this material. As a further condition of employment, they must agree to submit to a lie-detector test if requested."

"Another part of the order requires everyone with access to "Sensitive Compartment Information" to sign a nondisclosure agreement that provides for prepublication review... Other recent orders allow the CIA and the FBI to shadow political groups and other American citizens who may not even be suspected of breaking any law."

The San Francisco *Chronicle* carried a William Raspberry column about the Justice Department's languid investigations of civil rights violations. "Jesse Jackson persuaded Brad Reynolds (Assistant Attorney General for Civil Rights) to come to Mississippi and hear for himself what was going on." Reynolds spent two days listening to violations that Jackson had complained about in May, 1981. Reynolds said he was "shocked" to hear about "discriminatory redistricting, access to the circuit clerk being denied and intimidation at the ballot box."

The New York *Times* carried an AP story out of Washington that began, "The Central Intelligency Agency recommended today that its files on intelligence agents be placed completely off limits to people using the Freedom of Information Act in efforts to declassify Government secrets."

The Los Angeles *Times* reported that, "A Los Angeles-based group charged that Central Americans being held at the federal detention camp for illegal aliens in El Centro are being maltreated. The group, including seven nuns and an attorney, released a report which claimed that 'scores of detained refugees' have recounted beatings, denial of proper medical care and arbitrary use of isolation cells."

In reviewing a documentary about the McCarthy era, *Times* TV critic Howard Rosenberg mentioned "rumblings that TV's *Lou Grant* was cancelled last season less for its ratings than for Ed Asner's outspoken opposition to government policy in El Salvador." Rosenberg asked Howard Suber, a UCLA professor in the film department if blacklisting could again be as widespread in the entertainment business. Suber's reply: "The only safe thing you can say about blacklists is that we've not seen the last of them."

Of course, not everything that marks intrusion into our lives makes the daily paper. Every working day (June 22 being no exception) the following occurs:

Equifax, Inc. prepares 85,000 reports on individuals' lifestyles for corporate clients. These are based on interviews with neighbors and assumptions made from city directories.

America's direct mail industry enters households by mailing out 110,000,000 pieces of junk mail.

At least 4,100 telephone conversations are being overheard by federal and state law enforcement wiretaps, and perhaps ten times as many private wiretaps are also in place.

TRW Credit Data processes 86,000,000 credit reports. Some 200 inquiries came from consumers wanting to check their reports, at least a third of whom will complain about the information they discover.

The FBI has in its National Crime Information Center databank 200,000 wanted persons, 25,000 missing persons and 2,151,150 criminal history records of so-called "multi-state offenders."

In seeking out ways in which our lives resemble Orwell's vision, we tend to be captivated by the technological methods government and business use to intrude on us. We note television cameras watching us in banks, in shopping centers, along freeways—even in some corporate restrooms—and we nod knowingly that "Orwell was right. Big Brother *is* watching Us."

While this is very true, another of Orwell's warnings is even more to the point. While *1984*'s protagonist, Winston Smith, is being tortured, his inquisitor, O'Brien, orders him to repeat an important Party slogan: "Who controls the past controls the future; who controls the present controls the past."

The U.S.S.R. and Nazi Germany (and, sporadically, the People's Republic of China), repeatedly rewrote the past for their own purposes. Ironically, on the day this introduction was being written, the U.S.S.R. was rewriting the present and informing the world that the United States government was responsible for its having shot down a commercial airliner and having killed 269 innocent people.

Our government hasn't rewritten the past as of this writing, but this book does focus on the ways in which America has forgotten the guarantees of personal and intellectual freedom to which its citizens are entitled. This book was written precisely because this country's promise has always been to be a refuge against newspeak, against doublethink, against all the threats to individual liberty which the phrase "Big Brother" implies.

Can the past be rewritten here? Big Brother doesn't have that answer; you do.

ROBERT ELLIS SMITH   DAVID CROOK
DEBORAH CAULFIELD   MICHAEL GERSHMAN

November, 1983 Los Angeles, California

ADMINISTRATION TO EASE CURBS ON CIA. — NEWS ITEM.

CHAPTER 1

THE CENTRAL INTELLIGENCE AGENCY: NABOBS OF NATIONAL SECURITY

"Constitutional scrutiny of Intelligence Services is largely an illusory concept. If they're good, they fool the outsiders — and if they're bad they fool themselves."

—John Le Carre, introduction to *The Philby Conspiracy*, as quoted in *Portrait of a Cold Warrior*

YOUR TAX DOLLARS AT WORK

Among other covert and overt activities, the Central Intelligence Agency has:

- Tried to obstruct the FBI investigation of the Watergate break-in
- Made a hard-core porn movie, *Happy Days*, starring an actor who looked like President Sukarno of Indonesia for "blackmail purposes." (Howard Hughes aide Robert Maheu made his bid for Hollywood stardom by serving as casting director make-up man, cameraman and director)
- Provided women for King Hussein of Jordan and paid them with federal funds
- Opened, read and re-sealed first class mail for twenty years
- Provided the White House "Plumbers" with spy paraphernalia (for break-ins)
- Spied on American citizens in the United States and compiled a computerized list of 300,000 people and organizations
- Trained local police forces in lock picking, safe-cracking burglary, covert photography, surveillance and bugging

A BAKER'S DOZEN: 13 DIRECTORS OF THE
CENTRAL INTELLIGENCE AGENCY (CIA)

1. Rear Adm. Sidney W. Souers (1/23/46-6/10/46) Two days after being named director of CIA's forerunner, the Central Intelligence Group (CIG), Souers attended a party in his honor hosted by President Truman. Truman handed out black hats, cloaks and mock wooden daggers as party favors.
2. Lt. Gen. Hoyt Vandenberg (6/10/46-5/1/47) Vandenberg expanded the Agency's intelligence operations and tripled its personnel. His greatest feat was transferring the 1,000-person Strategic Services Unit of the War Department to the CIG and renaming it the Office of Special Operations (OSO.)
3. Rear Adm. Roscoe Hillenkoetter (5/1/47-10/7/50) He oversaw the transition from the CIG to the Central Intelligence Agency upon passage of the National Security Act in July, 1947. Hillenkoetter started CIA covert operations against foreign governments when he ordered the OSO to try to prevent a Communist victory in the 1948 Italian elections.
4. Gen. Walter Bedell Smith (10/7/50-2/9/53) He was Ike's chief of staff during WW II and ran the agency at the height of the Red Scare. He once said, ''I believe there are Communists in my own organization.''
5. Allen Welsh Dulles (2/26/53-11/29/61.) The most convivial Director of Central Intelligence, he did not shrink from ordering the assassination of foreign leaders like Patrice Lumumba of the Congo. Soviet pamphleteer Ilya Ehrenburg said in *Pravda*, ''If the spy, Allen Dulles, should arrive in Heaven through somebody's absent-mindedness, he would begin to blow up the clouds, mine the stars and slaughter the angels.''
6. John A. McCone (11/29/61-4/28/65) After leaving the Agency, McCone became a board member of International Telephone and Telegraph (ITT) and was heavily involved with CIA machinations in Chile in 1970.
7. Vice Adm. William F. Raborn Jr. (4/28/65-6/30/66) His was probably the unhappiest appointment of a CIA Director. Within the Company, it was said that, ''Allen Dulles ran a happy ship, John McCone a taut ship and Raborn's running a sinking ship.''

8. Richard Helms (6/30/66-2/2/73) He is regarded as a tight-lipped professional and bureaucrat *par excellence;* in 1965, he received the National Civil Service League's award for ''significant contributions to excellence in government.'' He pleaded ''nolo contendere'' to charges of perjury regarding CIA involvement in Chile and received a suspended sentence.

9. James Schlesinger (2/2/73-7/2/73) He was resented by CIA conservatives for purging them and promoting the liberals. When his portrait was hung at CIA headquarters, a special closed-circuit TV camera was secretly trained on it and monitored by a guard, lest some disgruntled employee deface it.

10. William Colby (9/4/73-1/30/76) The man who didn't keep the secrets. Many Agency people felt he was too forthcoming with the Rockefeller Commission, the group appointed by President Ford to investigate CIA activities in the U.S. and abroad.

11. George Bush (1/30/76-1/20/77) The current Vice President and the least controversial Director in CIA history. He did restore internal morale, which was important after the Rockefeller hearings.

12. Adm. Stansfield Turner (3/9/77-1/20/81) He is blamed for the intelligence failure that led to the taking of the hostages in Iran, one of the most blatant miscues in Agency history; however, President Carter had had ample warnings of the consequences of admitting the Shah of Iran but yielded to the pressures put upon him by Henry Kissinger and David Rockefeller.

13. William J. Casey (1/28/81-   ) He has led the agency through Reagan's machinations in Central America. The former Securities Exchange Commission (SEC) chairman was under fire in mid-1983 for not putting his investments in blind trusts while serving as Agency Director as well as his involvement in the ''Debategate'' scandal.

Regardless of the outcome of these controversies, they won't be chiseling Casey's name in stone at Langley (CIA headquarters in Virginia). It is a sad but inevitable fact of secret life that almost every Agency Director has lost the confidence of his President and has been fired or replaced—Hillenkoetter by Truman, Smith by Eisenhower, Dulles by Kennedy, McCone and Raborn by Johnson, Helms by Nixon, Colby by Ford, Bush by Carter, and Turner by Reagan.

HOW SENIOR OFFICIALS RATED 5 CIA DIRECTORS

A clue as to how CIA officials viewed their bosses is provided by David Atlee Phillips, a retired former high-ranking CIA official, in his book, *The Night Watch*. Phillips, who set up and heads the Organization of Retired Intelligence Agents, asked 57 high-ranking colleagues the following questions with rankings as indicated.

Judging from the results, the old CIA hands wanted to be with gentleman spy Allen Dulles in convivial circumstances; the more hard-nosed Helms was their choice when the crunch came:

Q: ''If I were to be shipwrecked on a desert island, a pleasant one with abundant food, a good climate, a supply of scotch and every hope a ship would pass by, I would choose to be with...''

1. Allen Dulles
2. Richard Helms
3. John McCone
4. William E. Colby
5. Admiral ''Red'' Raborn

Q: ''If I were to be shipwrecked on a terrible desert island, with little food and no amenities, with scant hope for survival and I wanted to escape badly, I would choose to be with...''

1. Richard Helms
2. William E. Colby
3. Allen Dulles
4. John McCone
5. Admiral ''Red'' Raborn

ALLEN DULLES' 11 CRITERIA FOR A GOOD INTELLIGENCE OFFICER

In *The Craft of Intelligence*, Dulles lists 11 ideal characteristics of the would-be intelligence officer:

1. Be perceptive about people
2. Be able to work well with others under difficult conditions
3. Learn to discern between fact and fiction
4. Be able to distinguish between essentials and non-essentials
5. Possess inquisitiveness
6. Have a large amount of ingenuity
7. Pay appropriate attention to detail

8. Be able to express ideas clearly, briefly and, very important, interestingly
9. Don't be overambitious for personal reward in the form of fame or fortune
10. Have an understanding for other points of view
11. Learn when to keep your mouth shut

***

12 CELEBRATED OSS ALUMNI (AND ONE ALUMNA)

The Office of Strategic Services (OSS) was the U.S. intelligence arm from June 13, 1942 to Sept. 20, 1945. It was the forerunner of the CIA, and its intrepid members are given major credit for helping to win World War II. The OSS obtained Nazi and Japanese codes, set up dozens of local resistance groups and secretly air dropped millions of tons of weaponry and communications equipment.

Since its personnel was drawn overwhelmingly from the ranks of the Eastern Establishment, many people have suggested that the letters "O.S.S." stood for "Oh So Social."

1. Stewart Alsop—political columnist
2. James Angleton—later head of CIA counterintelligence and the basis for fictional characters in *The Rope Dancer* by former CIA agent Victor Marchetti and *Orchids For Mother* by Aaron Latham
3. Tom Braden—political columnist and talk show host
4. Michael Burke—future president of Madison Square Garden
5. Julia Child—cooking expert
6. William Colby—future CIA director
7. Allen Dulles—future CIA director
8. Arthur Goldberg—Supreme Court justice
9. Richard Helms—future CIA director
10. Arthur Schlesinger—prize-winning historian
11. Walt Whitman Rostow—President Johnson's national security adviser
12. Herbert Marcuse—political theorist
13. David Bruce—former U.S. ambassador to Great Britain

THE HIGHEST OF THE HIGH

Whether it was called the 10/2 Panel (later 10/5 Panel) in 1948, the 5412/Special Group in 1954, the 303 Committee (after a room number in the Executive Office Building) in 1964 or the 40 Committee—from the 1970 NSC document defining its membership and responsibilities—there has always been a "highest of the high," a National Security Council subcommittee chosen by the President to make final decisions on intelligence activities.

In 1974, its members were the President's assistant for national security, the Deputy Secretary of Defense, the Under Secretary of State for Political Affairs, the Director of the Central Intelligence Agency and the Chairman of the Joint Chiefs of Staff. In February, 1976, it became the Operations Advisory Group.

One official familiar with its workings said, "They were like a bunch of schoolboys. They would listen and their eyes would bug out. I always used to say that I could get five million dollars out of the 40 Committee for a covert operation faster than I could get money for a typewriter out of the ordinary bureaucracy."

ALL THIS COSTS MONEY, YOU KNOW: 1974 SIZE AND COST (APPROXIMATE) OF U.S. INTELLIGENCE COMMUNITY

Organization	Personnel	Budget (in millions)
Central Intelligence Agency	16,500	$750
National Security Agency*..........	24,000	1,200
Defense Intelligence Agency*.......	5,000	200
Army Intelligence*.................	35,000	700
Naval Intelligence*................	15,000	600
Air Force Intelligence*.............	56,000	2,700
State Department (Bureau of Intelligence and Research)	350	8
Federal Bureau of Investigation (Internal Security Division)	800	40
Atomic Energy Commission (Division of Intelligence)	300	20
Treasury Department	300	10
TOTALS	153,250	$6,228,000,000

*Department of Defense agency

Source: *The CIA and the Cult of Intelligence*

BIG BROTHER'S BLATANT BUNGLES

The CIA has proved adept at covert operations and toppling left-leaning foreign governments; however, its record at providing intelligence has left much to be desired, to wit:

1. Knowing that China had amassed 200,000 troops in Manchuria in 1951, the Company failed to predict the Chinese intervention in Korea.
2. The day before the outbreak of the 1973 Arab-Israeli war, Secretary of State Henry Kissinger received a CIA memo assuring that war in the Middle East was "unlikely."
3. Despite repeated demonstrations and anti-government violence, the Company failed to predict the Islamic Revolution of Iran in 1978 and 1979.
4. The capture of agents John Downey and Richard Fecteau inside China.
5. The failure to discover that KGB agent Heinz Felfe was the head of the West German intelligence service (*Bundes Nachrichten Dienst*).
6. An attempted coup against Indonesian President Sukarno in 1958 failed miserably and had embarrassing repercussions.
7. Early in 1971, CIA told the White House that the North Vietnamese in Laos didn't have enough reserves to repel an attack. They did, and the result was a disaster with more than 600 U.S. helicopters hit, and more than 100 shot down.

***

CIA TRIUMPH: THE KHRUSHCHEV SPEECH

At the 20th Congress of the Soviet Communist Party in February, 1956, Party Chairman Nikita Khrushchev's speech denounced Joseph Stalin's long list of crimes and called for an end to the "Cult of Personality."

CIA Director Allen Dulles placed the agency's highest priority on obtaining a copy. According to Andrew Tully, author of *CIA: The Inside Story*, it came about six weeks later with help from Mossad, the Israeli secret service; however, *Covert Action Information Bulletin*, a magazine about CIA activities, contends the speech was obtained through a domestic wiretap placed on American Communists.

Whichever version is correct, the speech was authenticated. One version was given to Secretary of State John Foster Dulles; he gave it to the New York *Times*, which published it June 4, 1956.

***

DOING UNTO OTHERS: 11 GOVERNMENTS WHICH HAVE FALLEN WITH THE SUPPORT OF THE CIA

1. Iran—supported overthrow of Mohammad Mossadegh in August, 1953.
2. Guatemala-backed rebellion forcing ouster of Jacobo Arbenz in May, 1954.
3. Costa Rica—backed opposition for 1958 electoral defeat of Jose Figueres.
4. Cambodia—aided 1970 Lon Nol coup deposing Prince Sihanouk.
5. Greece—financed Colonel Papadopoulos' 1967 military takeover.
6. Ecuador—aided in overthrow of Jose V. Ibarra (1961); Carlos J. Arosemena (1963)
7. Chile—backed overthrow of Allende government in 1973.
8. Congo—tried to assassinate and helped engineer a coup against premier Patrice Lumumba.
9. Dominican Republic—provided weapons for the Trujillo assassination (1961), support for the army's ouster of President Juan Bosch (1963), and a cover story to justify U.S. intervention to prevent his return to office (1965.)
10. Brazil promised support and supplies to army generals involved in ouster of President Goulart (1964.)
11. Guyana—operated through labor unions to remove leftist government of Cheddi Jagan in 1953.

Source: *Superspies*

***

"The assassin, mercenary, Godfather, secret agent and cowboy all operate on the borders of some literal or figurative frontier, a lawless place of fabulous extremes and dangers."
—Author Jim Hougan in *Spooks*

"TRUTH *IS* STRANGER THAN FICTION, DOUBLE OH SEVEN."

In the spring of 1960, then Senator and Mrs. John F. Kennedy hosted a dinner party for Ian Fleming, who was Kennedy's favorite author as well as a veteran of British intelligence; others attending included journalist Joseph Alsop and CIA's John Bross.

As coffee was being poured, Kennedy asked Fleming how James Bond would get rid of Cuban leader Fidel Castro. Fleming, who had drafted the organizational structure for CIA's forerunner, the Office of Strategic Services (OSS), said the approach to take was, "Ridicule, chiefly," according to Fleming biographer John Pearson in *Alias James Bond*. Tongue in cheek, he said the three things which mattered most to Cubans were money, religion and sex and suggested the following triple play:

1) The U.S. should send planes to scatter counterfeit Cuban money over Havana, accompanied by leaflets announcing that it came compliments of the United States.

2) Using the Guantanamo naval base, the U.S. should conjure up some religious manifestation—say, a cross of sorts—which would induce the Cubans to look constantly skyward.

3) The U.S. should drop leaflets, with compliments of the Soviet Union, to the effect that owing to American atom bomb tests, the atmosphere had become radioactive, that radioactivity is held longest in beards and that it makes men impotent. As a consequence, the Cubans would shave off their beards, and, without bearded Cubans, there would be no revolution.

All three of Fleming's spoof ideas were seriously considered and several were even attempted. CIA scientists developed a chemical to dissolve Castro's beard and ruin his macho image, and the Agency entered in a plot to flood Cuba with counterfeit money.

Finally, Air Force Major General Edward G. Lansdale (see p.230) had a plan to announce that the Second Coming of Christ was imminent and that Christ was anti-Castro. At the appointed time, an American submarine would surface off Cuba and send up some starshells. This would be a manifestation of the Second Coming and Castro would be overthrown. Some wag called this operation "Elimination by Illumination."

8 WAYS THE CIA TRIED TO KILL FIDEL CASTRO

1. In 1960 and 1961, the CIA's Technical Services Division prepared a box of cigars poisoned with botulism toxin to be given to Castro. The plan was abandoned when fears were raised that Castro might inadvertently hand them out to a group of visiting schoolteachers.

2. In August, 1960, the CIA took steps to enlist underworld figures with gambling syndicate contacts to aid in assassinating Castro. Writer Robert Sam Anson later commented, "It was inevitable: Gentlemen wishing to be killers gravitated to killers wishing to be gentlemen."

3. In April, 1961, the agency delivered a batch of botulism toxin pills to a Cuban, for use in Castro's coffee, highballs or sopa de frijol negro. The Cuban agent, who had been selected by Mafia figure John Rosselli to do the job, got cold feet and never followed through with the plot.

4. After the 1961 Bay of Pigs invasion, the CIA re-opened its contacts with underworld assassins. In January, 1967, columnist Drew Pearson met with Chief Justice Earl Warren and told him he had evidence that Castro had planned to murder John F. Kennedy. Pearson's source was Edmund Morgan, an attorney for underworld figure John Rosselli. On March 3rd, Pearson wrote, "President Johnson is sitting on a political H-bomb, an unconfirmed report that Sen. Robert Kennedy may have approved an assassination plot which then possibly backfired on his brother."

5. In early 1963, the Agency considered placing an exploding conch seashell in an area of the sea where Castro often went scuba diving. Dissenters to the plan asked how the CIA could be sure that Castro would be the one to find it. And, they added, the assassination was supposed to look like an accident; Castro blowing up on the ocean floor would undoubtedly cast suspicion on the United States.

6. The suggestion was made that Castro be presented with a contaminated diving suit. CIA technicians bought a suit and contaminated the breathing apparatus with a virulent strain of tuberculosis bacilla and the suit with fungus spores that

would cause madura foot, a chronic disease. The plan was to send it to Cuba with American attorney James Donovan, who was negotiating the release of the Bay of Pigs prisoners. An unwitting Donovan would present it to Castro as a gift from the U.S.

That plan was deep-sixed (a Navy term for sunk), so to speak, when the Agency decided that there was the possibility that Donovan might try the diving suit on. More importantly, the plan was tossed out when the Agency realized that a poisoned wet suit as an official gift might not go over so well when it was discovered. Ironically, Donovan gave Castro a diving suit as a present.

7. On Nov. 22, 1963, the day of President Kennedy's murder, Rolando Cubela, a highly placed Cuban official who was displeased with Castro, was given a ballpoint pen rigged with a hypodermic needle in the clicking mechanism that would inject a lethal poison. Cubela was told to procure the toxin Blackleaf 40 for the job. Cubela was dissatisfied with the pen, calling it a "toy." He insisted that the Agency surely could develop something more "sophisticated."

8. Early in 1965, AM/LASH (Cubela's code name) met with the leader of an anti-Castro group and was given a pistol with a silencer that was to be used to kill Castro.

The CIA also plotted to destroy Castro's public image by spraying his broadcast booth with "super-acid," a chemical producing effects like LSD, treating his cigars with a chemical producing temporary disorientation, and dusting his shoes with thallium salts, a depilatory that would cause his beard to fall out.

After these failures against Castro personally, the CIA persevered in trying to overthrow his government by

- spreading non-lethal chemicals in sugar fields to sicken cane cutters
- sabotaging Cuban factories
- contaminating sugar exports
- circulating counterfeit money and ration books
- attacking oil storage facilities

NO SHORTAGE OF EXCUSES, THOUGH

All these failures against Castro were overshadowed by the Bay of Pigs fiasco in 1961, which resulted in the deaths of four U.S. pilots and hundreds of anti-Castro Cubans. In its aftermath, a bulldozer buried all records from the Guatemala training camp used to train the Cuban "freedom fighters."

President Kennedy asked a four-man committee for a report on the fiasco. General Maxwell Taylor, Attorney General Robert Kennedy, CIA Director Allen Dulles and Chief of Naval Operations Arleigh Burke concluded that failure was due in part to "a shortage of ammunition."

YES VIRGINIA, THERE REALLY IS A SMERSH

Ian Fleming popularized SMERSH as "the official murder organization of the Soviet government." He wasn't making the whole thing up; SMERSH actually did exist. It's a contraction of *smert shpionom!* which means, "Death to spies!" in Russian.

In 1921, the Cheka, a forerunner of Russia's KGB, established units in the Soviet army called *osobyi otdel* (special section.) These units spied on on the military and rooted out disloyal elements; the Russian people knew them as "Double-O" sections.

During World War II, the Double-O sections were expanded and renamed SMERSH; their mission was tracking down agents of the Gestapo and the Abwehr.

THE DEVIL'S PLAYGROUND

In *Superspies,* author Jules Archer details three deadly devices the not-so-idle minds of the CIA's Health Alteration Committee invented for use in assassinations:

1. A heat-sensitive engine bolt for cars that releases poisonous vapors into the passenger compartment
2. A battery-powered dart gun capable of firing a poisoned missile 300 feet; the dart would then dissolve on impact and leave no trace
3. A fluorescent light which emitted poisonous substances when turned on

5 FOREIGN LEADERS THE CIA TRIED TO KILL

In his introduction to *Alleged Assassination Attempts Against Foreign Leaders*, part of the Church Committee report, reporter Clark Mollenhoff outlined attempted assassination attempts:

1. Fidel Castro, Premier of Cuba: ''The White House has had a contract out on his life almost continuously from 1960 on...''
2. Patrice Lumumba, Premier of Congo (Zaire): ''Lumumba and two of his aides were killed by political opponents on or about Jan. 17, 1961. For at least five months before, the CIA was deeply involved in a number of plots to assassinate him to to deliver him into the hands of his enemies. The Senate Intelligence Committee gives the CIA and the president the benefit of the doubt, absolving them of responsibility for the death of Lumumba. Because of the lack of specific information on the circumstances of Lumumba's death the denial is plausible, but barely so.''
3. Rene Schneider, Chilean Army Commander-in-chief: Schneider was murdered on Oct. 22, 1970. Before his death, Schneider was the chief obstacle to the Chilean military's U.S.-backed plan to overthrow Allende. ''If President Nixon launched the CIA effort to 'remove' General Schneider, and if those who killed him were supported or encouraged by anyone from the CIA, then Nixon would be as legally responsible for the murder as if he had pulled the trigger of the gun.''
4. Ngo Dinh Diem, president of South Vietnam: Diem was killed on Nov. 2, 1963, during a CIA-encouraged coup by a cadre of Vietnamese generals. ''In seeking to absolve U.S. officials of responsibility for Diem's death, the Senate Intelligence Committee dealt charitably with the administration of the U.S. President who was assassinated twenty days after Diem's death.''
5. Rafael Trujillo, dictator of the Dominican Republic: During both the Eisenhower and Kennedy administrations, the CIA continued to aid and encourage dissident groups attempting to overthrow the Trujillo regime. He was murdered on May 30, 1961, with weapons supplied by the American government.

"Immediately following the assassination, the State Department cabled the CIA station in the Dominican Republic to destroy all records concerning contacts with the dissidents..."

There is also ample evidence of CIA attempts or plots against the lives of President Sukarno of Indonesia and "Papa Doc" Duvalier of Haiti. Former CIA Deputy Director of Plans (DDP) Richard Bissell told the Church Committee on June 11, 1975 that "the assassination of Sukarno was contemplated."

Similarly, Walter Elder, former executive assistant to Agency Director John McCone, told the committee on August 13, 1975 that arms were furnished to Haitian dissidents "to help [them] take what measures deemed necessary to replace the government," which would include Duvalier's untimely death.

13 THEY TRIED TO KILL WITH KINDNESS

On Feb. 18, 1977, the Washington *Post* revealed that the CIA had paid King Hussein of Jordan every year since 1957, because he "permitted U.S. intelligence operations to work freely in Jordan." A follow-up story in the New York *Times* named 13 other foreign leaders as having been paid by the CIA, according to *Post-Watergate Morality:*

1. Chiang Kai-shek
   Nationalist China (Taiwan)
2. Ramon Magsaysay
   Philippines
3. Syngman Rhee
   South Korea
4. Mobuto Sese Seko
   Zaire
5. Eduardo Frei Montalva
   Chile
6. Ngo Dinh Diem
   & Nguyen Van Thieu
   South Vietnam
7. Luis Echeverria Alvarez
   Mexico
8. Carlos Andres Perez
   Venezuela
9. Archbishop Makarios
   Cyprus
10. Jomo Kenyatta
    Kenya
11. Holden Roberto
    Angola
12. Forbes Burnham
    Guyana
13. Willy Brandt
    West Germany

11 FOREIGN BENEFICIARIES OF CIA LARGESS

1. Center for Studies and Documentation (Mexico)
2. Congress for Cultural Freedom (Paris)
3. Foreign News Service Inc.
4. Institute of Political Education (Costa Rica)
5. Interamerican Federation of Newspapermen's Organizations
6. International Federation of Free Journalists
7. International Journalists
8. International Student Conference
9. Public Services International
10. World Assembly of Youth
11. World Confederation of Organizations of the Teaching Profession

Source: *The Invisible Government*

A BISSELL COVERT ACTION MAYBE?

Richard Bissell served as the CIA's Deputy Director of Plans from 1958 to 1962 and planned the Bay of Pigs invasion among others. Addressing the Council on Foreign Relations in 1968, he defined covert action as follows, according to *The CIA File:*

1. Political advice or counsel
2. Subsidies to individuals
3. Financial support and "technical assistance" to political parties
4. Support of private organizations including labor unions, businesses, etc.
5. Covert propaganda
6. "Private" training of individuals and exchange of persons
7. Economic operations
8. Paramilitary or political action operations like the Bay of Pigs

ON SECOND THOUGHT, FORGET THE BISSELL

Author Jules Archer's description of CIA secret operations in *Superspies* differs drastically from Bissell's:

1. Rigging foreign elections
2. Framing anti-American labor and student leaders

3. Promoting riots
4. Directing goon squads
5. Teaching foreign police and military officers how to sabotage dissent
6. Developing counterrevolution
7. Assassinating targeted foreign figures

***

A CIA DICTIONARY

agent of influence—one who can be used to influence foreign individuals, opinion molders, organizations or pressure groups to advance U.S. aims.

asset—a person, group, relationship, instrument, installation or supply at the disposition of an intelligence agency.

backstopping—CIA term for providing appropriate verfication and support for an alias used by an agent.

bigot lists—restrictive lists of persons who have access to a particular and highly sensitive class of information.

black—used to indicate reliance on illegal concealment of an activity when an alias is not being used.

black propaganda—propaganda which appears to come from a source other than its true one, particularly ''the other side.''

blow—to expose, sometimes unintentionally, personnel, installations or other aspects of a clandestine activity or organization.

brush pass—a planned public collision which allows two agents to exchange documents while they are ''bumping'' into one another.

confusion agent—an individual dispatched by his sponsor to confound another intelligence apparatus rather than collect and transmit information.

Cookie factory—an in-house slang name for the Agency. (See Pickle factory.)

cover for action—activity that explains by some believable story, other than the truth, why a spy sees certain people, lives a certain way, etc.

cover for status—an activity or profession that gives a person a viable ostensible reason for being in a certain country when the real reason is espionage or other clandestine activity.

cut-out—a person used to conceal contact between members of a clandestine activity or organization, particularly an agent or intelligence officer.

dangle operation—one in which something or someone of interest is intentionally put into the path of another intelligence service with the hope that it will bite.

dark gray propaganda—propaganda attributed to a source usually hostile to the United States.

dead drop—public but usually unobserved receptacles where papers or packages can be hidden and picked up later.

denied area—a closed society such as Cuba, the USSR or Soviet Bloc countries.

executive action—short for assassination.

flaps and seals man—an expert in opening and closing letters.

flash alias documentation—fictitious identification which can only be ''flashed.'' For more intense scrutiny, backstopping (see above) is required.

gray gray propaganda—propaganda which is attributable to a neutral source, or, does not specifically identify its source.

hard targets—the Soviets, Cubans and other Communist countries.

jock strap medals—decorations awarded CIA officers in Clandestine Services; so named because that's the only piece of clothing on which they can be worn. They're kept in a safe at Langley until resignation or retirement.

light gray propaganda—propaganda attributed, not to the United States, but to nations known to be friendly towards it.

live drop—a person used, without his or her knowledge, to transmit information between agents and intelligence officers.

Nonskids—slang term for directives of the National Security Council (NSCD's.)

notionals—fictitious, private commercial entities which exist on paper only; serve as the ostensible employers of intelligence personnel.

Pickle Factory—a slang term for the CIA used by Company employees.

pissing contest—bureaucratic infighting waged over the cable or telex wire.

pocket litter—business cards or other material used to verify identification.

processing the take—reviewing all the materials provided by telephone taps.

proprietaries—a term used to designate ostensibly private commercial entities established and controlled by intelligence services.

putting in the plumbing—providing the operational support capabilities which must be installed prior to any significant operation.

sheep-dipping—improving the cover of an agent before sending him or her overseas to increase credibility.

snuggling—broadcasting at a frequency directly next to that of an official source so unwary listeners will think they are listening to the government version of the facts, particularly during civil war.

soft targets—non-aligned nations.

sterile telephone—one which cannot be located even after checking with the telephone company.

street man—an officer who specializes in meeting and recruiting spies as opposed to operations officers who are desk men.

target study—a compilation of everything known about a person who is or may become a subject for recruitment.

terminate with extreme prejudice—assassinate.

tweep—a slang acronym for *terminate with extreme prejudice.*

watch list—list of words—names, entities or phrases—which can be employed by a computer to select out required information from a mass of data.

wet job—intelligence work involving bloodshed or assassination.

white propaganda—news releases extolling the successes of the U.S.

***

"THE FAMILY JEWELS"

In May 1973, newly appointed director James Schlesinger asked Company employees to forward to him their records of any CIA activities which they considered to be illegal or improper.

The CIA's own ombudsman, the Inspector General, collected 693 pages of "potential flap activities," which were promptly labeled "the family jewels."

Included were Operation CHAOS—the massive operation directed against the domestic anti-war movement: the surveillance and bugging of American journalists, connections with the Watergate burglars and the White House "Plumbers," and the agency's mail interception program.

Presidents Nixon and Ford and National Security Advisor Henry Kissinger were never informed about them until after reporter Seymour Hersh asked questions about "the jewels" in December, 1974.

When details about "the jewels" were requested under the Freedom of Information Act, the Agency refused to release one word, explaining that making them public would reveal "intelligence sources and methods."

THE ROCKEFELLER COMMISSION

After Seymour Hersh's first article about CIA domestic activities appeared in the New York *Times* on Dec. 22, 1974, President Gerald R. Ford established the Commission on CIA Activities within the United States on Jan. 4, 1975.

The commission was chaired by Vice President Nelson A. Rockefeller and was directed to "determine whether any domestic CIA activities exceeded the Agency's statutory authority and to make appropriate recommendations."

It consisted of future President Ronald Reagan; John T. Connor, then Chairman and CEO of Allied Chemical Corp.; former U.S. Solicitor General Erwin Griswold; Lane Kirkland, Secretary-Treasurer of the AFL-CIO; General Lyman L. Lemnitzer, former Chairman of the Joint Chiefs of Staff and Dr. Edgar F. Shannon, President of the University of Virginia from 1959 to 1974.

After appearing before the Commission, CIA Director William Colby was taken aside by Vice President Rockefeller. He said, "Bill, do you really have to present this material to us? We realize that there are secrets that you fellows need to keep and so nobody here is going to take it amiss if you feel that there are some questions you can't answer quite as fully as you seem to feel you have to."

BIG BROTHER'S BOOKSHELF

1. *The Invisible Government*

Published in 1964, this was the first full-scale expose of CIA covert activities. Prior to publication, the Agency obtained a set of bound galleys—without authorization—and was shaken by David Wise and Thomas Ross's well-researched and fast-paced narrative.

CIA's legal division actually spent some time studying whether to buy up the entire first printing of 15,000 books. Bennett Cerf, president of Random House, said he'd be delighted, then added that, of course, he would immediately order another printing for the public.

What the Agency most wanted to protect was the existence of the Special Group which showed that Presidents had approved secret political warfare around the world. After publication, *Time* magazine planned a cover story based on the book; the Agency was successful in quashing that idea.

Finally, all CIA stations were sent phony book reviews for planting in local media. One part of the book review read, ''Our democracy is a representative democracy and not a debating society.''

2. *The CIA & the Cult of Intelligence*

After the CIA had surreptitiously obtained a copy of Victor Marchetti's manuscript, it asked for a federal injunction to delay publication which was granted in 1972. CIA asked that 339 specific portions be deleted based on ''national security'' objections but finally settled for 168. Alfred A. Knopf finally published the book in 1974 with blank spaces for 168 deletions, making this the first case of pre-publication court-ordered censorship in U.S. history.

3. *The Politics of Heroin in Southeast Asia*

In July, 1972, the Agency acquired and screened an unauthorized copy of the manuscript, which dealt with Agency complicity in Indochinese drug traffic. Following an eight-page CIA critique and a letter from CIA counsel Lawrence Houston, it was published as written by Alfred W. McCoy in the middle of August.

4. *A Decent Interval*

The CIA sued former agent Frank Snepp, whose book was critical of CIA involvement in Vietnam. Eventually, the Supreme Court ordered Snepp to give the CIA $140,000 in proceeds from the book.

In an ironic turnabout, former Agency Director Stansfield Turner's memoirs of *his* years at the agency have been extensively edited by the CIA's Publications Review Board, against his vigorous protest; Turner headed the Agency at the time of the Snepp case.

5. *Deadly Deceits: My 25 Years in the CIA*

Former agent Ralph W. McGehee's recently published book includes an appendix entitled, ''This Book and the Secrecy Agreement,'' about Agency efforts to delay publication. He submitted the manuscript for CIA review in accordance with a recent Supreme Court ruling and, while rewriting, discovered the Agency was deleting material it had already cleared.

He went public with his complaints, following which the Agency ''reconsidered'' its actions and became more reasonable. The CIA might find less reasonable McGehee's main finding that it produces information policymakers want to hear and suppresses the bad news.

***

10 WAYS CIA TRIED TO STOP ''ON COMPANY BUSINESS'' FROM REACHING AN AUDIENCE

A three-part Public Broadcasting System documentary by Allan Frankovich called ''On Company Business,'' later released in theaters, was severely critical of the CIA. Here are ten ways the Agency reacted, according to Frankovich:

1. Pressured the Public Broadcasting System; PBS never aired parts two and three
2. Tried to link Frankovich to international terrorism
3. The U.S. embassy in Australia pressured the National Executive of the Australian Labor Party to have them cancel their invitation for him to screen the film to their national leadership, then in opposition

4. In 1980, had the chairman of the Senate Intelligence Oversight Committee attempt to question Frankovich about non-existent Soviet links
5. Pressured foreign television executives
6. Protested the film's release and Frankovich's presence in Nicaragua as a hostile act through embassy channels to the foreign ministry
7. Tried to suggest through a newspaper in Nicaragua that he had worked and was still working for the CIA
8. Helped arrange for the insertion of articles attacking Frankovich and the film in newspapers, including the foreign press. Robert Moss, the author of a CIA-funded book defending the overthrow of the Allende government, was the author of one
9. Helped the late Rep. Larry MacDonald (D-Ga.) with a speech he inserted into the Congressional Record insinuating the film was a communist terrorist conspiracy
10. Suggested that there were legal problems with the film after attorneys for both the corporation for Public Broadcasting and the Public Broadcasting affiliate in New York had stated there were none

***

GET A JOB: 23 PROFESSIONS IN CONSTANT DEMAND AT THE NATIONAL SECURITY AGENCY

1. Cryptanalyst—code breaker
2. Traffic Analyst—ferrets useable intelligence information from foreign (or domestic) radio communications
3. Collection Officer—operates listening posts
4. Linguist—language expert
5. Computer Systems Analyst—designs and monitors NSA computer systems
6. Communications Security Analyst—tries to keep them from doing to us what we do to them
7. Engineer
8. Physical Scientist
9. Engineering Specialist

10. Telecommunications Officer
11. Mathematician
12. Cryptologic Mathematician—maker and breaker of codes
13. Signals Analyst—deals with all types of communications
14. Signals Conversion Officer—attempts to locate and intercept communications purposely hidden in radio interference
15. Telemetry Specialist—listens to machines talk to other machines
16. Conversion Specialist
17. Electronic Signals Specialist
18. Communications Signals Specialist
19. Special Research Analyst
20. Information Science Analyst
21. Industrial Production Officer
22. Logistician
23. Education and Training Officer

Source: *The Puzzle Palace*

***

24 GROUPS THAT RECEIVED FUNDS DIRECTLY OR INDIRECTLY FROM THE CIA

1. African American Institute
2. American Council for International Commission of Jurists
3. American Federation of State, County and Municipal Employees
4. American Friends of the Middle East
5. American Newspaper Guild
6. American Society of African Culture
7. Asia Foundation
8. Association of Hungarian Students in North America
9. Committee for Self-Determination
10. Committees of Correspondence
11. Committee on International Relations
12. Fund for International Social and Economic Education
13. Independent Research Service
14. Institute of International Labor Research
15. International Development Foundation

16. International Marketing Institute
17. National Council of Churches
18. National Education Association
19. Paderewski Foundation
20. Pan American Foundation (University of Miami)
21. Frederick A. Praeger, publishers
22. Radio Free Europe
23. Synod of Bishops of the Russian Church Outside Russia
24. United States Youth Council

Source: *The Invisible Government*

***

"We may find that the FBI and the CIA...were far more dangerous to the health and legitimacy of American society than the Communists. If it had not been for the FBI, the Communist Party in the United States might well have disappeared 20 years ago. The machinations of the CIA around the world... have done an enormous amount to reinforce the legitimacy of communism."
—Univ. of Michigan professor Kenneth E. Boulding to the American Bar Assn. in 1975, as quoted in *Superspies*

***

33 PRINCIPAL CONDUITS OF CIA FUNDS

1. Andrew Hamilton Fund
2. Beacon Fund
3. Benjamin Rosenthal Foundation
4. Borden Trust
5. Broad-High Foundation
6. Catherwood Foundation
7. Chesapeake Foundation
8. David, Joseph and Winfield Baird Foundation

9. Dodge Foundation
10. Edsel Fund
11. Florence Foundation
12. Gotham Fund
13. Heights Foundation
14. Independence Foundation
15. J. Frederick Brown Foundation
16. J.M. Kaplan Foundation
17. Jones-O'Donnell
18. Kentfield Fund
19. Littaur Foundation
20. Marshall Foundation
21. McGregor Fund
22. Michigan Fund
23. Monroe Fund
24. Norman Fund
25. Pappas Charitable Trust
26. Price Fund
27. Robert E. Smith Fund
28. San Miguel Fund
29. Sidney and Esther Rabb Charitable Foundation
30. Tower Fund
31. Vernon Fund
32. Warden Trust
33. Williford-Telford Fund

In addition to those listed above, the M.D. Anderson Foundation, of which Watergate special prosecutor Leon Jaworski was a trustee, was also a CIA recipient. Others included the Whitney Fund via John Hay Whitney, publisher of the New York *Herald Tribune;* the Hobby Foundation, administered by Houston *Post* publisher Oveta Culp Hobby; the San Jacinto Fund through oilman John Mecom, Jr. and the Hoblitzelle Foundation via Judge Sarah T. Hughes, who administered the oath of office to President Johnson.

***

"I always felt the real key was that you were offering something
special—a real secret life...Everybody has a little of Walter
Mitty in him."
—Former CIA agent John Stockwell,
quoted in *The Search for the Manchurian Candidate*

WE HEAR OAKLAND'S TRYING TO GET
A FRANCHISE THROUGH EMINENT DOMAIN

While the CIA's charter assigns it the task of foreign intelligence
gathering, the Agency hasn't forgotten the folks at home. According to *The Espionage Establishment*, the CIA maintains (at least) 15
offices in the U.S. with the following phone numbers helpfully
provided by the Bell system.

1. New York (212) 755-0027
2. Chicago (312) 353-2980
3. Los Angeles (213) 622-6875
4. Boston (617) 354-5965
5. Detroit (313) 226-4469
6. Philadelphia (215) 627-6872
7. San Francisco (415) 986-0145
8. Miami (305) 445-3658
9. Pittsburgh (412) 281-4009
10. Houston (713) 229-2739
11. St. Louis (314) 621-6902
12. Atlanta (404) 221-6969
13. Seattle (206) 442-0824
14. Denver (303) 388-3728
15. Minneapolis (612) 726-9011

A NATIONAL SECURITY CHRONOLOGY

1918

May 6—The forerunner of the National Security Agency is established by the War Department. Its $100,000 annual budget
consists of $60,000 not authorized by Congress.

1939

Apr. 24—U.S. Signal Intelligence Service is formed and becomes the first agency authorized to intercept radio and telephone communications.

1942

June 13—President Franklin D. Roosevelt establishes the Office of Strategic Services (OSS) under General William J. Donovan.

1945

Aug. 18—ITT, Western Union and RCA protest a post-war government request that they monitor all international cables and telephone calls but later comply.

Sept. 20—President Harry S. Truman disbands OSS.

1946

Jan. 22—Truman establishes the Central Intelligence Group, forerunner of Central Intelligence Agency, to plan and coordinate ''all Federal foreign intelligence activities.''

1947

July 17—Truman okays plan to wiretap citizens for national security reasons.

Sept. 18—National Security Act establishes the CIA, creates the National Security Council and unifies the armed services into the Department of Defense.

Dec. 16—Defense Secretary James Forrestal assures presidents of ITT and RCA of immunity from prosecution if they continue to provide copies of international cables and telegrams to security agencies. Western Union is told the same a month later.

Dec. 19—The National Security Council holds its first meeting and resolves to use the CIA as an ''active tool'' in the Cold War. It decides that the CIA will undertake a broad range of covert activities to prevent a Communist victory in the upcoming Italian elections.

1949

June 20—The Central Intelligence Agency Act is passed, exempting the CIA from "publication or disclosure of the organization, functions, names, official titles, salaries or number of personnel." It is even allowed to spend money "without regard to the provisions of law and regulations relating to the expenditure of Government funds."

1950

Apr. 20—CIA director Roscoe Hillenkoetter approves Bluebird, an interrogation project teaming up a psychiatrist, a polygraph expert trained in hypnosis, and a technician. He authorizes the use of unvouchered funds to pay for the most sensitive areas of this behavior-control program.

1952

Oct. 24—President Truman signs a seven-page "top secret" presidential memorandum (stamped with a code word that was itself classified) establishing the National Security Agency.

Nov. 4—National Security Agency begins operations.

1953

Apr. 3—Future CIA director Richard Helms proposes a CIA program for "covert use of biological and chemical materials."

Apr. 13—Director Allen Dulles approves a program using chemical and biological warfare in covert operations. He names it MKULTRA, gives it a $300,000 budget and orders the Agency's bookkeepers to pay the costs without question.

May 28—Iran Premier Mohammed Mossadegh attempts to blackmail the U.S. by warning he will seek help elsewhere if the U.S. cuts off aid. The CIA sends Brig. Gen. H. Norman Schwartzkopf, an old friend of the Shah's, to see him despite Soviet protests.

June 17—2,000,000 East Germans defy the Soviet dictatorship, fighting tanks, ripping open jails to free political prisoners and beating Communist officials to death. CIA gives aid and comfort—but no material help—to the rebels.

Aug. 13—The Shah of Iran orders Mossadegh's ouster. On Aug. 19th, the Premier is arrested.

1954

June 8—Secretary of State Dulles says at a press conference that "beheading of all anti-communist elements in Guatemala" is imminent.

June 18—A CIA coup overthrows Guatemalan president Jacobo Arbenz, who had nationalized the property of the United Fruit Company. Secretary of State John Foster Dulles's law firm wrote contracts for UFC and Guatemala in the 30's, and his brother, CIA director Allen Dulles, had been president of United Fruit.

1956

June—U-2 overflights of USSR begin.

Oct. 22—Hungarian students and workers revolt in Budapest and make 16 demands of their Soviet bosses. Radio Free Europe, a CIA front, keeps repeating the message, "America will not fail you," even as Soviet troops were crushing the revolt.

1960

Mar. 17—President Dwight D. Eisenhower authorizes the secret training of Cuban exiles for an invasion of Cuba.

May 1—The Soviet Union shoots down U-2 pilot Francis Gary Powers. A State Department spokesman says a "weather observation" plane is missing over Turkey.

May 11—President Eisenhower assumes responsibility for the U-2 incident.

Oct. 31—CIA bugs the Las Vegas hotel room of comedian Dan Rowan, who is involved with Phyllis McGuire, the girlfriend of Sam Giancana, the mobster the CIA paid to kill Fidel Castro.

Nov. 29—President-elect John F. Kennedy is briefed on secret plans to "liberate Cuba" and aid "freedom-loving exiles in delivering their homeland from a Communist regime."

1961

Jan. 31—The Samos II spy satellite is launched.

Apr. 8—U.N. Ambassador Adlai Stevenson is briefed guardedly about the impending U.S.-backed invasion of the Bay of Pigs in Cuba, although he later denies advance knowledge of the invasion.

Apr. 12—Five days before the Bay of Pigs invasion, President Kennedy says the U.S. won't send troops to Cuba.

Apr. 17—CIA-backed Cubans invade Cuba's Bay of Pigs.

Apr. 18—Four U.S. Navy pilots die in Bay of Pigs air battle.

Aug. 13—East Germany closes the Berlin border and begins building the Berlin wall.

Oct. 1—The Defense Intelligence Agency is established under Lt. Gen. Joseph Carroll, formerly a leding assistant to J. Edgar Hoover.

Dec. 7—The Colorado Springs *Gazette Telegraph* reveals that CIA-backed Tibetan guerillas are training in Leadville, Co. for an incursion into Red China.

1962

Feb. 10—Captured U-2 pilot Francis Gary Powers is exchanged for convicted Russian spy Rudolf Abel at the Glienecker Bridge in Berlin.

Feb. 11—CIA establishes the Domestic Operations Division.

May 15—The first radio satellite is launched.

Oct. 23—The U.S. blockades Cuba after it is revealed that Russian missile bases there are operational; five days later, Russia agrees to dismantle the missiles.

1963

Nov. 1—South Vietnamese generals overthrow Pres. Ngo Dinh Diem with CIA aid. Diem and his brother are captured and executed.

1964

Jan. 4-5—President Lyndon B. Johnson tells reporters Tom Wicker of the New York *Times*, Douglas Kiker of the New York *Herald Tribune* and Phil Potter of the Baltimore *Sun* of the CIA's "complicity" in the murders of Rafael Trujillo of the Dominican Republic and Ngo Dinh Diem of South Vietnam.

June 30—Henry Cabot Lodge tells the New York *Times*, "The overthrow of the Diem regime was purely a Vietnamese affair. We had nothing to do with it."

1967

Feb. 13—*Ramparts* magazine's story on the CIA funding of the National Student Association becomes public.

Mar. 22—President Lyndon B. Johnson receives the FBI document outlining CIA-Mafia plans to kill Castro.

August—CIA establishes the Special Operations Group (SOG) to monitor radical organizations in U.S. and to report on the antiwar movement.

1968

Jan. 23—North Koreans seize U.S. ship Pueblo in the Sea of Japan.

1969

July 1—NSA domestic wiretapping begins.

Sept. 6—Richard Helms confirms the importance of CIA's operation CHAOS in a memo which also established its funding.

1970

Feb. 26—Hoover ends relations with the CIA after an FBI agent tells a Denver CIA agent about a missing professor. He writes, "I want direct liaison here with CIA to be terminated and any contact with CIA in future to be by letter only."

Mar. 18—With U.S. approval, Lon Nol overthrows Prince Sihanouk as Cambodia's head of state. The next day, the U.S. announces that the question of recognition of the new government "does not arise."

Apr. 10—C. Jay Parkinson, Chairman of the Board of Anaconda, tells CIA officials he and other American companies are willing to pay $500,000 to block the election of Salvador Allende as President of Chile.

June 27—During a 40 Committee meeting, National Security Advisor Henry Kissinger approves a $500,000 contingency fund to influence the final vote of the Chilean Congress if Allende wins the Sept. 14th election. "I don't see why we have to let a country go Marxist just because the people are irresponsible," Kissinger says.

1970

Sept. 15—Nixon friend and Pepsi Cola chief Donald Kendall meets with Kissinger and Attorney General John Mitchell, prophesying disaster if Allende takes office in Chile. Nixon tells CIA Director Helms to prevent Allende's inauguration after he has been legally elected President of Chile.

1971

June 15—The first Big Bird Spy satellite, capable of spotting 8-inch object from a height of 90 miles, is launched.

1972

June 19—DCI Helms and aides discuss Watergate for the first time; CIA officer Lee Pennington, Jr. helps the wife of burglar James McCord burn his files.

Sept. 1—The New York *Times* reveals illegal Army Intelligence surveillance of the 1967 Pentagon march, the 1968 Democratic and Republican conventions, and the 1968 Poor People's march.

Dec. 17—The New York *Times* reports that the CIA provided training to 14 New York City policemen. A CIA spokesman says similar ''courtesies'' are extended to other American police departments.

1973

Jan. 24—In the wake of Watergate, Helms destroys all his personal files.

May 9—DCI James Schlesinger orders all CIA employees past and present to give information about activities ''which might be construed to be outside the legislative charter of the Agency,'' giving birth to ''The Family Jewels.''

July 10—The Washington *Post* reports the ''word 'perjury' was being uttered'' in Senate offices by those who heard Helms' testimony on Chile.

1974

Oct. 4—Ex-CIA agent Philip Agee publishes a list of 37 CIA agents working in Mexico in *Excelsior,* Mexico City's leading morning newspaper.

Dec. 22—Seymour Hersh's story in the New York *Times* reveals CIA "Operation CHAOS," which was approved in August, 1967 by President Johnson. The CIA spied on anti-war groups, underground press, black militants and others for "possible foreign funding." By 1973, CIA had list of 300,000 names.

Dec. 30—CIA tells President Gerald R. Ford it conducted illegal domestic intelligence activities against dissidents. The CIA compiled files on at least 10,000 citizens and conducted break-ins, wiretapping and mail-tampering.

1975

Jan. 4—President Ford appoints the "Rockefeller Commission" to study domestic CIA activities.

June 10—Rockefeller Commission reports the CIA engaged in "unlawful" activities that "constituted improper invasions upon the rights of Americans." The section of the report dealing with foreign assassinations is withheld from the public.

May 15—Defense Secretary James Schlesinger ends NSA's Project SHAMROCK which intercepted international telegrams from 1945-1975 and was by far the largest governmental interception program.

June 18—Testifying before the Senate Intelligence Committee, National Security Council aide Robert Johnson claims Pres. Eisenhower ordered the assassination of Congolese leader Patrice Lamumba at an NSC meeting in August, 1960.

Nov. 6—CIA Director William Colby acknowledges that in 1964 a CIA official prepared campaign material for President Johnson and reported regularly on campaign matter to the CIA.

Dec. 4—Senate Intelligence Committee says the CIA heavily aided a coup in Chile but couldn't show its direct involvement.

1975

Dec. 23—Having moved into the Athens residence of the former CIA station chief against advice, new chief Richard Welch is killed by three unknown terrorists shortly after his identity had been published in *Counterspy,* a magazine devoted to exposing CIA machinations. The murder was used as justification to make publishing the names of CIA officials a federal offense.

1976

Jan. 29—The House votes 246-124 not to release the Pike committee report investigating the intelligence agencies.

Feb. 18—Reporter Daniel Schorr effectively ends his CBS career after admitting that he furnished the suppressed House report on CIA covert activities to the *Village Voice.*

1977

Jan. 14—The Justice Department refuses to prosecute former CIA officials for opening mail, because no written record of executive approval existed to prove or disprove legality.

Nov. 4—Helms pleads ''nolo contendere'' to a charge that he lied to Church Senate Select Intelligence Committee about CIA's involvement in Chile. He received a suspended sentence and the Association of Retired Intelligence Officers passed the hat to pay his $2,000 fine.

1978

Jan. 24—President Jimmy Carter issues an order stating ''the CIA may not engage in any electronic surveillance within the United States.''

Feb. 8—Communications expert David Waters tells a Senate committee that the National Security Agency probably has ''thousands of remote wiretaps'' on private phone calls.

1980

Oct. 29—A six-year employee of the NSA is forced to sign a statement that he will tell his family about his homosexuality.

1983

May 11—The New York *Times* reveals the Defense Intelligence Agency set up a special unit for intelligence gathering. The Army Intelligence Support Activity was established during the hostage crisis, because the Pentagon was dissatisfied with CIA intelligence data. No Congressional committee was advised of the unit's existence, as required by law.

June 22—CIA Director William E. Casey becomes the fourth Reagan official known to have had possession of former President Carter's briefing papers before the Carter-Reagan debate.

Memo From H. R. Haldeman to the President

POLITICS AND OTHER DIRTY TRICKS

"Every government is run by liars and nothing they say should be believed."

—I.F. Stone, in the film, *I.F. Stone's Weekly*, 1974

THAT'S PROGRESS

In 1972, before the Watergate revelations, an opinion poll showed that fully 38 percent of Americans were willing to believe that their leaders had consistently lied to them. By the spring of 1975, over two thirds (68%) were convinced, according to *Superspies*.

***

"I hate to think what would happen if any of you ever got out of this . . . and got involved in U.S. politics. These kinds of dirty tricks must never be used in internal U.S. politics. The whole system would come apart."
—Psychwar expert Paul Linebarger lauding the tactics of agent E. Howard Hunt to a class of new CIA recruits, as quoted in *Portrait of a Cold Warrior*

BLACK MIND, BAD LYRICS

Linebarger used as an example of Hunt's "black mind" the following anecdote. While on assignment in Mexico City, Hunt learned that a local Communist front would be holding a reception for Soviet visitors. He obtained an invitation, had 3,000 more printed and distributed them widely, causing the front to run out of food and liquor and close its doors.

In Mexico City, Hunt "ran" (i.e. controlled) then-contract agent William F. Buckley. Hunt assigned Buckley to translate a book by a disenchanted Chilean Marxist, *The Yenan Way* by Eudocio Ravines, and they became friends. (Buckley is the godfather of Hunt's three children and was named executor of Dorothy Hunt's estate after she was killed in a plane crash.)

Hunt had the confidence of CIA director Allen Dulles and is said to have quietly collaborated with Dulles on his book, *The Craft of Intelligence*. While Hunt was doubtless an effective agent, other CIA higher-ups had little confidence in him. A CIA station chief told agent (and later author) David Atlee Phillips, "Listen to the music when he sings, but don't pay any attention to his lyrics."

***

"I want every son of a bitch in the State Department polygraph-
ed until you find the guy.... It's more important to find the
source of these leaks rather than to worry about the civil rights
of some bureaucrats."
—President Richard Nixon to Egil (Bud) Krogh, Jr.,
August, 1971

THE "PLUMBERS" (NIXON'S SPECIAL INVESTIGATIONS UNIT)

President Nixon formed the "Plumbers" unit in response to the New York *Times'* publication of the Pentagon Papers on June 13, 1971. The unit, which reported to John Ehrlichman, was originally told to investigate media leaks and consisted of Hunt; former FBI agent G. Gordon Liddy; David Young, Henry Kissinger's appointments secretary; and unit chief Egil (Bud) Krogh, a long-time Ehrichman friend and aide.

The "Plumbers" were responsible for the Sept. 3, 1971 break-in at the Beverly Hills office of Dr. Lewis Fielding, Daniel Ellsberg's psychiatrist. The unit also manufactured phony State Department cables, hoping to implicate President John Kennedy directly in the assassination of Vietnamese president Ngo Dinh Diem and also investigated the fatal automobile accident at Chappaquiddick and Teddy Kennedy's involvement in the incident.

THE SKY ABOVE, THE CROWD BELOW

Bill Gulley, head of the White House Military Office under presidents from Johnson to Ford, reports in *Breaking Cover* that the Nixon White House continually complained that Washington, D.C. police overestimated the size of anti-war demonstrations in the capital.

On White House orders, the Military Office detailed the Pentagon to take aerial photos of demonstrations from a U-2 spy plane. When counts they got from the U-2 pictures turned out to be considerably lower than police estimates, the White House press office began releasing the figures but never explained publicly how they got them.

***

17 JOURNALISTS AND GOVERNMENT AIDES WHOSE PHONES WERE TAPPED ON HENRY KISSINGER'S ORDERS IN 1969

William H. Sullivan, ambassador to Laos under President Johnson, close aide to Kissinger during Paris peace talks on Vietnam.

Helmut Sonnenfeldt, National Security Council staff member.

Richard L. Sneider, Foreign Service officer, later Deputy Assistant Secretary of State.

Hedrick Smith, correspondent with the New York *Times*.

John P. Sears, then a deputy Presidential counsel in charge of liaison with local Republicans.

William Safire, White House speechwriter, now columnist with the New York *Times*.

Robert E. Pursley, an Air Force lieutenant general, then top military aide to the Secretary of Defense.

Richard F. Pedersen, close aide to the Secretary of State.

Richard Moose, National Security Council staff member under Presidents Johnson and Nixon.

James W. McLane, White House aide responsible for anti-inflation policy.

Winston Lord, National Security Council staff member and later a close assistant to Kissinger.

Anthony Lake, National Security Council staff member who later joined Edmund Muskie's campaign.

Marvin Kalb, CBS diplomatic correspondent, also a member of White House "enemies list" and a biographer of Kissinger.

Morton Halperin, planning expert on the National Security Council staff, one of the few victims to sue Kissinger and President Nixon.

Daniel L. Davidson, NSC staffer formerly involved in Paris peace talks. He commented of Kissinger, "He was the man who held himself out to be my friend. But to invade my privacy and my wife's privacy is outrageous."

Henry Brandon, Washington correspondent for the Sunday *Times of London*.

William Beecher, then a New York *Times* reporter, later appointed Deputy Assistant Secretary of Defense.

Source: *The American Police State*

***

THE OFFICIAL ENEMIES LIST

In *The Night Watch*, a CIA agent evaluates Charles Colson as follows: "He lacks the essentials of greatness." He did not lack a taste for partisan politics, however, and submitted a potential "enemies list" to White House counsel John Dean on Sept. 9, 1971. Dean delivered the final list to the Senate Watergate Committee on June 27, 1973.

1. Arnold M. Picker, United Artists Corp., New York.
2. Alexander E. Barkan, AFL-CIO Committee on Political Education, Washington.
3. Ed Guthman, Los Angeles *Times*.
4. Maxwell Dane, Doyle Dane Bernbach, New York.
5. Charles Dyson, Dyson-Kissner Corp., New York.
6. Howard Stein, Dreyfus Corp., New York.
7. Allard Lowenstein, former congressman, New York.
8. Morton Halperin, Common Cause, Washington.

9. Leonard Woodcock, United Auto Workers, Detroit.
10. S. Sterling Munro Jr., congressional aide, Washington.
11. Bernard T. Feld, Council for a Liveable World, Washington.
12. Sidney Davidoff, mayoral aide, New York.
13. John Conyers, congressman, Detroit.
14. Samuel M. Lambert, National Education Assn., New York.
15. Stewart Rawlings Mott, philanthropist, New York.
16. Ronald Dellums, congressman, Berkeley, Calif.
17. Daniel Schorr, CBS News, Washington.
18. S. Harrison Dogole, Globe Security System, Philadelphia.
19. Paul Newman, actor, Los Angeles.
20. Mary McGrory, newspaper columnist, Washington.

Many others were proposed but didn't make the top 20. Dean says they included Rev. Eugene Carson Blake, conductor Leonard Bernstein, 12 black congressmen, 6 other members of the House of Representatives, 10 senators, Alabama Gov. George Wallace, Mayor John Lindsay, 56 reporters and news executives, 14 labor officials, 48 businessmen, 24 academics, and 18 organizations ranging from the Black Panthers to Common Cause.

***

WOODSTEIN, INC.

Washington *Post* reporters Bob Woodward and Carl Bernstein turned their coverage of a third rate burglary into a first rate industry. In "Watergate, Inc.", (*Playboy*, July, 1982) authors Tom Passavant and Conan Putnam estimated that works of the two journalists have been responsible for grossing nearly $80 million. Here's a breakdown:

"All the President's Men"

Playboy excerpt	$ 30,000
Advance	55,000
Book sales (hardcover and paperback)	12,143,050
Movie rights (to Simon & Schuster)	450,000
Movie box office gross	58,000,000

"The Final Days"

Newsweek excerpt	$ 65,000
Hardcover sales	5,475,000
Paperback reprint rights	1,500,000

Lectures

Woodward	$ 450,000
Bernstein	450,000
TOTAL	$79,618,050

***

CAN'T GET ENOUGH OF IT

According to Passavant and Putnam, the Library of Congress card catalogue lists 169 book titles under the heading "Watergate." They also counted 286 bylined "Watergate" magazine articles by free-lance writers in the *Readers' Guide to Periodical Literature* and the *Popular Periodicals Index.* They estimate that the public has paid more than $70 million for Watergate writings.

Here is a list of some notable non-Woodstein Watergate books:

	AUTHORS' TAKE	RETAIL TAKE
Blind Ambition, John W. Dean III	$300,000	$4,778,000
Born Again, Charles W. Colson	50,000 (to charity)	5,800,000
The Company, John Ehrlichman	N/A	2,200,000
The Ends of Power, H.R. Haldeman	600,000	400,000
Mo: A Woman's View of Watergate, Maureen Dean and Hays Gorey	150,000	488,790
The Palace Guard, Dan Rather and Gary Paul Gates	N/A	3,200,000
The Presidential Transcripts	N/A	2,940,000
RN, The Memoirs of Richard Nixon	2,000,000	N/A

***

12 WATERGATE FIGURES AND HOW MUCH THEY MADE ON THE LECTURE CIRCUIT

1. Bernard Barker (burglar) $40,000
2. Samuel Dash (Ervin Committee counsel) $350,000
3. John Dean (White House counsel).......at least $700,000
4. Sam Ervin (Senator, committee chairman) $1,000,000
5. E. Howard Hunt (Plumber, conspirator) $300,000
6. G. Gordon Liddy (Plumber, conspirator) $840,000
7. Jeb Stuart Magruder (deputy
      campaign manager CREEP) $200,000
8. Eugenio R. Martinez (burglar)....................$40,000
9. James W. McCord Jr. (burglar) $200,000
10. Elliot Richardson (Attorney General).............$225,000
11. Fred Thompson (Ervin Committee
      minority counsel)............................$300,000
12. Frank Wills (Watergate Building guard) $2,000

Source: "Watergate, Inc.," *Playboy*, July, 1982

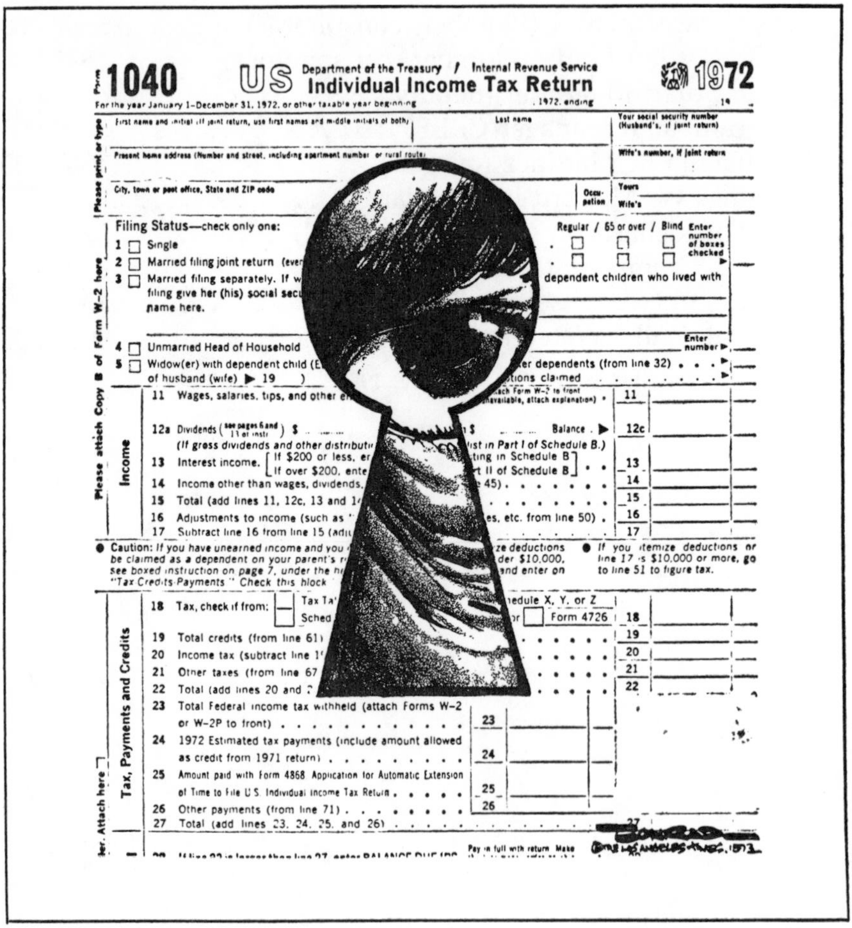
Form 1040
US Department of the Treasury / Internal Revenue Service
Individual Income Tax Return
1972
For the year January 1–December 31, 1972, or other taxable year beginning , 1972, ending 19
Filing Status—check only one:
1 Single
2 Married filing joint return
3 Married filing separately.
4 Unmarried Head of Household
5 Widow(er) with dependent child
Income
11 Wages, salaries, tips, and other
12a Dividends
13 Interest income.
14 Income other than wages, dividends,
15 Total (add lines 11, 12c, 13 and 14
16 Adjustments to income
17 Subtract line 16 from line 15
Tax, Payments and Credits
18 Tax, check if from:
19 Total credits (from line 61)
20 Income tax
21 Other taxes (from line 67
22 Total (add lines 20 and 21
23 Total Federal income tax withheld (attach Forms W-2 or W-2P to front)
24 1972 Estimated tax payments (include amount allowed as credit from 1971 return)
25 Amount paid with Form 4868 Application for Automatic Extension of Time to File U.S. Individual Income Tax Return
26 Other payments (from line 71)
27 Total (add lines 23, 24, 25, and 26)
©THE LOS ANGELES TIMES, 1973

CHAPTER
3

THE INTERNAL REVENUE SERVICE: BIG BROTHER & THE WITHHOLDING COMPANY

"Taxes are the price we pay for civilization."

—Oliver Wendell Holmes, inscription on the IRS building in Washington.

CONGRESSMAN GEORGE HANSEN'S LIST OF POWERS RESERVED SOLELY FOR THE IRS

In *How the IRS Seizes Your Tax Dollars and How to Fight Back*, Rep. George Hansen (R-Ida.), says only the IRS can:

1. Attach 100% of your wages or property.
2. Inspect your bank records and credit ratings without obtaining a court order.
3. Seize your property without obtaining a court order.
4. Try your case, should you want to fight, in a special court it oversees.
5. Order production of documents, records, and other materials without a court case being in existence.
6. Make public your tax debt with impunity.
7. Put you under electronic surveillance without a court order.
8. Waive rights such as those under the Statute of Limitations through its power of arbitrary assessment.
9. Use extralegal coercion. Threatening witnesses with audits regularly produces whatever evidence the IRS asks for.
10. Legally violate a written agreement it has with you.
11. Maintain lists of citizens guilty of no crime for the sole purpose of harassment or surveillance.

CONGRESSMEN HARASSED BY THE IRS DURING RE-ELECTION CAMPAIGNS

1. In 1968, Former Senator Ed Long (D-Mo.) lost his bid for re-election after his tax returns were leaked to *Life* magazine. Long had just spent three years investigating the IRS in his Senate subcommittee. He was later cleared of any tax irregularities.
2. Former Senator Joseph Montoya (D-N.M.) investigated the IRS in committee and also had his tax returns leaked to the press shortly before he sought re-election. In Montoya's case, the IRS discovered that it owed *him* money.
3. Congressman George Hansen found the IRS leaked the fact that his tax returns contained "certain irregularities" shortly before his re-election campaign in 1976. Hansen, who wrote an anti-IRS book in 1981, was indicted by a Washington, D.C. grand jury in April, 1983 for an alleged "failure to report financial information to the government." He has termed the indictment "phony and trumped-up" and claims he is being persecuted for his political beliefs.

***

THE BUREAUCRATIC MIND AT WORK

The following are recent IRS proposals designed to crack down on alleged tax cheaters, according to the Los Angeles *Times*, August 21, 1982.

1. Calling in all $100 bills periodically so that drug traffickers, gamblers and others who "need a highly liquid, anonymous form of wealth" could be identified.
2. Creating a master computer list of real estate transactions in order to find home sellers holding "take-back" mortgages and receiving interest payments on them.
3. Increasing the maximum reward for persons who inform on tax evaders from $50,000 to $250,000.
4. Awarding citizens "a souvenir note and/or gift from the President" if they voluntarily contributed extra tax dollars to reduce the national debt.

***

IN YOUR HEART, YOU KNOW HE'S RIGHT

Sen. Barry Goldwater (R-Ariz.) was so outraged after the Senate Intelligence Committee's 1975 investigation of IRS abuses that he made the following remarks in a separate statement and added it to the Committee's final report:

"Nowhere has the perversion of domestic intelligence been more vividly demonstrated than [in our] investigation of the Internal Revenue Service.... Intelligence components of the IRS have indiscriminately investigated hundreds of thousands of taxpayers and have amassed reams of information wholly irrelevant to the IRS' narrow responsibility for collecting taxes...

"In 1961, for instance, the IRS initiated a program to conduct a test audit of various 'right-wing' organizations. Termed the 'Ideological Organizations Audit Program,' the project attempted intensive investigation of 10,000 tax-exempt organizations that was far removed from even-handed enforcement of the internal revenue laws.

"Precedent having been established, a Special Services Staff was organized in 1969 to conduct audits of 'activist' and 'ideological' taxpayers... the 'special service' rendered the nation was the unwarranted targeting of 18,000 individuals and 3,000 groups.

"... the IRS next established an 'Information Gathering and Retrieval System'... during its two years of life, some 465,442 individuals and organizations were examined before the program was terminated in 1975.

"Abuses uncovered in connection with the IRS' Operation Leprechaun... are as profoundly contemptuous of the American taxpayer as they are characteristic of the IRS' perennial efforts to transform itself into a repository of domestic intelligence."

* * *

VOLUNTARY COMPLIANCE

During its short life (1969-1973), the IRS's Special Services Staff:

1. Used informants to collect political intelligence information. From mid-1970 through August, 1973 the IRS received bimonthly intelligence digests from a Washington, D.C. informant who had infiltrated anti-war groups.

2. Established blind post office "drop boxes" to collect information that might relate to activist political organizations and persons.
3. Gathered intelligence material from other IRS units, particularly field offices, service centers and the files of divisional intelligence centers.
4. Collected intelligence-type information from other government agencies, particularly from the FBI. The IRS received 11,818 separate reports from the agency. 6,000 were classified information, mainly from the FBI's COINTELPRO (Counter-Intelligence Program) activities. Other agencies assisting the IRS included the Social Security Administration, the Department of the Army and Congressional Internal Security committees.
5. Developed files on political individuals and groups. By 1973 the IRS had political and tax intelligence files on 8,585 individuals and 2,873 groups. 41% of the organizations were composed of blacks or other minorities. 11% of the groups were categorized as "New Left" and 15% as right-wing or racist.
6. Compiled political activity lists as a basis for initiating tax audits. A targeted individual's tax file usually contained a report on political affiliations, an FBI report and tax returns.
7. Distributed tax returns to other government agencies, such as the Department of Justice.

Source: *Abuses of the Intelligence Agencies*

***

11 FASCINATING IRS COVERT OPERATIONS

Investigative reporter David Wise has been turning his searchlight on covert government activities since he illuminated secret CIA maneuvering in *The Invisible Government* (with Thomas B. Ross) in 1964. In *The American Police State*, Wise uncovers 11 covert IRS operations, as follows:

1. Operation Leprechaun: From 1972 to 1975, the Miami IRS office investigated suspected tax violators through a group of 62 paid informants, the best known of whom was Mrs. Elsa

Guitierrez (code named "Carmen"). As part of her $200-a-week position with the IRS, Guitierrez was "to have drinks and sexual relations with individuals for the purpose of gathering tax information." The IRS maintained a membership for her in the Miami Playboy Club, so she could mingle with her affluent targets. "Leprechaun" was suspended after Guitierrez testified to congressional investigators in 1975.

2. Project Haven: Also conducted by the IRS Miami office, this operation was conducted from 1973 to 1975 by agent Richard Jaffe and his informant, known only by the code name TW 24. They attempted to obtain information on trust accounts established overseas by Americans. Their greatest coup was obtaining photocopies of 450 pages of records of a bank in the Bahamas. IRS agents apparently copied the documents when a bank official visited Miami and went to dinner with a woman friend of the informant.

3. Operation Tradewinds: A nine-year effort to obtain the names of Americans maintaining secret accounts in banks in the Bahamas.

4. Operation Sunshine: For a year and a half, IRS undercover agent Harry C. Woodington hung around bars in Miami and Fort Lauderdale gathering allegations about 913 people. He was trying to identify persons who might be bribing IRS agents. In 1975, Woodington, sometimes known by his code name "Harry the Hat," collected $55,000 for his efforts, which resulted in not one single case of corruption.

5. Operation Mercury: In the '60's, the IRS was alerted when anyone sent a money order of $1,000 or more through Western Union. In many cases, the IRS investigated the person's tax status.

6. Scorpio: A probe into profits of politicians' irregular practices.

7. Operation P: An investigation of "pimps, panderers, prostitutes, pornography and massage parlors."

8. Project a Go-Go: A "compliance check of go-go dancers."

9. Chain Link: An effort to "identify and determine compliance of local fences."

10. Operation Rabbit: Investigations of police shakedowns in Chicago.

11. Operation Scalpel: An attempt to determine the compliance rate among physicians.

IT'S A TOUGH GIG

According to a 1980 FBI report, 74% of all threats and 41% of all assaults on federal workers were directed at IRS employees.

***

EXCUSES, EXCUSES

The IRS had a handy explanation when it was discovered that 25% of the people found on Nixon's Enemies List were audited (compared with a national average of 2%.) According to the Los Angeles *Times* of Jan. 1, 1974, the IRS told Associated Press:

- People on the list tended to be involved in a wider range of business activities than average persons with the same income.
- Many of the people on the list were writers and journalists who (in the IRS' words) "tend to have large deductions for business expenses, which automatically subject them to closer scrutiny."
- The list contained many who were contributors to political campaigns and this also tended to bring close IRS checking.

The article concluded by stating "but except for random computer selection, actual audits are made only when IRS personnel feel they can get additional revenue."

***

ENEMIES: 16 PEOPLE AUDITED AT THE REQUEST OF THE NIXON WHITE HOUSE

1. Rep. Bella Abzug (D-N.Y.)
2. Mortimer Caplin, Democrat who formerly headed IRS
3. Clark Clifford, Democratic strategist and former Sec. of Defense
4. Richard Dougherty, McGovern campaign press secretary
5. Henry Kimelman, McGovern chief fund raiser and finance chairman
6. Shirley MacLaine, actress and active Democrat
7. Lawrence O'Brien, Democratic Party National Chairman
8. Pierre Salinger, journalist and Kennedy administration press secretary

9. Polly Bergen, actress
10. John Kenneth Galbraith, economist and former ambassador to India
11. Gene Hackman, actor
12. Gilman Kraft, brother of columnist Joseph Kraft
13. Burt Lancaster, actor
14. Norman Lear, producer
15. Paul Newman, actor
16. Joanne Woodward, actress

Source: *The American Police State*

***

MORE ENEMIES: INDIVIDUALS TARGETED BY THE NIXON IRS'S SPECIAL SERVICES STAFF

Sherman Adams, assistant to President Eisenhower
Stewart Alsop, political columnist
Julie Andrews, actress
Joan Baez, singer
Jimmy Breslin, writer
James Brown, singer
Godfrey Cambridge, comedian
Sammy Davis Jr., entertainer
Former Rep. Charles Diggs (D-Mich.)
Former Sen. Charles Goodell (R-N.Y.)
Former Sen. Ernest Gruening (D-Alas.)
Aaron Henry, Mississippi civil rights activist
Kareem-Abdul Jabbar, basketball player
Jesse Jackson, Chicago civil rights activist
John Lindsay, former mayor of New York
Coretta Scott King, widow of Dr. Martin Luther King, Jr.
Norman Mailer, author
Linus Pauling, Nobel Prize-winning chemist
Tony Randall, actor
Connie Stevens, singer
Elizabeth Taylor, actress

Sources: Tax Reform Research Group/ABC News

AND MORE: KNOW A MAN BY HIS ENEMIES

These prominent personalities were found among a list of 575 names of political enemies submitted by the Nixon White House to the IRS for possible audits; most appeared to be contributors to George McGovern's presidential campaign:

California Assemblyman Willie Brown
Sen. William Proxmire (D-Wisc.)
Paul Conrad, Los Angeles *Times'* political cartoonist
Angier Biddle Duke, London, former U.S. Chief of Protocol
Max Factor, cosmetics scion
Ralph Gleason, San Francisco *Chronicle* jazz critic
Hugh M. Hefner, Playboy publisher
Sen. Howard M. Metzenbaum (D-Oh.)
Stewart Mott, General Motors heir
Max Palevsky, industrialist
Mr. and Mrs. Joseph Robbie, owner of the Miami Dolphins
Dr. George Wald, Harvard professor
Harold Willens, organizer, Businessmen against the War
Patrick Caddell, pollster
Frederick G. Dutton, University of California regent and a Kennedy associate
Frances (Sissy) Farenthold, liberal Texas politician
Lt. Gen. James M. Gavin
Sen. Gary Hart (D-Co.)
Frank Mankiewicz, McGovern campaign director
Paul C. Warnke, SALT talks negotiator

Source: Los Angeles *Times,* Dec. 21, 1973

***

ON THE OTHER HAND...

Sen. Lowell R. Weicker, Jr. (R-Conn.), a member of the Senate Watergate Committee, announced he had documents to show that IRS tax intelligence had been used to protect such ''White House friends'' as evangelist Billy Graham and movie star John Wayne after tax audits on them began, according to the Los Angeles *Times, Apr. 7, 1974.*

6 MAGAZINES TARGETED FOR INVESTIGATION BY THE IRS IN THE NIXON ADMINISTRATION

Commonweal
Human Events
The National Observer (defunct)
New York Review of Books
Rolling Stone
Washington Monthly

Sources: Tax Reform Research Group/ABC News

***

4 MAGAZINES CURRENTLY UNDER IRS INVESTIGATION

Politically motivated IRS investigations of magazines were supposed to have died a well-deserved death when Richard Nixon left the White House. Apparently, someone forgot to put a silver spike through the heart of the beast.

Mother Jones, the San Francisco-based magazine published by a non-profit foundation, is in the fourth year of a fight to save its tax exemption. Others being audited currently are *Ms.* magazine, *The Guardian*, a radical newsweekly, and *NACLA Reports*, published by the North American Congress on Latin America, composed mainly of academic Latin American specialists.

The IRS district office in New York recommended revoking the latter's exemption for failing to present ''a full and fair exposition of pertinent facts.'' One of their sins, says their lawyer, was an article critical of the Rockefeller family.

Sources: *The Progressive*, June, 1983/*Organizing Notes*, Jan.-Feb., 1983

> ''I know everybody's income and what everybody earns; And I carefully compare it with the income-tax returns; To everybody's prejudice I know a thing or two; I can tell a woman's age in half a minute - and I do! Yet everybody says I am a disagreeable man! And I can't think why!''
> —King Gama in Gilbert and Sullivan's *Princess Ida*

13 RELIGIOUS GROUPS
TARGETED FOR IRS INVESTIGATION
BY THE NIXON WHITE HOUSE

American Jewish Committee
American Jewish Congress
Associated Catholic Charities
Baptist Foundation of America
B'nai B'rith Anti-Defamation League
Christian Beacon, Inc.
Christian Echoes Ministry, Inc.
Church League of America
Founding Church of Scientology
The Nation of Islam, Chicago
National Council of Churches of Christ
Protestants and Other Americans United for Separation of
    Church and State
Unitarian-Universalist Association

Sources: Tax Reform Research Group/ABC News/Senate Intelligence Committee

14 BUSINESSES, FOUNDATIONS & PROFESSIONAL
GROUPS TARGETED BY THE IRS UNDER NIXON

American Library Association
American Law Institute
Carnegie Foundation
Conservative Book Club
Ford Foundation
Fund for the Republic
Legal Aid Society
National Education Association
National Student Association
Peace Foundation
Playboy Foundation
Louis M. Rabinowitz Foundation
University of North Carolina
U.S. Civil Rights Commission*

* Staffers in the Nixon White House were apprently unaware that a
government agency doesn't pay taxes.
Sources: Tax Reform Research Group/ABC News

19 POLITICAL GROUPS
MARKED FOR INVESTIGATION BY NIXON'S IRS

American Civil Liberties Union
American Nazi Party
Americans for Democratic Action
Committee for a Sane Nuclear Policy
Common Cause
Communist Party
Fair Play for Cuba Committee
John Birch Society
Liberty Lobby
Life Line Foundations, Inc.
The Minutemen
National States Rights Party
Progressive Labor Party
Revolutionary Action Movement
Socialist Workers Party
Students for a Democratic Society
United Republicans of America
W.E.B. Dubois Clubs
Young Socialist Alliance

Sources: Tax Reform Research Group/ABC News

***

AT IRS, THE PUNISHMENT FITS THE CRIME

In 1972, vocal tax protester Ronald C. Miller, a Fresno, Calif. cab driver, was convicted of filing a false W-4 form that claimed six dependents when he was actually entitled to only one. The false form was in effect for a total of 18 days, and Miller's total tax liability was just $5. He was sentenced to one year in prison.

STRONG BACK, GOOD TEETH, FULLY EQUIPPED

In 1975, the IRS attempted to collect $200,000 in back taxes from the defunct Birmingham Americans of the World Football League, according to the Los Angeles *Times*, March 11, 1975. The team's only assets were the contracts of 59 players; the IRS auctioned the contracts.

''We're handling this particular transaction as we would any other delinquent taxpayer's,'' said an IRS official. ''If they have any assets, and we have reason to believe they do, we have authority to seize those assets and put them up for sale.''

Settling a tax bill of another WFL team, the Portland Storm, two years earlier, the IRS auctioned 23 parkas, 81 pairs of football shoes, 129 white uniform pants, 40 green practice jerseys, 27 white practice jerseys, 64 white game jerseys, 54 towels, 76 footballs, 96 jock straps, several footlockers, one cart of socks and towels, one lot of leg socks and another of pads, one blue tote bag of dirty green game jerseys and another of dirty pants and four laundry bags of dirty clothes.

15 MINORITY GROUPS & PROGRAMS TARGETED BY THE IRS UNDER NIXON

Black Economic Development Conference
Black Student Union
Black Panther Party
Brown Berets
Congress of Racial Equality
Har-You
Headstart Program
Los Angeles Black Congress
Malcolm X Society
The Medgar Evers Rifle Club
NAACP
National Urban League, local chapters
Republic of New Africa
Southern Conference Education Fund
Student Nonviolent Coordinating Committee of Atlanta

Sources: Tax Reform Research Group/ABC News

AMERICA'S "VOLUNTARY" TAX SYSTEM

On Aug. 2, 1979, Mr. and Mrs. Stephen Oliver of Fairbanks, Alaska, were confronted on the street by six IRS agents, who demanded that the Olivers turn over their battered 1970 Volkswagen in partial satisfaction of a disputed tax lien of $3,300.

The incident is reported by Ernest Volkman and John Cummings in "The New American Gestapo" (*Penthouse*, April, 1981). They go on to recount that the Olivers refused, and the agents proceeded to smash the windows of the car with nightsticks and dragged the Olivers out bodily. The couple had insisted that no government agency had the authority to seize their property without a court order.

They were wrong. Congress has granted the IRS the "power of distraint and seizure by any means" without court orders. This power is the only known legal exception to the Fourth Amendment's ban against warrantless searches and seizures.

AT&T: TOO FAT TO TAX?

Over a 10-year period, the IRS has failed to collect at least $2.9 billion in income taxes owed by American Telephone & Telegraph. According to the Los Angeles *Times* (Nov. 9, 1976) the IRS budget prevented it from fully auditing the returns of a corporation with revenues of $26 billion.

"The error continues with each advancing year, growing larger as the physical plant grows," says Lawrence Sloan, a former valuation engineer for IRS. In its annual report for 1975, AT&T valued its plant facilities at $87.6 billion.

The IRS said it would like to comment but was prevented by law from discussing the tax affairs of a corporation or a person.

THE W-2 BLUES

IRS officials would like the public to believe that the W-2 forms filed by employers give the government a foolproof system of checking on the income of most wage earners.

The truth is that the IRS routinely throws away without examination most of the W-2's and 1099's (dividend and interest income forms) that it receives each year. The Los Angeles *Times* reported on Apr. 13, 1976 that only 14% of the total forms were matched up with individual income tax returns in 1974.

IRS officials pointed out that the matching program was only one of several factors that could trigger a tax audit.

WHY INTERNAL REVENUE AGENTS GET IN TROUBLE

- Falsification or distortion of reports and other paperwork
- Personal misconduct
- Failure to pay proper taxes
- Failure to discharge duties properly
- Unauthorized outside activity
- Embezzlement, theft, bribery, extortion, acceptance of gratuities
- Divulgence of confidential information

Source: *Inside IRS*

AN IRS CHRONOLOGY

1862

July 1—Congress passes the first income tax to help pay the Civil War debt.

1912

Mar. 12—Congress begins discussion of a ''special excise tax'' for individuals. The 16th Amendment is passed, and the IRS is born.

1943

July 1—Paycheck withholding of income tax begins.

1947

Dec. 4—Attorney General Tom Clark begins the Attorney General's list of subversive organizations. By January, the IRS is checking the charitable status of any organization listed.

1965

July 26—IRS Commissioner Sheldon Cohen tells a Senate subcommittee that IRS conference rooms in 22 cities have concealed microphones.

1967

Feb. 1—CIA asks IRS to examine *Ramparts* magazine which is about to reveal CIA funding of the National Student Association.

1969

June 25—President Nixon asks IRS to investigate "dissident and extremist" groups for tax-exempt funding.

July 2—IRS establishes its "Activist Organizations Committee" to investigate left-leaning political groups "taking advantage of tax shelters."

1971

Aug. 15—White House counsel John Dean outlines for Nixon his "Political Enemies Project" and how best to "screw our political enemies."

Dec. 22—Nixon aide Alexander Butterfield requests an "up-to-date IRS record check" on Missouri Gov. Warren Eastman Hearnes, a leading candidate to be Sen. Edmund Muskie's running mate.

1972

Aug. 10—U.S. District Judge William T. Beeks rules it is unlawful for the IRS to withhold its in-house manuals and statistics from the public.

Sept. 11—Dean summons IRS Commissioner Johnnie M. Walters and gives him a list of 579 McGovern contributors with a request to have their returns investigated.

1973

Jan. 28—The joint U.S. House-Senate Committee on Internal Revenue Taxation votes to investigate charges that the Nixon White House used the IRS for political purposes.

Aug. 9—IRS Commissioner Donald Alexander says the special unit investigating so-called "extremist" organizations will be disbanded. Organized in 1969, the unit reportedly collected information on 3,000 organizations and 8,000 individuals from leftist and rightist organizations.

1974

Apr. 1—After refusing to comply with the Freedom of Information Act for seven years, IRS establishes a Disclosure Division.

1975

Dec. 31—Warren Bates, the IRS's Assistant Commissioner for Inspection (Internal Security) tells Congressman George Hansen the IRS uses armed agents to go to taxpayers' homes and demand their tax returns. IRS claims it uses lists of people they deem to be "violent."

1976

Apr. 21—The U.S. Supreme Court rules that the Fourth Amendment's guarantee of privacy does not prevent the government from obtaining a bank's microfilmed records of a customer's account.

1983

Jan. 24—Los Angeles *Times* reports that IRS is resuming its covert intelligence operations—dormant since the mid '70s—with special emphasis on developing major criminal cases against drug dealers.

May 9—The St. Louis IRS office begins a computerized calling service that telephones tax delinquents every 30 minutes, 12 hours a day, until the alleged delinquent agrees to pay the outstanding tax bill.

May 29—William Bradford Reynolds, Assistant Attorney General for Civil Rights, says the Supreme Court has granted the IRS the power to deny tax exemptions to churches that support the nuclear freeze, hospitals that support abortion and single-sex private schools. Reynolds based his statement on the Court decision a week before that granted the IRS the authority to withhold tax exemptions for private schools that practice racial discrimination.

EVERY SUCCESSFUL REVOLUTION PUTS ON IN TIME THE ROBES OF
THE TYRANT IT HAS DEPOSED.   — BARBARA TUCHMAN

THE LAW—MAKERS AND BREAKERS

"Mr. Justice Holmes called wiretapping dirty business,' in 1928. Since that time 'dirty business' has become the apt phrase describing the regime under which we now live. . . I am indeed morally certain that the Conference Room of this Court has been 'bugged;' and President Johnson during his term . . . asserted to me that even his phone was tapped."

—Justice William O. Douglas, dissenting in
In re Grand Jury Witness Heutsche v. U.S. (1973)

AND THAT'S *WITH* DIRECT DIALING

From 1975 to 1982, the average cost of a court-ordered wiretap nearly tripled to $21,686. New Jersey has the dubious distinction of being the state in which judges authorized more wiretap applications than another state—for the fourth consecutive year. Illinois spent $428,444 on a 214-day tap investigating racketeering. Florida, New Jersey and New York account for more than half the wiretaps, according to the Administrative Office of the U.S. Courts.

***

LOCALITIES WITH THE MOST LAW-ENFORCEMENT WIRETAPS IN 1982

Suffolk County, N.Y.
Hudson County, N.J.
(Jersey City, Hoboken)
Buffalo, N.Y.
New York City
Nassau County, N.Y.
Newark, N.J.
Elizabeth, N.J.

Atlanta, Ga.
Orlando, Fla.
Omaha, Neb.
Baltimore, Md.
Miami, Fla.
Ft. Lauderdale, Fla.
Jacksonville, Fla.

Sources: Administrative Office of the U.S. Courts/*Privacy Journal*

"In some respects, wiretapping involves a greater invasion of privacy than a search."
—Attorney General Robert F. Kennedy in testimony before a Senate committee in 1962, as quoted in *Superspies*.

BIG (LITTLE) BROTHER'S BIG EAR: WIRETAPS OFFICIALLY AUTHORIZED BY ATTORNEY GENERAL KENNEDY

1. Lloyd Norman, *Newsweek*'s Pentagon and military-affairs correspondent [allegedly ordered by President Kennedy].
2. Hanson W. Baldwin, Jr., New York *Times'* military-affairs specialist. Baldwin wrote a story about photographic surveillance of Soviet missiles which caused the Soviet Union to increase their concealment.
3. Baldwin's secretary.
4. Robert Amory, Jr., former top CIA official and close friend to President Kennedy. Amory was also close to an official at the Yugoslavian Embassy who was an undercover intelligence officer. Amory was falsely accused later of having passed classified information to the Yugoslavian.
5. Surrey and Karasik—This law firm lobbied for Dominican Republic sugar interests and was under investigation for trying to raise U.S. sugar quotas.
6. The chief clerk to the House Agriculture Committee which handled the sugar-quota legislation.
7. Bernard Fall, a French historian who wrote seven books on Vietnam and who maintained contact with North Vietnam President Ho Chi Minh.
8. Rev. Martin Luther King, Jr.
9. Frank Capell, a right-wing author who wrote *The Secret Story of Marilyn Monroe*. The book, published in 1964, suggested a relationship between Robert Kennedy and the late actress.
10. Malcolm X, the black nationalist.

Sources: *The Final Days/Robert Kennedy and His Times*

UNCLE SAM'S TAPPED OUT

Even though the federal government is the nation's leading wiretapper, Uncle Sam can't guarantee the security of his own phones, according to *Privacy Journal*, March, 1976.

In a memorandum to all federal agencies, the General Services Administration said, ''Agencies are specifically advised that the FTS [Federal Telecommunications System] normally does not have security features to protect against either loss of, error in or interception of information. Therefore, the security and confidentiality of information transmitted over the FTS is not ensured.''

***

WIRETAP APPLICATIONS FILED BY U.S. PROSECUTORS SINCE 1968 *

1968	Johnson	0 (half year)
1969	Nixon	33
1970	Nixon	182
1971	Nixon	285
1972	Nixon	206
1973	Nixon	130
1974	Nixon-Ford	121
1975	Ford	108
1976	Ford	137
1977	Carter	77
1978	Carter	81
1979	Carter	87
1980	Carter	79
1981	Reagan	106
1982	Reagan	130

* Necessitated by passage of the Federal wiretap law in 1968
Source: Administrative Office of the U.S. Courts

***

THE OTHERS USE PSYCHICS

Questionnaires sent to 400 of *Fortune*'s list of largest companies supported the American Polygraph Association's contention that *one fourth* of all U.S. corporations now use polygraphs, according to ''Polygraph Usage Among Major Corporations'' by John Belt and Peter Holden in *Personnel Journal*, Aug. 1978.

***

SNOOPERBOWL

The National Lawyers Guild held a fundraiser January 17, 1982 in Detroit and called it Snooperbowl I, according to *Privacy Journal,* Jan. 1982. The group urged people to bring the dossiers they had obtained from Michigan State Police ''red squads '' under a 1981 court order and charged everyone coming to the event $19.84.

THE OPENED DOOR POLICY:
BREAK-INS OF THE '70 S

1. FBI informer Timothy J. Redfearn broke into the Denver offices of the Socialist Workers party on July 7, 1976. Boxes of stolen documents were immediately delivered to the local FBI office.
2. On the evening of Sept. 3, 1971, three Cuban-Americans broke into the Los Angeles office of Dr. Lewis Fielding, psychiatrist of Daniel Ellsberg, then accused of leaking the Pentagon Papers to the New York Times.
3. In November 1971, unknown burglars broke into the Manhattan office of Dr. Robert Akeret, a psychoanalyst treating Patricia (Mrs. Daniel) Ellsberg.
4. On May 28, 1972, the Watergate burglars made their first illegal entry into the office of the Democratic National Committee in Washington.
5. On Feb. 5, 1973, burglars entered the New York office of Dr. Constantine D.J. Generales, a distinguished cardiologist and expert on space medicine. The burglars took a set of keys, a TV set and a cassette tape recorder containing the tape of a conversation held months before when a woman identifying herself as a CIA agent asked the doctor to spy for the agency.
6. Sen. Howard Baker (R-Tenn.) had his home burglarized in August 1975, while serving on the Church committee investigating intelligence agency abuses.
7. Another member of the intelligence committee, Sen. Charles McC. Mathias (R-Md.) was burglarized in November 1975.
8. William Watts, president of the liberal Potomac Associates think tank, made an early draft of the Nixon Enemies list in 1971. In June 1973, he made somebody's list, and his Washington office was burglarized. Authorities speculated that burglars may have been installing or removing electronic

listening devices. His office was broken into twice more in 1974.

9. Beginning in August 1971, the FBI conducted a surveillance operation against the Institute for Policy Studies, a Washington liberal research center. FBI surveillance included numerous burglaries over a two-year period.

10. During the weekend of May 6-7, 1972, the Watergate building offices of the Bank Operations Division of the Federal Reserve Board were broken into. File cabinets were pried open but nothing was found to be missing. (See p.137 for break-ins of media people.)

Source: *The American Police State*

***

THEY GOT THE OTHER TWO THIRDS RIGHT

On October 26, 1982, Congress's Office of Technology Assessment issued a report that sharply documented inaccuracies in the FBI's National Crime Information Center, according to *Privacy Journal*. The report said that one third of all the arrest records in the NCIC's Computerized Crime History file do not include a court disposition, although federal law requires it.

About 20% of the records were inaccurate, OTA concluded after attempting to verify 400 records chosen at random in 1979. Researcher Kenneth N. Laudon, who conducted the study, said FBI statisticians challenged OTA findings when the report was being prepared but came up with essentially the same figures. Laudon says, ''The FBI spent more money trying to attack the figures than the $20,000 OTA spent to compile them.''

In September, 1982, Congress passed a law mandating the bureau to include missing children in the NCIC, meaning a police officer querying the system may get a ''hit'' and think he has encountered a criminal suspect, not the victim of a crime or a runaway. It also means that the majority of names in the NCIC may belong to innocent people.

***

STATES WHERE PATIENTS HAVE NO RIGHT TO SEE THEIR OWN MEDICAL FILES

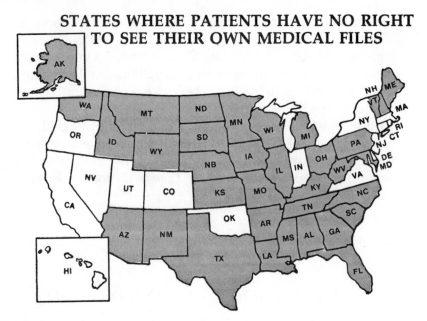

Source: *Compilation of State & Federal Privacy Laws,* 1981

STATES IMPOSING LOYALTY OATHS ON THEIR EMPLOYEES IN THE '50s

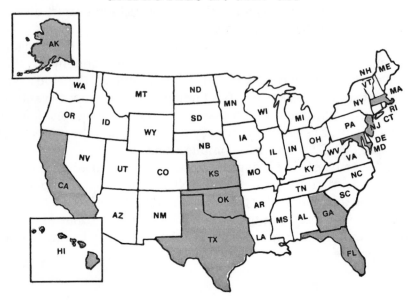

Source: *The Great Fear*

These maps indicate just how widely the states vary the way they treat civil liberties and privacy by statute. In all cases, the shaded states are those which, either in the recent past or currently, infringe on personal liberties.

STATES EXCLUDING THE COMMUNIST PARTY FROM THE BALLOT IN THE '50s

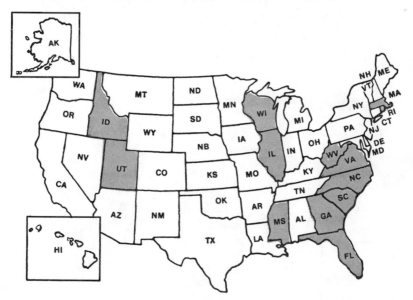

Source: *The Great Fear*

STATES WHERE FORNICATION IS ILLEGAL *

* defined as voluntary sexual intercourse by an unmarried person
Source: *Privacy, How To Protect What's Left of It*

STATES WHERE ADOPTED PERSONS DON'T HAVE THE AUTOMATIC RIGHT TO SEE THEIR BIRTH CERTIFICATES

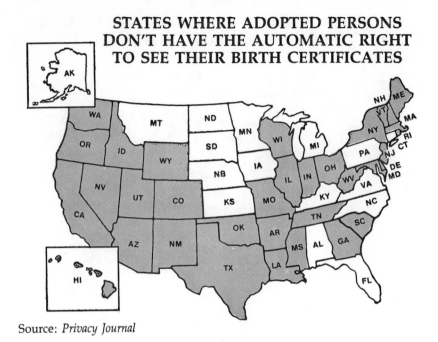

Source: *Privacy Journal*

STATES NOT PERMITTING PEOPLE TO SEE INFORMATION ABOUT THEMSELVES IN STATE AGENCY DATA BANKS

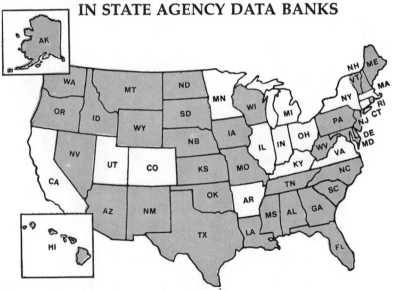

Source: *Compilation of State & Federal Privacy Laws,* 1981

STATES THAT PERMIT EMPLOYERS TO USE POLYGRAPHS ("LIE DETECTORS") ON THEIR EMPLOYEES

Source: *Compilation of State & Federal Privacy Laws,* 1981

STATES THAT DON'T PROTECT THE RIGHT OF PRIVACY IN THEIR CONSTITUTIONS.

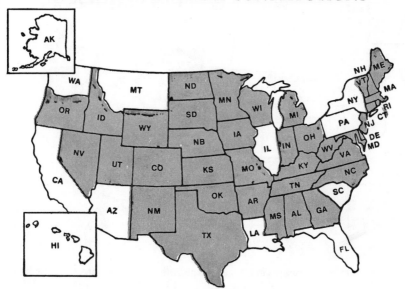

Source: *Compilation of State & Federal Privacy Laws,* 1981

STATES WITH NO EXISTING OR PENDING LEGISLATION PROTECTING CITIZENS' PRIVACY FROM INTRUSION BY TWO-WAY CABLE-TV SYSTEMS

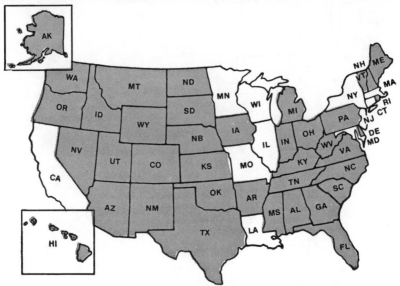

Source: *Cablevision*, "Who's Watching Whom", June 6, 1983/*Privacy Journal*

STATES WHERE COHABITATION* IS A CRIME

* Defined as two persons living together as husband and wife without being married. The offense is a misdemeanor, except in Arizona, where it is a felony and carries a three-year maximum sentence. Census figures show that at least two million persons live together in this manner.

Source: *Privacy, How to Protect What's Left of It*

STATES ADMITTING VOICEPRINTS AS VALID EXPERT EVIDENCE

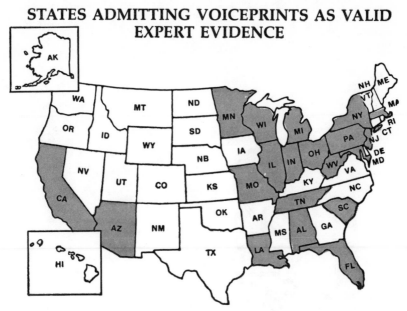

Source: *Privacy, How to Protect What's Left of It*

SCIENCE AND TECHNOLOGY

"The electronic technology at the disposal of the federal government is ... awesome... Scattered throughout the massive bureaucracy right now are some 11,000 computers, which have access to information from over 4,000 data systems, and the government is acquiring new systems at the rate of 1,500 a year... Together, these systems contain almost 4 billion records on individuals—20 different dossiers for each man, woman and child."

—Edward Rasen, "High-Tech Fascism," *Penthouse,* March, 1980

GOVERNMENT DATA BANKS WITH MORE THAN 10 MILLION NAMES

Bureau of Census
Social Security master file
Social Security earnings records
U.S. Savings Bonds office
Internal Revenue Service look-up file
Internal Revenue Service master file
Immigration and Naturalization Service index
Patent and Trademark Office
Federal Bureau of Investigation identification index
Selective Service list of registrants
Old Age Assistance Recipients
Office of Personnel Management file
Recurring Check Issuing
Department of Treasury records on Recurring Check Issues
Veterans and Dependents Files
Social Security claims
Medicare Enrollment
Veterans Administration education file
Department of State

Copyright Applications
Supplemental Security Income program
Secretary of Defense medical claim history files
Federal Communication Commission licensees and applicants
Office of Personnel Management recruiting
Office of Personnel Management retirement
Railroad Retirement Board
Defense Logistics Agency MARDAC Data Base
Office of Workers Compensation Programs
Social Security claims
Department of Army medical prescriptions

Source: Annual Report, Privacy Act of 1974, Office of Management & Budget

***

NSA'S GOOD NEIGHBOR POLICY

The National Security Agency (NSA) has astounding capabilities for capturing and evaluating data. Its machines can scan 300,000 radio communications siimultaneously. An array of telegraphs and telexes relay written words directly into data banks where they are scanned for key words.

One reason for NSA's incredible reach is the physical location of its equipment. In *The Puzzle Palace*, author James Bamford lists the Communication Satellite Corp.'s international telecommunications satellite earth stations and nearby NSA listening posts that intercept COMSAT traffic.

1. Etam, W. Va.: COMSAT's massive earth station has three satellite dish antennas, which transmit and receive more than half the international phone calls, cables, telex messages, data transmissions and other satellite communications entering and leaving the U.S.	1. Less than 60 miles from Etam, near Sugar Grove, W.Va., NSA has built a spectacular array of receiving dishes ranging in size from 30 to 150 feet in diameter. "The NSA dishes should be able to pick up every earthbound whisper destined for Etam, as well as every pulse sent skyward."

2. Andover, Me.: COMSAT's No. 2 communications center for trans-Atlantic traffic.	2. 125 miles from Andover is the Naval Security Group Activity Center, which Bamford says "would serve as an excellent platform from which to intercept signals" to and from Andover.
3. Brewster, Wash.: COMSAT's earth station is located on the Columbia River halfway between Seattle and Spokane.	3. In the early'70s, the NSA opened a $3.5-million facility just 100 miles to the south— on an isolated tract of land on the Army's Yakima Firing Range.
4. Jamesburg, Calif.: COMSAT's other Pacific Coast terminal is located near this tiny village on the edge of the Monterey National Forest.	4. Bamford says the Army Security Agency intercept station at Two Rock Ranch, 130 miles to the north is a possible location for an NSA tap.

Bamford concludes: "...(By) having four strategically placed satellite antenna fields located near the COMSAT earth terminals and several average microwave receiving horns stuck on a rooftop or hanging on the side of an obscure tower near the cable heads, the NSA should be able to monitor continuously nearly *every international telephone conversation or message to or from anyone in the United States.* Such a power could have been fantasized only by Orwell— and never dreamed of by [J. Edgar] Hoover."

"I can see myself all laid out in a rectangle of computer capitals; my entire existence is displayed on the dark field of a monitor, to one side of the bureau person's window, as a meager system of squarish characters of laminated layers of light. 'But there are some things that don't show up on there,' I say with some energy. 'I'll give you just one example of my mother's kindness'..."
—John Hersey, *My Petition for More Space,*
as quoted in *Privacy Journal,* February, 1975

19 GOVERNMENT AGENCIES THAT USE ELECTRONIC AND OTHER ESPIONAGE METHODS ON U.S. CITIZENS

1. FBI
2. CIA
3. Food and Drug Administration
4. Internal Revenue Service
5. Postal Inspection Service
6. State Department
7. Treasury Department
8. Justice Department
9. Drug Enforcement Administration
10. Bureau of Alcohol, Tobacco and Firearms
11. Secret Service
12. Naval Investigative Service
13. Defense Mapping Service
14. Department of the Army
15. Department of Agriculture
16. Coast Guard
17. Atomic Energy Commission
18. Civil Service Commission
19. Customs Service Bureau

Source: *Superspies*

***

AN EPIC BATTLE AGAINST DRUGS

The El Paso (Tex.) Intelligence Center (EPIC) is the central command post for the government's war on drugs entering from Latin America. This multi-million-dollar facility features the most sophisticated electronic communications and detection equipment in the U.S. arsenal.

According to "High-Tech Fascism" by Edward Rasen (see above), EPIC includes computers, teletypes, coded telephones, satellites, microwave scanners, vapor detectors, and forward-looking infrared modules. The facility provides information immediately accessible to government agencies as diverse as the Mississippi Narcotics Bureau and the North American Air Defense Command.

Those agencies represented are listed below.

1. Drug Enforcement Administration
2. Coast Guard
3. Immigration and Naturalization Service
4. Bureau of Alcohol, Tobacco and Firearms
5. Customs Service
6. Internal Revenue Service
7. Federal Aviation Administration
8. National Security Agency

YES, BUT ARE THEY A NIELSEN FAMILY?

Senior citizen residents at Rossmoor's Leisure World in Mesa, Arizona, not only can't turn off their TV sets, but their TV sets can be turned on without their knowledge or control, according to *Privacy Journal*, May, 1974.

Every new home is wired for two-way TV—a TV set and TV camera—along with a fire detector, emergency call alarm and a burglar alarm. Burglar and fire monitors could automatically turn on to "see" inside the residence in the event of an emergency—or in the case of a curious snooper at the "headend" of a two-way system—even if the resident were not home.

> *"It just gets crazier and crazier. They have records upon records, but for all the records, no one knows what the hell is going on."*
> —Herman Cosman, after the Social Security Administration computer insisted he was dead and ceased Medicare benefits, while Medicare premiums kept being deducted from his Social Security check. Quoted by UPI, Nov. 26, 1975

BIG BROTHER'S MEDICINE CHEST

While Big Brother always keeps a weather eye and ear out to detect drugs coming into the United States, the CIA has either developed or stockpiled at least 26 dangerous drugs and toxins:

1. Acontine nitrate (wolfbane)—causes severe abdominal discomfort and, in large quantities, death.

2. anthrax—fatal when inhaled; symptoms resemble pneumonia.
3. BZ—blocks nerve impulses and causes death.
4. Carbachol—causes flushing, colic, diarrhea, salivation and nausea.
5. *Chondodendron toxicoferum*—a paralytic agent, "absolutely lethal in high doses."
6. Cinchonine—overdoses result in severe nausea, vomiting and heart malfunction.
7. Cobra venom—kills by paralyzing the nervous system.
8. Cogentin—"wide range of debilitative, physiological effects"
9. Colchicine—can cause muscle paralysis and fatal respiratory failure.
10. Cyanide—blocks body's absorption of oxygen, resulting in death by asphyxiation.
11. dehydroacetic acid—"causes vomiting and convulsions"
12. encephalitis
13. intestinal flu
14. Jamaica dogwood—a plant used to stun fish so they can be easily captured
15. M-246—produces paralysis
16. neurokinin—"produces severe pain"
17. phencyclidine—"high dosage leads to disorientation and death"
18. rabbit fever
19. S-341—similar to BZ, but more powerful.
20. Saxitoxin (shellfish toxin)—causes failure of respiratory, cardio-vascular, nerve and muscle systems.
21. *Staph. enterotoxin*—a mild form of food poisoning that incapacitates its victim for three to six hours.
22. Strychnine—paralyzes nerve-muscle junctions.
23. TB
24. "2-4 pyrolo"—causes temporary amnesia.
25. *Venezuelan equine encephalomyelitis*—a virus that immobilizes a person up to five days. Can be mistaken for the grippe.
26. *yage*—what author William Burroughs described as "the final fix."

***

BLACKBOARD JINGLE

When you scribble nasty words on a blackboard, make sure it's not the Gemini 100 Electronic Blackboard now being marketed by Bell Telephone. Your words can be broadcast through a nationwide electronic network, according to *Privacy Journal*, March, 1980.

The surface of this special blackboard converts ordinary chalk marks into electronic signals that are transmitted over a telephone line. At the receiving end, the signals are displayed as written information on a standard television screen. Erase the chalk marks and the image on the TV screen—across the country or down the hall—is erased as well. The writing on the blackboard can also be stored on tape for later retrieval.

> *"As every man goes through life he fills in a number of forms for the record, each containing a number of questions... There are thus thousands of threads in all... They are not visible, they are not material, but every man is constantly aware of their existence... Every man, permanently aware of his own invisible threads, naturally develops a respect for the people who manipulate the threads."*
> —Alexander Solzhenitsyn, *Cancer Ward*

11 STEPS FOR INTERCEPTING TELEPHONE CALLS WITHOUT BREAKING AND ENTERING

According to *The Puzzle Palace*, the Mitre Corporation prepared this primer on high-tech bugging for the Ford White House:

1. Locate the microwave repeater sites for the route of interest.
2. Acquire the use of a small farm along the route with sufficient line-of-sight access to the radiated energy.
3. Set up radio interception equipment including a sufficiently large antenna... in a barn to avoid being observed.
4. Place call between accomplices and put tracer signals on the circuit.
5. Scan the microwave channels to find tracer signals.
6. Telephone accomplice from farm either when tracer is found or no tracer tone can be found (accomplice must have second main station telephone to receive such a call.) Have him end call and place a new call with the tracer tone.

7. Begin monitoring the channels on which tracer signals were found.
8. Continue search for trunk circuits until the portion of the trunk group carried by the microwave route has been apppoximately identified.
9. Terminate use of tracer calls and continue to monitor the circuits for desired information.
10. Program micro-computer equipped with inband signaling decode device to automatically scan the groups of interest. In the event that either of the two targeted telephones is dialed, the scanning device will either signal the intercepter to listen, or automatically connect a recorder to the conversation.
11. Recorded conversations can either be analyzed for relevant communications in situ or transported to an information extraction facility.

11 SCHEMES USED TO DETERMINE IDENTITY

1. Fingerprints—used by law enforcement agencies and the military
2. Voice prints—employed by law enforcement in cases like kidnapping
3. Body weight—used extensively in computer facilities
4. Signature—a mainstay of banks and credit card companies
5. Pressure applied to a writing instrument—banks and computer facilities
6. "Hand geometry"—used by school cafeterias. The University of Tennessee has students place their hands on "readers." These devices measure the bone length of each finger and the web of skin between each finger.
7. Passwords—used by military and intelligence agencies
8. Identity Cards—a perennial of food stamp and insurance programs
9. Personal questions—banks use them over the phone (mother's maiden name)
10. Magnetic strips on cards or other media—credit cards
11. Eye scanners to trace the pattern of blood vessels—computer facilities

Source: *Privacy Journal*

A SCIENCE AND TECHNOLOGY GLOSSARY

ARPA—The Defense Advanced Research Projects Agency is the foremost sponsor of research into computers and surveillance systems.

ARS—The Advanced Record System was designed by the General Services Administration to handle messages for government agencies; shortcomings in the system have prompted proposals to upgrade the ARS for computer communications.

Biocybernetics—The study of ways to link men and computers is now being sponsored by ARPA and other government agencies.

EFTS—Electronic Fund Transfer Systems are being used by banking and credit card companies to permit merchants and customers in widely dispersed areas to use central computers to handle financial transactions without cash.

Elsur—Electronic Surveillance comes in three basic forms: bugging picks up conversations via hidden microphones, wiretapping picks up conversations directly from telephone lines, and radio interception picks up messages sent by air including long-distance phone calls relayed by microwave towers.

message switching—New computer technology has made it possible for telecommunications networks to transmit and store messages across the country; the FBI wants to utilize this technology to coordinate state and local police information.

microwave—From ovens to telephones, the technology of using microwaves is making life more efficient; but when microwaves are used to relay long-distance telephone calls it becomes very easy for anyone with the proper radio equipment to listen in.

ZARF—This term is used to describe teams of military computer experts who test the security of computers by trying to penetrate supposedly secure systems—and usually do so.

Zenith—This code name was used to describe the efforts during the Nixon Administration to upgrade the White House computer operation.

Source: *Technospies*

"I won the Nobel Prize for Literature. What was your crime?"

MIND CONTROL & BEHAVIOR MODIFICATION

"The development of a refined technology of behavior control in modern society is inevitable. [By 1984] the means at hand will be more sophisticated and efficient than Orwell ever dreamed, and they will be in at least modest use... not by the will of tyrants but by the invitation of all of us, for we have been schooled to readiness for all these things and will demand their benign use regardless of their potential risk."

—Perry London, *Behavior Control*

THIS EXPERIMENT COULD REALLY HAVE BOMBED

In the spring of 1943, the Office of Strategic Services (OSS) had heard repeatedly that German scientists were experimenting with "truth drugs," specifically to get information from captured enemy agents. In retaliation, the OSS set up a "truth drug" committee.

Deciding that *cannabis indica* (marijuana) showed the most promise, the committee began a testing program using people involved with the Manhattan Project, the effort to build an atomic bomb.

A Project official says, "Our secret was so great, I guess we were safer than anybody else." A dozen test subjects were asked to swallow concentrated, liquid marijuana. The subjects all leaned over and vomited; they disclosed no secrets and one subject wound up in the hospital.

> *"It was fun, fun, fun. Where else could a red-blooded American boy lie, kill and cheat; steal, deceive, rape and pillage with the sanction and blessing of the All Highest?"*
> —CIA scientist George White, as quoted in
> *The Search for the "Manchurian Candidate"*

WHERE WAS MARCUS WELBY WHEN WE NEEDED HIM? THREE OF THE CIA'S MIND-CONTROL PIONEERS

Stanley Lovell first began conducting experiments for the intelligence community during the days of the OSS and began the government's search for a method of mind control. The Boston industrialist was dubbed "Dr. Moriarty" (after the fiendish professor in Sherlock Holmes stories) and was said to like the title.

One colleague said of him, "He could invent anything under the sun with great enthusiasm. I mean, he threw himself into inventing flying bats with fire bombs attached to their wings [authors' note: an actual World War II program] or whatever he invented, with such enthusiasm that it was infectious, and no scheme or no idea was too wild for him to consider."

Lovell said his job was "To stimulate the 'Peck's Bad Boy' beneath the surface of every American scientist and to say to him, 'Throw all of your normal law-abiding concepts out of the window. Here's the chance to raise merry hell.'"

George White, hired by Lovell, led the mind control search for two decades. A long-time Narcotics Bureau investigator (who was involved in busting Billie Holliday), White made a smooth transitionfrom confiscating drugs to distributing them. He workedwith a "Truth Drug Committee" at St. Elizabeth's Hospital in Washington, D.C. The committee experimented unsuccessfully with mescaline, scopalomine and marijuana on unwitting victims.

Under White, the CIA set up a safehouse in San Francisco for more testing of drugs on unwitting subjects, this time setting up a self-contained brothel with built-in bugging equipment. Things went so well, the Agency opened a branch office in Marin County and tested stink bombs, itching and sneezing powders and diarrhea inducers by secretly doping drinks, food or cigarettes.

In 1963, CIA Inspector General John Earman stumbled across the safehouses during a routine audit and succeeded in shutting them down despite the active opposition of rising CIA official Richard Helms, who had suggested such programs originally.

John Gittinger, a CIA psychologist, devised a Personality Assessment System which was used to try to gauge the trustworthiness of agents and potential agents. His system was hailed within intelligence circles, but, no one else could interpret the variables as well as he could, limiting the system's usefulness.

During the Cuban missile crisis, the White House called on Gittinger's psychological expertise to ask how Chairman Khruschev would react to American pressure. He later profiled the Shah of Iran and found him to be a brilliant but dangerous megalomaniac whose problems stemmed from an overbearing father, the humiliation of serving as a puppet ruler and his inability for many years to produce a male heir.

***

SONS OF THE PIONEERS

In 1971, the CIA's medical office prepared a profile of Daniel Ellsberg at the request of White House "Plumber" David Young. To get raw data, the White House authorized a break-in at the office of Ellsberg's psychiatrist, Dr. Lewis Fielding in Beverly Hills, California.

According to testimony by then-CIA director Richard Helms, this was the first time the CIA was asked to put together a psychological profile of an American citizen. Produced in the third week of August, 1971, the CIA study found that Ellsberg had been motivated by "what he deemed a higher order of patriotism."

Dr. Bernard Malloy, a CIA psychologist, said Ellsberg was a brilliant and highly motivated man who considered himself "as having a special mission. There's no suggestion that [Ellsberg] thought anything treasonous in his act." The White House was not pleased with the report.

***

UNCLE SAM AND THE ACID TRUTH

The CIA was convinced that the Russians were working on LSD when they started their own experiments. This concern extended to paranoia, although agents said they never saw direct proof of Soviet involvement with the drug.

When the Agency received intelligence from Switzerland claiming that Sandoz Laboratories was about to put 100 million doses of LSD on the market, the agency was prepared to buy the entire shipment. It was later discovered that the information was wrong; only 100 doses had been manufactured.

UNCLE SAM, HIPPIE

The CIA spent millions of dollars on LSD-related research at colleges and universities world-wide. According to LSD guru Timothy Leary, who participated in research when he was still a Harvard professor, "The CIA funded and supported and encouraged hundreds of young psychiatrists to experiment with this drug. The fallout was that the young psychologists began taking it themselves and discovered it was an intelligence-enhancing consciousness-raising experience."

***

LSD EXPERIMENTERS FUNDED BY THE CIA

- Harold Abramson—Mt. Sinai Hospital and Columbia University, New York
- Carl Pfeiffer—University of Illinois Medical School
- Harris Isbell—Addiction Research Center, Lexington, Ky.
- Louis Jolyon West—University of Oklahoma
- Harold Hodge—University of Rochester

Source: *The Search for the "Manchurian Candidate"*

***

UNCLE SAM AND THE ACID TRUTH 2

On Nov.19, 1953, Dr. Frank Olson of the Army Chemical Corps' Special Operations Division unknowingly ingested LSD put into a drink of Cointreau by a CIA doctor, according to *The Search for the "Manchurian Candidate"*. After a period of agonizing self-examination, he committed suicide on the 28th, jumping through a tenth floor window of New York's Statler Hotel.

CIA officials later told Olson's wife that he jumped or fell out the window, but never mentioned the LSD. Even Olson's closest co-workers let his wife believe the suicide was caused by stress. In June, 1975, the Rockefeller Commission finally revealed the CIA-LSD connection. After 22 years of silence, the U.S. government apologized and paid Mrs. Olson $750,000 in compensation.

***

LSD EXPERIMENTERS ALLEGEDLY FUNDED BY MILITARY SECURITY AGENCIES

- Amadeo Marrazzi—University of Minnesota and Missouri Institute of Psychiatry
- Henry Beecher—Harvard University and Massachusetts General Hospital
- Charles Savage—Naval Medical Research Institute
- James Dille—University of Washington
- Gerald Klee—University of Maryland Medical School
- Neil Burch—Baylor University
- Paul Hoch & James Cattell—New York State Psychiatric Institute

Source: *The Search for the "Manchurian Candidate"*

***

THEY PROBABLY HATED THE FOOD

According to *The Search for the "Manchurian Candidate"*, CIA and Navy scientists trained dolphins to attack enemy frogmen with huge needles attached to their snouts. The dolphins carried tanks of compressed air on their backs which would instantly kill the frogmen by forcing air into their lungs. A scientist confirms that dolphins were sent to Vietnam and a number went AWOL.

***

MEMORIES ARE MADE OF THIS

At a Gothic estate known as "Ravenscrag" in Montreal, Dr. Ewen Cameron conducted CIA-funded experiments at the Allan Memorial Institute of Psychiatry of McGill University, according to an ABC News Closeup called "Mission: Mind Control."

Cameron experimented in two areas that he called "psychic driving" and "depatterning." "Psychic driving" consisted of giving patients intensive electric shock treatment and injections (with drugs, one of which was LSD) in order to make the patient regress deeply and to become forgetful. Then Cameron would try to implant new ideas in the patient's mind.

After the first step was completed, Cameron would play endless tape recordings and give the patient more drugs to, in his words, "make direct, controlled changes in personality."

Cameron's "depatterning" experiments involved breaking up existing behavior patterns by means of intensive electroshock therapy with prolonged periods of sleep. He used this combined sleep-electroshock treatment on patients as long as 30 days and in one case, he kept a patient asleep for 65 days.

A follow-up study conducted by his successor showed that 60% of the patients who had undergone depatterning experienced amnesia for periods of anywhere from six months to 10 years.

***

"H" IS FOR HELPER

The U.S. Public Health Service Hospital in Lexington is the nation's main center for detoxification of heroin addicts. Its director in the '50s, Dr. Harris Isbell, was funded indirectly by the CIA to experiment on his captive audience with numerous drugs, many of them relatively untested, according to *The Mind Manipulators*.

Experimenters seemed to have no trouble finding recruits, however. According to testimony given a Senate subcommittee by former inmate James H. Childs, the volunteers were paid off with the narcotics they were supposed to be kicking.

Childs says, "You knock on this little door, and the guy would look out... and I would say, 'I want 15 milligrams.' He would say, 'Where do you want it? In your arm, your skin or your vein?' Everybody that was on the research... got the payoff of the drug." His testimony was corroborated by Edward M. Flowers who, at the time of the research and heroin payments, was 19 years old.

***

"The day has come when we can combine sensory deprivation with drugs, hypnosis, and astute manipulation of reward and punishment to gain almost absolute control over an individual's behavior."
—Prof. James McConnell of the University of Michigan in *Psychology Today*, April, 1970

ULTRA MANIPULATION

The MKULTRA Program, established in 1953, was the CIA's umbrella for finding "avenues to the control of human behavior" and is described in depth in *The Mind Manipulators* by authors Alan W. Scheflin and Edward M. Opton, Jr.

MKULTRA included research in anthropology, psychology, psychiatry, sociology, innocuous fields like lipreading and graphology, and the less innocuous—radiation, electroshock, or development of substances which would:

- "Promote illogical thinking and impulsiveness to the point where the recipient would be discredited in public."
- "Produce amnesia for events preceding and during their use."
- "Produce physical disablement such as paralysis of the legs, acute anemia, etc."
- "Alter personality structure in such a way that the tendency of the recipient to become dependent upon another person is enhanced."
- "Lower the ambition and general working efficiency of men when administered in undetectable amounts."

Under MKULTRA, CIA scientists also sought to develop a knockout pill which could "surreptitiously be administered in drinks, food, cigarettes, as an aerosol, etc., which will be safe to use, provide a maximum of amnesia, and be suitable for use by agent types on an ad hoc basis."

The ultimate goal was a material which can be "surreptitiously administered by the above routes and which in very small amounts will make it impossible for a man to perform any physical activity whatsoever."

The search for these seven substances formed the nucleus of only one of 149 MKULTRA subprojects.

***

"There will be in the next generation or so, a pharmacological method of making people love their servitude, and producing . . . a kind of painless concentration camp for entire societies."
—Aldous Huxley, quoted in
The Search for the "Manchurian Candidate"

I LOST IT AT THE MOVIES

In the summer of 1975, Dr. Thomas Narut of the U.S. Naval Hospital in Naples, Italy told a NATO conference on stress that the Navy was working on techniques to produce assassins who would be free of anxiety.

Author Peter Watson was present and later recounted the incident in *War On The Mind*. According to Watson, Dr. Narut told the conference that convicted murderers from military prisons were made to watch films of mutilations and industrial accidents repeatedly, with their eyes held open. After multiple exposure to such films, the subjects would supposedly become capable of killing with emotional detachment.

MEANWHILE, BACK IN THE U.S.S.R.

Uncle Sam is a neophyte in mind control compared to Uncle Ivan, as the following items about the Soviet Union will illustrate:

TRY A LITTLE TENDERNESS

Eight common Communist coercive methods for eliciting individual compliance, according to the U.S. Group for the Advancement of Psychiatry's 1956 special symposium on indoctrination:

Method	Variants	Effects
1. Enforcing trivial demands	• Enforcement of rules and schedules • Forced writing	• Develops habit of compliance
2. Demonstrating "omnipotence" and "omniscience"	• Confrontations • Demonstrating complete control over victim's fate • Tantalizing with possible favors	• Suggests futility of resistance
3. Occasional indulgences	• Unpredictable favors • Rewards for partial compliance • Promises of better treatment	• Provides positive motivation for compliance • Reinforces learning • Impairs adjustment to deprivation

4. Threats	• Of death, torture, or non-repatriation endless isolation and interrogation	• Cultivates anxiety
5. Degradation	• Prevention of personal hygiene • Filthy, infested surroundings • Taunts and insults • Denial of privacy • Demeaning punishments	• Makes continued resistance seem more threatening to self-esteem than compliance • Reduces prisoner to concern with "animal" values
6. Control of perception	• Darkness or bright light • No books or recreations • Barren environment • Monotonous food • Restricted movement	• Fixes attention on predicament • Fosters introspection • Frustrates all actions not consistent with compliance
7. Isolation	• Complete physical isolation • Semi-isolation • Isolation of small groups	• Develops intense concern with self • Deprives victim of social support • Makes victim dependent on interrogator
8. Induced debilitation and exhaustion	• Semi-starvation • Exposure • Exploitation of wounds • Sleep deprivation • Over-exertion	• Weakens physical and mental ability to resist

***

UNPERSONALITY

Telephone directories are in short supply in the Soviet Union. Accordingly, to locate an address or phone number one stops at a government-run "inquiry office."

Dissidents Alexander Ginzburg and Yuri Galanskov were tried for "circulating anti-state literature." After Pavel Litvinov's denunciation of the trial was broadcast in Russian on the BBC, many admirers tried to contact him in Moscow, according to *Soviet Dissidents*; however, when they went to the inquiry office, they were told tha⁺ no such person existed.

Litvinov once inquired about himself and received official notification of his non-existence. The notice informing him of this bad news was confiscated in a later search of his apartment.

***

"PLEASE GET UNDER THE COUCH, THE DOCTOR WILL SEE YOU NOW."

Soviet dissidents leave themselves open to government interpretation of their "mental illnesses." Commiting those acts not countenanced by the Russian government leads to typical "analyses" like the following:

Name	Symptoms	Diagnosis
Alexander Esenin-Volpin	• Writes and reads unorthodox poems	• Schizophrenia
Vladimir Bukovsky	• Organized exhibitions of Western artists; xeroxed Yugoslavian critique of Communist bureaucracy, *The New Class*	• "Lives in unreal world, reacts inadequately to the world around him"
Yuri Galanskov	• Collected material rejected by recognized publishing houses; printed selections in magazine	• Held for observation
Alexei Dubrovolsky	• Contributed to dissident magazines	• Held for observation
Victor Fainberg	• Publicly protested Soviet invasion of Czechoslovakia	• "Schizo-dissension, delusions of reform"

Natalya Gorbanevskaya	• Collection and dissemination of anti-social literature in *Chronicle of Current Events*	• "Deep psychopathy, possibility of sluggish schizophrenia"
Zhores Medvedev	• Wrote critique of discredited geneticist T.D. Lysenko; involved in two unrelated areas; science and "publicist activities"	• "Paranoid delusions of reforming society, split personality"
Mikhail Kukobaka	• Distributed copies of the Universal Declaration of Human Rights	• Suffered from "a mania for the reconstruction of society"

Source: *Soviet Dissidents: Their Struggle for Human Rights*

***

DEPARTMENT OF REMOTE POSSIBILITIES

Dr. Ralph Schwitzgibel of Harvard University is the Thomas Edison of remote control behavior modification. According to *The Mind Manipulators,* he has used wristwatch-like devices to monitor the pulse rates and locations of juvenile delinquents and recommends methods for keeping people away from at least two vice-ridden activities.

After the good doctor conditions a subject to get nauseous upon hearing a certain tone while drinking alcoholic beverages, that tone can be broadcast to him in a barroom via walkie-talkie.

Dr. Schwitzgibel also has a unique way to monitor sex offenders, which can also be used to keep tabs on athletes in training, priests in temptation, or anyone else in imminent danger of having a good time. His device, used in the laboratory to measure penile erection, can be linked to a portable transmitter to broadcast precisely where the action is.

***

"If we are going to lock up our old people, or our ugly people, or anyone else, we should do it without leaning on you... In the current clamor for law and order... our behavioral experts are willing to diagnose a wider and wider spectrum of so-called misfits as 'dangerous.' The effect is to implement a system of preventive detention and to ignore civil liberties."
—Chief Judge David Bazelon, D.C. Court of Appeals
to the American Psychiatric Association, July, 1970

WIRED WORLD OF SPORTS

In 1971, National Security Agency computer specialist Joseph A. Meyer took some of his "Puzzle Palace" training and sought to apply it to America's persistent crime problem, according to *The Mind Manipulators.*

Meyer suggested that the 25 million or so people who have been arrested (including traffic offenders) be made to wear electronic tracking devices or "externalized consciences" as he called them. These "transponders" would then communicate the location of potential perpetrators to regional computers.

Not only would possible crime targets like banks be alerted to danger in their vicinity, but the computerized records of each individual's whereabouts would make alibis impossible. "The aim," says Meyer, "is to constrain criminals and arrestees into behaving ... At night, they will stay close to home, to avoid being implicated in crimes."

Meyer even figured out a way to keep the ornery critters from removing the devices. In Meyer's wired wired world, such action would become a felony.

***

HE WAS JUST A LITTLE AHEAD OF HIS TIME

Hopefully, Meyer has had a chance to read that the city of Albuquerque is testing an "electronic leg iron" strapped to the ankle to keep track of the movements of probationers.

A story transmitted over the UPI wire on January 16, 1983 adds that the miniature radio transmitter, about the size of a pack of cigarettes, signals a receiver in the probationer's home. The receiver, plugged into a phone jack, sends a record of the subject's movements to a central computer, which prints out warnings whenever the probationer strays more than 1,000 feet from the receiver; the receiver can also tell if the transmitter is removed.

The device is being marketed by a company called National Incarceration Monitor and Control Services. If the six-month test is a success, the firm's Michael Goss says he hopes to be operating in several Western states in—you guessed it, 1984.

In a related matter, *The Texas Observer* reports that the Austin, Tex. police department has added a cattle prod to its repertory. The device, called "The Source" by its Florida manufacturer, delivers a 3500-volt shock and is currently being used by police in South Africa.

THIS ONE HAS A MONKEY ON HIS MIND

California isn't about to lose its status as a Big Brother trend-setter. Not if Robert Weigle, chief probation officer of Santa Clara County has his way. Weigle has proposed installing brain implants in recently released drug addicts to see if they are back on narcotics.

An AP story on March 18, 1983 quotes Weigle as saying, "There are a lot of moral and ethical questions that have to be answered, and I want to get the ball rolling." While not advocating the use of personality-altering drugs at the moment, Weigle says, "I wouldn't eliminate them either."

GREAT MILESTONES IN MIND CONTROL

1942

Spring—Gen. William "Wild Bill" Donovan, chief of the OSS, sets up a working group of psychiatrists and biochemists to find a drug to induce people "to tell the truth about matters where it would be contrary to [their] interests."

1943

May 24—Ex-narcotics agent George White experiments with "truth drugs" on behalf of the OSS, and, according to his diary, knocks himself out.

1944

March—Movie actress Frances Farmer is committed to a mental hospital by leading conservative Superior Court Justice John Frater of Washington state, after her mother complained about her playing the radio too loudly.

1948

Oct.—Walter Freeman, the "father of the lobotomy," performs the operation on Farmer at Western Washington State Hospital.

1949

Feb.—After months of imprisonment, culminating in hypnosis while under the influence of "SHE" (Scopalomine-Hukatine-Ephatomine) Josef Cardinal Mindszenty, Catholic Primate of Hungary, "confesses" to spying for the U.S.

1950

Apr. 20—CIA director Roscoe Hillenkoetter approves BLUEBIRD, an interrogation project teaming up a psychiatrist, a polygraph expert trained in hypnosis, and a technician. He authorizes the use of unvouchered funds to pay for the most sensitive areas of this behavior-control program.

Sept.—CIA employee and journalist Edward Hunter coins the term "brainwashing" in a Miami *Daily News* article on Chinese "thought reform." It soon becomes the explanation for disloyal statements by U.S. POW's held in North Korea.

1951

Dec.—As part of Project BLUEBIRD, Morse Allen of the CIA's Office of Security, proposes experiments with electroshock and electrically-induced sleep as aids to interrogation.

1952

Feb.—The CIA's Office of Scientific Intelligence proposes allocating $100,000 to develop neurosurgical techniques in connection with BLUEBIRD.

1953

Apr. 13—Director Allen Dulles approves a program using chemical and biological warfare in covert operations. He names it MKULTRA, gives it a $300,000 budget and orders the Agency's bookkeepers to pay the costs blindly.

June 18—A CIA memo indicates U.S. prisoners, recently released by North Korea, had a "blank period, or period of disorientation, while passing through a special zone in Manchuria."

Nov. 28—Dr. Frank Olson commits suicide after being given LSD by the CIA without his knowledge.

1961

June—The Army tests LSD on nine foreigners and a black American soldier named James Thornwell, who is accused of stealing classified documents. His captors threaten to "extend the state indefinitely, even to a permanent condition of insanity," according to Army documents. Thornwell later sued for $30 million.

1967

Apr. 7—Presidential aspirant George Romney says he got "the greatest brainwashing that anyone can get" from U.S. generals and diplomats in Vietnam. The remark effectively terminates his candidacy.

1972

Sept. 17—The New York *Times* reports that, under the sponsorship of the National Institute of Mental Health, an inmate at Maryland's Patuxent Prison is dosed with female hormones to correct "supermasculine aggressiveness."

1974

Jan.—Sen. Sam Ervin (D-N.C.), chairman of the Subcommittee on Constitutional Rights, questions the head of the Law Enforcement Assistance Administration (LEAA) on federal spending for psychosurgery and other behavior modification programs in the absence of clear guidelines for the protection of subjects.

Feb. 14—LEAA head Donald Santarelli announces cancellation of all funding for psychosurgery projects.

1976

Feb. 23—Former CIA drug experimenter Dr. L.J. "Jolly" West testifies on behalf of Patty Hearst. He says that she was subjected by the Symbionese Liberation Army to an ordeal much like that of the Korean War POW's who made false confessions of germ warfare use.

1979

Nov. 1—Calling forced medication "an affront to human dignity," Federal Judge Joseph A. Tauro rules in a suit filed by Boston State Hospital patients that a mental patient, unless violent, has the right to refuse tranquilizing medication.

CHAPTER 7

BIG BUSINESS & BIG BROTHER

"In the past you had to be famous or infamous to have a dossier. Today there can be a dossier on anyone. Information systems, with a seemingly limitless capacity for storing and sorting information, have made it practical to record and transfer a wealth of data on just about everyone."

—IBM board chairman Frank T. Cary,
as quoted in *Superspies*

SOME EMPLOYERS WHO HAVE INSISTED THAT THEIR WORKERS TAKE LIE DETECTOR TESTS

Adolph Coors, brewers
Carson Pirie Scott & Co., operators of Chicago department stores and restaurants
Foremost-McKesson drug and liquor distributors in San Francisco
Zayre's department stores (see below)
Gimbel's department stores
Alexander's department stores
Duane Reade Drugs, New York
U.S. Department of Defense
U.S. Central Intelligence Agency
U.S. National Security Agency
Peoples Drug Stores
Brink's Inc.
Avis Rent-a-Car System Inc.
Seven Eleven Food Stores
Chicago Art Institute
Sun Banks in Florida
Dart Drug Corp. in Washington, D.C. area
General Telephone & Electronics Corp.
Montgomery Ward & Co.
McDonald's Corp.
Quality Inns
Marshall Field & Co., Chicago

The New York *Times* recently reported that David Ivey, an assistant store manager, was awarded $250,000 in a Florida court case for his firing by Zayre's on the basis of a polygraph exam. Ivey was forced to take the test when $500 was found missing from a company safe. He failed; another employee, later found to be responsible, had passed with flying colors.

Source: *Privacy Journal*

***

14 COMPANIES THAT SELL PERSONAL INFORMATION

1. American Security Council (claims six million cards on "subversive" troublemakers from the '60s and '70s)
2. Church League of America (claims "largest and most comprehensive files on subversive activity, with the single exception of the FBI," collects news clippings and group literature)
3. Equifax Inc. (millions of subjective files based on interviews with neighbors and co-workers and on assumptions based on Zip Code and neighborhood appearance, for insurors and employers)
4. Industrial Foundation of America (15,000 records on workers' compensation claimants, for employers)
5. Inn-Guard Inc. (travelers with unpaid hotel bills, theft or destruction of hotel property)
6. Landlord Credit Data Service of America (files on tardiness in rent payments, objectionable pets or partying, for landlords)
7. Law Enforcement Intelligence Unit (LEIU) (25,000 or more cards on political dissidents and other suspects, for local police detectives and intelligence units; funded by government money)
8. Medical Information Bureau (11 million computerized medical codes, for insurance companies)
9. National Registry of Insurance Agents (Social Security numbers and names of agents indebted to insurance companies)
10. Professional Exchange Service Ltd. (non-paying medical patients)

11. Renters Reference of America (lists of desirable and undesirable tenants)
12. Risks International (claims to have files on terrorists in U.S. and abroad, for corporate clients)
13. Telident (lists of persons filing malpractice claims, for doctors)
14. Western States Crime Intelligence Seminar (disseminates information on "traveling criminals" to local police detectives)

Privacy Journal, Feb., 1980 adds that reports cost client companies anywhere from $6.50 to $50 depending on the depth of the information desired.

***

YOU'VE GOT TO GIVE THEM CREDIT

The Associated Credit Bureaus of America (ACB) is composed of over 2,000 credit bureaus and 2,000 collection agencies, according to *Superspies*. Together they maintain files on an estimated 120 million Americans—more information than has been collected by the FBI and the CIA combined. Each year, approximately 7,500,000 dossiers are exchanged among ACB members.

***

THE 10 COMMANDMENTS
OF DEBT COLLECTION

According to the Debt Collection Act of 1977 (Public Law 95-109), a debt collector shalt not:
1. Telephone you at a time or place he should know is inconvenient, or, unless you tell him otherwise, after 8 p.m. or before 9 a.m.
2. Call or write you if you have referred the matter to an attorney.
3. Call at your place of employment if your employer has told him that such calls are prohibited.
4. Tell your employer or your neighbor about your debt.
5. Threaten harm to you, your reputation or your property.
6. Use obscene or abusive language.

7. Advertise the debt to coerce payment.
8. Continuously ring your telephone or engage you repeatedly in conversation over the telephone. (See IRS Chronology, p.60.)
9. Fail to identify himself and his company or falsely identify himself.
10. Communicate with others using a postcard or a return address or any other language that indicates a debt is at issue.

Source: *Privacy Journal*

DON'T BUG THE CUSTOMERS

Warning that 1984 may be fast approaching, a Federal judge fined a suburban Baltimore automobile dealer $7,500 for bugging his showroom in order to eavesdrop on customers.

According to the Philadelphia *Bulletin*, June 9, 1974, Tommy Thompson, general manager of a Lincoln-Mercury dealership, pleaded no contest to a charge of illegal electronic surveillance before U.S. District Judge Joseph H. Young.

Young called the eavesdropping an "odious violation. 1984 may not yet be here, but we are approaching it," he said.

Thompson's lawyer, John Henry Lewin, told the judge that, according to street talk, "every automobile agency set up in metropolitan Baltimore in the last five years had electronic equipment installed so that salesmen could listen in on customers during bargaining over car prices."

***

NOW HEAR THIS

Department stores now can play high-speed, barely audible messages over loudspeakers to encourage shoplifters to desist.

This "subliminal communications" technique is being used by retailers, employers and others to modify behavior. The theory is that sounds too quiet for the ears to hear or sights too fast for the eyes to see can nevertheless register responses in the brain according to the Dec., 1980 issue of *Technology News of America*.

Behavioral Engineering Corp., a Metairie, La. company headed by Hal C. Becker, Ph. D., markets a service that plays programmed messages at a level just below that of the background music in a store or factory. A store message might say, "I need to buy that" or "I will not steal." In a movie theater, it might say, "Buy more popcorn" or "I am thirsty."

The messages can be repeated 3,000 times an hour.

YOU'LL NEVER SHOP ALONE—
14 L.A. BUSINESSES THAT WATCH EVERYONE

In its Sept., 1983 issue, *Los Angeles* magazine asked a number of local stores and cultural attractions if their premises were under electronic surveillance. Those who answered in the affirmative included:

Abercrombie and Fitch
Brentano's
CBS Television City
Disneyland
The Forum
Hollywood Park
Joseph Magnin
KABC TV Studios
MGM/UA Studios
Neiman-Marcus
Sheraton-Universal Hotel
Universal Amphitheater
Universal Studios
Zoetrope Studios

Those who had no comment included:

The Beverly Hills Hotel	The Hotel Bel-Air
Burbank Studios	The Norton Simon Museum
California Institute of Technology	The Rodeo Collection

***

COMPANIES THAT OVERHEARD EMPLOYEE PHONE CALLS IN PORTLAND, OREGON

Braniff Airlines
Continental Airlines
Doctors Official Telephone Service
GMA Research Corp.
General Services Administration (U.S.)
Hilton Reservation Service
Institute for Public Affairs Research
Internal Revenue Service
Northwest Natural Gas Co.
The Oregonian
Pacific Northwest Bell Telephone Co.
Pan Am
Police Emergency Communications
Portland General Electric Co.
Salem *Statesman*
Sears, Roebuck & Co.
Superior Answering Service
Tri-Met
United Airlines
Wallace Security Agency

This list was published by Willamette *Week*, a Portland area newspaper and reprinted in *Privacy Journal*, June, 1977. Under federal and state law, electronic surveillance is legal if one party to the conversation provides consent. An employer's decision to overhear conversations on office telephones has been regarded as adequate "consent."

Companies say they use the monitoring to assure that accurate and courteous service is being provided. In Georgia, users of such equipment must be listed publicly, but in Oregon and most other states, there are no such lists.

***

CORPORATE HEAD GAMES

A survey of 1,200 corporate executives conducted by the *Harvard Business Review* in 1974, revealed the following:

- 24 percent reported their firms used "locker searches"
- 46 percent use "package checks"
- 39 percent use "electronic surveillance of high risk areas"
- 52 percent use "personality tests that measure chracteristics"
- 10 percent use lie detector tests.
- 49 percent use "drug abuse detection checks"
- 10 percent use handwriting analysis in screening applicants

Source: *Mindcontrol*

***

COMPANIES THAT MONITOR CONVERSATIONS BETWEEN THEIR EMPLOYEES AND CUSTOMERS

Various companies (and government agencies like the IRS and Veterans Administration) listen in when their employees talk to customers. The practice is called "service monitoring" and is used by the following:

United Parcel Service
Continental Airlines
Pacific Telephone (and most of the Bell System operating companies)
Macy's
Sears, Roebuck & Co.
Avon Products
Atlanta *Constitution*
Portland *Oregonian*
Florida Power Corp.
Hilton Hotels
Insurance companies
Credit bureaus and collection companies
Major airlines

Source: *Privacy Journal*

SELECTED CATEGORIES OF PERSONS FOR WHOM COMMERCIAL MAILING LISTS ARE AVAILABLE

Some of the bigger mailing list companies are Dependable List, Dun & Bradstreet, Inc., Doubleday & Co., American Student Lists, *Newsweek, Time* and *Playboy.* The categories listed below and other classifications of people are readily available, usually for about five cents per name:

Women 35 to 44 years of age with teenagers, a cat and an interest in astrology

Scotch drinkers born in July

Seventh Day Adventists with more than one telephone

Persons purchasing sexual aids

Snowmobile owners in affluent census blocks

Donors to Democratic causes who consider themselves moderates

Girls in the Denver area between ages of 12 and 18 who respond to TV advertising (with telephone numbers)

Females 45 to 55 years old living in Nielsen "B" counties with incomes of $12-20,000 and a history of buying through the mail

Persons who supported Richard Nixon during the impeachment process and to the present

Persons who voted in the past four elections, along with party affiliation and telephone number, arranged in street order

Time magazine readers who are department heads and work in communications

Citizens against gun control and for abortion

Retired military officers who patronize religious book stores

Persons, by race and age, who have had wallpaper installed recently

Suburban families,with ages of each member and amount of recent mail purchases

Clergy in affluent zip codes

Scotch drinkers who have purchased sensual clothing

Any combination of the above

Sources: *Direct Mail Lists Rate & Data/Privacy Journal*

***

THIRD DOWN AND 110 TO GO

In addition to playing rough in the office, Big Brother is pretty hard-nosed on the gridiron. In "Pigskin Peeping" (*Privacy Journal*, Aug., 1975), William C. Strong reports that the NFL Player's Association has charged the National Football League with maintaining closed files on certain players, psychological testing, hiring ex-FBI agents to spy on players, etc.

Pete Gent, a former wide receiver for the Dallas Cowboys, wrote a novel, *North Dallas Forty*, about a player who is drummed out of the league after a hired investigator reports on his private life. Gent likens this episode to the summary firing and public humiliation of eight San Diego Chargers in 1974 for what NFL Commissioner Pete Rozelle called violation of the league's "drug code," a non-existent document Rozelle produced from his grab-bag of discretionary authority.

Rozelle sent two investigators to talk to Charger players, who had been assured that whatever information that emerged would be kept in-house. In a matter of days, eight players were notified they were in violation of the "NFL drug code." After persuading the players to waive a hearing, Rozelle issued a press release naming the players involved and their fines.

Gent says he was tailed during the 1967-68 season by a Dallas law enforcement officer and says fellow players were questioned in an effort to investigate his private life. Former player Rommie Loudd, later player personnel director for the New England Patriots, says he often solicited information from call girls, desk clerks, girl friends and anyone else who could shed light on a player's mental and physical condition.

The NFL's director of security, Jack Danahy, admits the NFL has agents in every football town to protect the players and league from organized gambling. He says he's never had a request from a player to see his file. Were he to receive such a request, he says, "I'll cross that bridge when I come to it."

***

"I think it's about time they take those cameras off the bank customers and aim them at the bank presidents."
—Johnny Carson, "The Tonight Show," August 10, 1977, on the investigation of Bert Lance, Director of the Office of Management and Budget under President Carter

IF YOU'VE GOT THE MONEY, HONEY...

Those automatic teller machines now sport cute (perhaps too cute) names like Tillie the Alltime Teller, Ginny the Green Machine, Buddy System, Sam the Superteller and All Day All Night Marianne, according to *The Nilson Report*, a newsletter for credit card executives.

Nevertheless, several of them also sport built-in cameras, according to *Privacy Journal*. One machine snaps a photo of the customer using the teller plus the time, date and transaction number. A competitive machine produces two photos, one at the beginning of the transaction, one at the end.

The photos were originally intended to stop fraudulent use of your bank card by people who find out your identification number. Now, they are kept on file for short periods of time and are also made available to law enforcement officials if the machine is damaged or there is reason to believe a crime has been committed.

CHAPTER 8

PRIVACY—AND OTHER RARITIES

"Privacy is no luxury. It's as indispensible as the dark earth where a seed hides itself before it sprouts into a plant or a tree. Or the quiet of the womb where life hides getting ready to sprout into a human being."

—From *First Monday in October*, by Jerome Lawrence
and Robert E. Lee, as quoted in *Privacy Journal*

LICENSED TO KILL

Privacy Journal reports that in 1978, a man who had been bothering a Tempe, Arizona woman discovered her name and address by taking her license plate number to the state Department of Motor Vehicles. He went to her home, shot and killed her and then committed suicide.

The woman's father, who witnessed the tragedy, campaigned in the state legislature for an amendment to the law that permitted easy access to motor vehicle information. In 1981, the Arizona legislature passed a law that in essence limits such information to organizations with proper identification.

In the past five years, California and Indiana have placed restrictions on the release of drivers' records. Similar legislation has been introduced in Kansas, Minnesota, New Jersey, New York, Oregon, Pennsylvania, Texas, and Vermont. Bills in Illinois and Iowa would prohibit the release of a person's age from state files, according to the Direct Marketing Association, the trade association of the direct-mail business.

JURY RIGGING

In the yellow pages of every major city's phone book are listings of perfectly respectable firms which will search to uncover the possible biases of prospective jurors, according to *Privacy Journal*.

These firms are generally listed as "Investigators," and, depending on the service, their costs range from $200 a day plus expenses on up. They guarantee discretion so that prospective jurors will never know that somebody has investigated them.

What gets searched? Everything that's public, according to Paul Mapes in the Los Angeles *Daily Journal*. Birth, death, marriage, political affiliation, occupation, schooling, credit rating, taxes paid, property owned, medical ailments, employment of relatives and whether or not the person was ever quoted in a local newspaper and what was said.

Things not in public records are also looked at. These can include: places a prospective juror frequents; whether he or she is a militant feminist, environmentalist, or conservative; ethnic background, prejudices and sexual preference. The extent of the inquiry depends upon available funds.

Godfrey Lehman of San Francisco has challenged these investigations as an invasion of privacy. During jury selection, Lehman refused to answer a lawyer's question about his occupation, claiming it was an unreasonable search under the Fourth Amendment. The judge threatened Lehman with a jail term for contempt, then struck him from the jury rolls.

The persistent Lehman got himself appointed to the Governor's Commission on Personal Privacy in California and was instrumental in having the Juror Privacy Act of 1983 introduced in the California legislature.

***

GREAT MOMENTS IN THE STORAGE OF SENSITIVE INFORMATION

1977: One of Charles Manson's female followers picks up credit card carbons from trash cans in California department stores and uses the information to order merchandise fraudulently.

April, 1978: A U.S. appeals judge says, "It seems more prudent to put only genuine trash, not secrets, in garbage cans," in upholding an FBI search of a man's trash that uncovered coin wrappers and coin trays and led to his convictions for stealing $3000 in coins from nearby banks.

September, 1978: An employee of the San Francisco Police Department records room is arrested after fellow police officers find in her home a police report naming her boyfriend as a criminal suspect. The report should have been filed in departmental files.

October, 1978: Payroll records of 24,000 employees of the Ontario Health Ministry are found in the garbage by two people who take them to a local radio station.

May, 1979: An investigative reporter finds account records, balance sheets, deposit slips, customers' monthly statements, and confidential bank memoranda in the trash bin in front of the Soviet-owned Eurobank in Paris.

June, 1979: MasterCharge records from the Bank of Montreal are found spilled on a street in Montreal. Included are names of persons refused credit cards.

1979: A Sydney, Australia, school teacher distributes computer paper for students to draw on. On the reverse side are confidential data prepared by a computer service company.

1980: For a month, police detectives segregate the garbage of one man from that of his neighbors in Milwaukee and find evidence of an illegal gambling operation.

February, 1981: Sailors pick through tons of rotting garbage to retrieve classified documents on nuclear propulsion that were mistakenly sent from the Orlando Naval Training Center to a dump, instead of to a paper shredder.

May, 1981: *Parade* magazine reports that hundreds of printouts with information about delinquent debts in upstate New York showed up as packing material for a shipment from Ohio. A credit bureau in New York had made the paper available to a trash collector, who apparently recycled it.

1981: A federal court in Illinois rules that a company may use as evidence in its price-fixing lawsuit against another company the correspondence between the defendant and its attorney. The first company found the letters after two years of monitoring the trashbin of the defendant. The court says that the defendant company could have found other means to dispose of the materials if it considered them sensitive.

February, 1982: A fellow of the International Institute for Applied Systems Analysis in Austria delivers a lecture at the University of Maryland on "Consumption and Rubbish in America." He is the author of *Rubbish Theory: The Creation and Destruction of Value.*

1982: A three-year-old boy is cited for littering because his name appears on an insurance form found in a trash bag dumped 22 blocks from his home in Philadelphia.

January, 1983: A New York man pleads guilty to fraudulent use of altered and stolen credit cards with the names of active customers. Information about the customers was gathered from carbons found in garbage cans behind retail stores.

Source: *Privacy Journal,* June, 1983

WE'D LIKE TO KNOW A LITTLE BIT ABOUT YOU FOR OUR FILES...

If a person wanted to find out whatever he could about you and build a dossier on you, here are some things he might do, according to Jules Archer in *Superspies:*

1. Obtain a copy of your driver's license to get your address, license number, height, eye color and age.
2. If he has you under surveillance or has your car's license number, he could find out through the department of motor vehicles about any arrests, where you are employed and how long you have been employed.
3. Through the county clerk's office, he could find out about loans from banks or finance companies, whether you have any judgments against you and what addresses you use.
4. Also through public files, he can check your birth certificate, marriage licenses, death notices (if you were dead), liquor licenses and police accident reports.
5. If you have an unlisted telephone number, he could get your address through the tax collector's office.
6. Checking with a finance company on the premise of a credit inquiry, he could find out your earnings, names and addresses of relatives and where you bank.
7. While still making a credit inquiry, he could direct inquiries to places where you shop or ask questions of your landlord.

QUESTIONS ONCE ASKED ON A WELFARE APPLICATION FORM IN SOUTH DAKOTA

"When and where did intercourse first occur?"
"Frequency and period of time during which intercourse occurred?"
"Was anyone else present?"
"If yes, give dates, names and addresses?"
"Were preventive measures used?"

Source: *Privacy, How to Protect What's Left of It*

> "The first thing to go in a totalitarian society is the right to privacy."
> —David F. Linowes, chairman of the Privacy Protection Study
> Commission, January 22, 1976, as quoted in *Privacy Journal*

HOW THE PROS DO IT

Years after the fact, former Nixon aide John Ehrlichman is still explaining why his approval of a covert operation to secure Daniel Ellsberg's psychiatric history did not *necessarily* mean authorizing a break-in. In an interview in Santa Fe, Ehrlichman said he merely "approved an operation to get information," according to *Privacy Journal*.

"I have tried personal injury cases for about 12 or 15 years for insurance companies," said the former Seattle attorney, "and when you do that it's important for you to know what the physical condition of the plaintiff is. One of the ways that you find out is to get the confidential records of the plaintiff. And the way you do that is the adjuster goes out, sweet-talks the nurse at the hospital, or hires a doctor who talks to the plaintiff's doctor and says, 'Can I look at Tillie Jones' records ?'

"There are probably 15 ways that insurance adjusters get a look at so-called privileged records. So, if you had asked me at the time, 'Is there a way for those fellows [the White House "Plumbers"] to do this without violating somebody's civil rights or breaking into somebody's office? I'd have said 'sure.' In my experience there are all kinds of ways."

***

WHAT UNCLE SAM TELLS EMPLOYERS ABOUT YOU

The armed services used to put a numerical code on each discharge certificate that indicated the reason for the discharge, even if it was voluntary. Veterans pointed out that the codes were subject to error and were often the reason that qualified veterans were denied employment.

In 1975, the armed forces began using Separation Program Designators (SPD). According to *Privacy Journal*, the new system does as much harm as the numerical codes due to the typing of military clerks. *KCC* means you were released due to a reduction in force beyond your control; *HKC* means homosexual misconduct. *KGM* means you left enlisted service to become an officer; *GMK* means you had "aberrant tendencies/sexual deviate, not homosexual."

There are persistent reports that the armed services surreptitiously circulate the code list to large employers so they may screen veterans without the applicants' knowledge.

CODE

BDK1—Military Personnel—Security Program
BFS1—Conduct Triable by Courts-Martial
BHJ1—Unsatisfactory Performance
BHK1—Substandard Performance of duty
BKC1—Misconduct Homosexual—(Class I)
BKC2—Misconduct—Homosexual—(Class II)
BKC3—Misconduct—Homosexual—(Class III)
BKE1—Misconduct—Chronic Default
BKK1—Misconduct—Drug Abuse
BMG1—Unsuitability—Alcohol—Abuse
BNC1—Unacceptable Conduct (Other)
BNC2—Unacceptable Conduct for Cause
CHK1—Substandard Performance of Duty
DFS1—Conduct Triable by Courts-Martial
FCM1—Conscientious Objector
GDK1—Military Personnel Security Program
GHJ1—Unsatisfactory Performance
GHJ2—Unsatisfactory Performance
GHK1—Substandard Performance
GKA1—Misconduct—Frequent Involvement

GKB1—Misconduct Conviction by Civil Authorities
GKC1—Misconduct—Homosexual (Class I)
GKC2—Misconduct—Homosexual (Class II)
GKC3—Misconduct—Homosexual (Class III)
GDK1—Misconduct—Absent Without Leave
GKE1—Misconduct—Chronic Default
GKF1—Administrative Separation of a Member Who has Deserted
GKG1—Misconduct—Fraudulent Entry
GKH1—Misconduct—Failure to Contribute
GKJ1—Misconduct—Shirking
GKK1—Misconduct—Drug Abuse
GKL1—Misconduct—Sexual Perversion
GMB1—Unsuitability—Personality Disorder
GMB2—Unsuitability—Personality Disorder
GMD1—Unsuitability—Inaptitude
GMG1—Unsuitability—Alcohol Abuse
GMH1—Unsuitability—Financial Irresponsibility
GMJ1—Unsuitability—Apathy, Defective Attitude or Inability to Expend Effort Constructively
GML1—Unsuitability—Homosexual tendencies
GMP1—Unsuitability—Unsanitary habits
GNC1—Unacceptable Conduct (Other)—Morally unqualified to perform
GNC2—Unacceptable Conduct—Unfitness
GPB1—Personal Drug Abuse

KEY

B—Discharge, General
C—Discharge under other than Honorable conditions
D—Bad Conduct Discharge
F—Dishonorable Discharge
G—Retirement Certificate (Excludes transfer to FMCR)

"In the beginning of my career—1932—I had a right to consider privacy my right—and so I fought for it. I thought the few people I knew could keep their mouths shut."
—Katharine Hepburn in Virginia Law Weekly,
DICTA, Vol. XVII #25, 1965

"When a reporter enters the room, your privacy ends and his freedom begins."
—Warren Beatty, telling the American Society of Newspaper Editors why he hasn't granted an interview in eight years, May, 1983

CALLING DR. KILDARE

A single data bank in Boston stores medical information on more than 13 million Americans—almost always without their knowledge.

According to *Privacy Journal*, the Medical Information Bureau was created as an alert system to warn insurers about potential insurance risks. 770 member companies continuously feed MIB coded data about health records, psychiatric disorders, drinking patterns and sexual behavior.

Senator William Proxmire (D-Wisc.) who headed a Senate sub-committee investigating MIB, said—only half jokingly—that if the White House had known about MIB, the "Plumbers" wouldn't have had to break in to get Daniel Ellsberg's records.

17 INVASION OF PRIVACY SUITS FILED BY FAMOUS PEOPLE OR THEIR FAMILIES

Muhammad Ali—stopped *Playgirl* magazine from running a drawing of a naked black boxer with a face almost identical to Ali's.

Ann-Margret—claimed a "skin magazine" misused a still photo of her from a movie in which she was partially nude.

Ed Asner—objected to the commercial use of a program he videotaped without fee under the assumption that it was to benefit a charity.

Johnny Carson—prevented an inventor from marketing "the world's foremost commodian," called "Here's Johnny."

Cher's father—claimed his daughter was wrong to reveal private facts in an interview.

Steve Garvey—settled out of court a magazine story about his marital problems.

Martin Luther King, Jr.'s heirs—prevented marketing of plastic busts of King without consent.

Hedy Lamarr—sued because the Mel Brooks' film *Blazing Saddles* made fun of her name.

Nathan Leopold—objected to a fictionalized account of the "thrill killing" of which he was convicted in a notorious Chicago trial in 1924.

Bela Lugosi's heirs—claimed they had a right to control future profits from the Count Dracula character he became identified with in the 30s.

Marilyn Monroe's heirs objected to portrayal of her in Norman Mailer's book *Marilyn*.

Ralph Nader—won damages from General Motors Corp. for hiring Fidelifacts' gumshoes to follow him and pry into his personal life.

Joe Namath—tried to prevent *Sports Illustrated* from using an action photo as part of a subscription promotion offer.

Jacqueline Kennedy Onassis—required a zealous photographer to keep his distance from her and her two children.

Elvis Presley's heirs—claimed profits from souvenirs with the singer's likeness.

Brooke Shields—sought to prevent use of photographs after her mother consented to their use.

Warren Spahn—collected damages from the publisher of a biography for young readers, that fictionalized aspects of his childhood and married life.

Source: *Privacy Journal*

***

AND BRING A NOTE FROM YOUR MOTHER

According to federal law, parental consent is required before school children can be asked about these areas in psychological testing:

- political affiliations
- psychological problems potentially embarrassing to the family
- sex behavior or attitudes
- illegal or anti-social behavior
- privileged relationships, as with clergy, doctors and lawyers
- family income

Source: Public Law 95-561

NOT TO MENTION THE HOLE IN THE DOUGHNUT...

The current Supreme Court feels the only areas of life considered worthy of privacy protection are these, according to *Privacy Journal*:

- procreation of children
- the rearing and education of children
- family life
- contraception
- the results of employment testing (maybe)

The Court has excluded from privacy protection the following: financial and tax information, homosexual and extramarital sexual activity, the drug prescriptions one uses, one's reputation in the community if not convicted of a crime.

***

GREAT MOMENTS IN ELECTRONIC SURVEILLANCE

1934: U.S. Supreme Court rules that telephone conversations are not protected by the Constitutional amendment against unreasonable searches and seizures. Only material things are protected. In dissent, Justice Louis Brandeis calls "The right to be let alone" the most comprehensive of rights and the right most valued by civilized man."

1934: In response, Congress passes the Federal Communications Act prohibiting the interception of telephone messages.

1961: The Supreme Court rules that intangibles, like conversations, may not be seized without a warrant, in effect reversing the 1934 case. The 1961 case involved a "spike mike" inserted several inches into the wall of a suspect's house.

1965: A witness before a Senate committee demonstrates an olive with a tiny transmitter in the center and an antenna for a toothpick, the first bug-in-the-martini.

1966: The Court sets out strict Constitutional guidelines for electronic surveillance by police, saying New York state's wiretap law isn't precise enough.

1967: The Court refutes the government's position that it may wiretap (without a warrant) a place like a telephone booth where there is not "expectation of privacy." The Constitution protects people, not places, says the Court.

1968: In response, Congress passes Title III of the Omnibus Crime Control Act, which permits the government to wiretap if it has a warrant, where there is consent or an emergency, or where the President is protecting the nation's security. The law prohibits non-consensual eavesdropping by private parties and bans the manufacture, sale, possession, or advertising of devices for that purpose.

1969: The Nixon Administration takes office, announcing its intention to utilize Title III to the maximum extent.

1972: The Supreme Court rejects the Administration's argument that it may use warrantless taps to investigate domestic groups that it views as a threat to the national security.

1972: Burglars representing the President's reelection campaign are caught installing listening devices in the Democratic National Committee office at the Watergate building.

1972: The market in electronic eavesdropping equipment sold to law enforcement reaches $400 million a year, according to the Electronics Industry Association. Most of the money comes from the Law Enforcement Assistance Administration, U.S. Department of Justice.

1976: A national commission created to study Title III reaffirms electronic surveillance as "an indispensible aid to law enforcement," but "a substantial minority" of the commission says, "Seven years of experience with the statute have cast serious doubt on that presumption."

1978: The Supreme Court rules that a "pen register," a device attached to a telephone to record numbers dialed to it is not subject to restrictions of Title III or any other law as long as there is no trespass when it is installed.

1978: Congress passes the Foreign Intelligence Surveillance Act to make sure that federal intelligence agencies get the consent of a special court before installing electronic surveillance even to protect national security.

1979: The FBI devotes $447,000 and 56 days wiretapping 700 persons as part of its BRILAB investigation of official bribery and racketeering in Louisiana. Eventually, two officials were convicted.

1982: The Supreme Court rules that police do not have to follow constitutional guidelines when attaching a tiny magnetized transmitter—a "bumper beeper"—to a vehicle under suspicion.

Source: *Privacy Journal*

***

"The Officers of Congress may come upon you now fortified with all the terrors of paramount federal authority... They may, unless the general government be restrained by the bill of rights,... go into your cellars and rooms, and search, ransack and measure every thing you eat, drink, and wear. They ought to be restrained within proper bounds."
—Patrick Henry, June 14, 1788

***

12 CITIES WITH "RED SQUADS"

Police departments of these twelve large cities regularly keep "dissidents" under surveillance:

New York
Chicago
Los Angeles
San Diego
Philadelphia
Washington
Seattle
Baltimore
Detroit
Memphis
Indianapolis
Houston

Source: *Privacy Journal*

6 PROPOSALS TO COMPUTERIZE AND CONSOLIDATE ALL THE GOVERNMENT'S PERSONAL INFORMATION

1. Federal Data Center (Bureau of the Budget, 1965)—This proposal was the outgrowth of a commission studying how to make the government's collection of personal information more efficient.
2. National Data Center (1966)—A variation of the original proposal, this proposal grew out of hearings chaired by Rep. Cornelius Gallagher (D-N.J.) who was very critical of it. Social critic Vance Packard testified and called it "a depersonalization of the American way of life."
3. FEDNET (Also called the "New Equipment Project" by the General Services Administration in 1974)—Uncle Sam's housekeeping arm suggested this as a way to consolidate the government's information systems; President Ford vetoed it in 1976.
4. AIDS (Automated Integrated Digital Services, 1976)—When FEDNET bit the dust, the GSA floated the proposal again under a different name, and Ford vetoed it again.
5. National Recipient System (Department of Health and Human Services, 1981)—This Reagan administration plan originated in the Department of Health and Human Services. Under the proposal, there would be a central government file for anyone receiving government assistance of any kind. After the plan was leaked to the House Ways and Means Committee, it created a furor and died a quiet death.
6. Long-Term Computer Matching Project (President's Council on Integrity and Efficiency, 1982)—The Inspectors General of every government department proposed that they prevent waste and fraud by exchanging computer media. Sen. William Cohen (R-Me.) pointed out correctly that, "Computer matching is just another way of creating a Federal Data Center."

Source: *Privacy Journal*

***

THE ACLU'S LIST OF 23 AGENCIES
THAT SPIED ON CITIZENS IN 1975

The American Civil Liberties Union says the following government agencies spent some of your 1975 tax dollars spying on you, according to the Los Angeles *Times*, Apr. 10, 1975.

1. FBI
2. CIA
3. IRS
4. U.S. Postal Service
5. Secret Service
6. Defense Mapping Agency
7. Defense Contracting Audit Agency
8. Army Criminal Investigation Command
9. Administrative Services Section, Joint Chiefs of Staff
10. National Security Agency
11. Bureau of Alcohol, Tobacco and Firearms
12. Naval Investigative Service
13. Defense Intelligence Agency
14. Defense Nuclear Agency
15. Defense Security Assistance Agency
16. Defense Supply Agency
17. Defense Civil Preparedness Agency
18. Defense Advance Research Projects Agency
19. Defense Investigative Service
20. Department of the Air Force
21. 502d Army Security Agency Group
22. Office of Deputy Chief of Staff for Intelligence
23. Investigation and Police Information Division, U.S. Army, Europe

"*This* is the unbiased, unslanted, tell-it-like-I-say-it-is news . . . ."

MEDIA: THE MINISTRY OF INFORMATION

"Personal secrets should stay secret almost all the time, while state secrets ought to stay secret almost never."

Nicholas Von Hoffman, Washington *Post*, September 22, 1976

THE ENEMY WITHOUT

The following books might not have been written if the Freedom of Information Act had not required the government to disclose information to the authors:

The Yellow Book Road: The Failure of America's Roadside Safety Program by Center for Auto Safety (1974)

The Lemon Book: How Not to Get Ripped Off When You Buy a Car, What to Do When You Get Ripped Off Anyway by Center for Auto Safety (1980)

Pills That Don't Work by Public Citizen Health Research Group (1981)

The Search for the "Manchurian Candidate" by John Marks (1977) *

The U.S. Crusade in China: 1943-1947 by Michael Schaller (1979)

Korea: The Untold Story of War by Joseph C. Goulden (1982)

China, American Catholicism and the Missionary by Thomas Breslin (1980)

Sideshow: Kissinger, Nixon and the Destruction of Cambodia by William Shawcross (1979) *

Bitter Fruit: The Untold Story of the American Coup in Guatemala by Stephen Schlesinger and Stephen Kinzer (1982)

Roosevelt and the Isolationists, 1932-1945 by Wayne Cole (1980)

Errol Flynn: The Untold Story by Charles Higham (1980)

Bodyguard of Lies by Anthony Brown (1975), about Hitler's reaction to D-Day

The Oil Cartel Case: A Documentary Study of Antitrust in the Cold War Era by Burton Kaufman (1978)

Strategies of Containment by John Lewis Gaddis (1982)

Ike's Spies by Stephen Ambrose and Richard Immerman (1981)

Perjury: The Hiss-Chambers Case by Allen Weinstein (1978)

Report on Human Rights in El Salvador by American Civil Liberties Union (1982)

Our Father Who Art in Hell: The Life and Death of Jim Jones by James Reston, Jr. (1980)

The Age of Surveillance by Frank J. Donner (1981) *

Spying on Americans: Political Surveillance from Hoover to the Huston Plan by Athan Theoharis (1978) *

The FBI and Martin Luther King Jr. by David Garrow (1981) *

China Scapegoat: The Diplomatic Ordeal of John Carter Vincent by Gary May (1979)

Puzzle Palace: A Report on America's Most Secret Agency by V. James Bamford (1982) *

(Editors note: Those books asterisked were particularly useful in the compilation of this book and the 1984 Big Brother Calendar, Price/Stern/Sloan, 1983.)

Source: *Former Secrets*

THE ENEMY WITHIN: 6 STORIES NOT PRINTED BY THE NEW YORK *TIMES* AT GOVERNMENT REQUEST

1. U-2 Flights Over Russia

The *Times* had knowledge of the U-2 flights *before* a plane was downed over Russia on May 1, 1960. In his memoirs, *On Press*, reporter Tom Wicker explains, ''Withholding publication in those days [seemed] responsible, since publication would have put an end to the profitable flights or resulted in a U-2 being shot down.''

2. Cuban Missile Crisis

A personal appeal from President Kennedy caused the fact that operational Soviet missile bases had been discovered in Cuba to be withheld from print. Kennedy first called Washington bureau chief James Reston, who advised the President to phone publisher Orvil Dryfoos. Dryfoos asked Reston and others their opinions, and the decision was made not to publish.

3. CIA Training of Tibetan Guerillas

Shortly after John McCone became DCI in December, 1961, the *Times* learned that the CIA was training Tibetan paramilitary units in Leadville, Co. for a possible invasion of Communist China. The Office of the Secretary of Defense "pleaded" with the paper to kill the story which it did. The Colorado Springs *Gazette Telegraph* subsequently ran the story on Dec. 7th, and the resultant furor caused the operation to be dropped.

4. The Bay of Pigs Invasion

On April 6, 1961, the *Times* had a story by Tad Szulc asserting that a Cuban exile army was being trained under CIA auspices in the U.S. and Central America for an "imminent" invasion. Managing editor Turner Catledge conferred with Reston, who declared the invasion was *not* imminent and, with Dryfoos' consent, changed a four-column headline to a one-column headline, deleted mention of the CIA and removed the "imminent" angle from his own reporter's story (but ran a mention of Stuart Novins' similar report on CBS Radio.)

President Kennedy later told Catledge and Dryfoos that "if you had printed more about the operation you would have saved us from a colossal mistake."

5. The Glomar Explorer

In 1973, a CIA official mentioned Project Jennifer to reporter Seymour Hersh, who learned about an attempt to pick up Russian intercontinental ballistic missiles test-fired into the Indian Ocean. Involved in the breaking Watergate story, Hersh forgot about it until CIA Director William Colby called him about Jennifer in February, 1974. Colby visited the *Times'* Washington bureau and was forthcoming about Watergate and related matters but asked Hersh to check with him if he intended to pursue Jennifer again.

A break-in at Howard Hughes' Los Angeles headquarters on June 5th was reported in the Los Angeles *Times* and partially revealed that the CIA had financed construction of the Glomar Explorer. (Two CIA officials persuaded Los Angeles *Times* editor William Thomas to downplay the story for reasons of national security.)

Hersh read the item, notified Colby he was on the story again and flew to Los Angeles to dig for details. Colby called publisher Arthur Sulzberger and told him of the Los Angeles *Times'* patriotic downplaying of the Glomar story. Sulzberger conferred with Managing Editor Abe Rosenthal who found that Hersh was not quite ready to write the story anyway.

He *was* ready early in March and was stunned to hear Rosenthal say it would be wrong to publish because of an "on-going intelligence operation" and suggested holding it. Washington bureau chief Clifton Daniel relayed the decision to Colby who even got a letter from the *Times* agreeing to hold the story. (Colby was equally successful in stalling *Time* magazine, the Washington *Post* and *Star*, NBC, ABC, *Newsweek* and *Parade*.)

Jack Anderson's colleague, Les Whitten, got wind of the story on March 18th and decided to have Anderson go with it that night on his radio program, informing Hersh of his ultimate decision (and following up on some leads provided by Hersh.)

When Daniel confirmed that Anderson would break the story before the *Times'* first edition hit the street, he decided to publish Hersh's account in the editions of March 19th.

6. Attempted Assassinations of Foreign Leaders

On January 16, 1975, President Gerald L. Ford had lunch with seven *Times* editors and reporters, Press Secretary Ron Nessen and Alan Greenspan, chairman of the Council of Economic Advisers in the Family Dining Room of the White House.

Rosenthal asked about the make-up of the Rockefeller Commission, recently named to investigate the CIA in the wake of Hersh's articles about domestic spying and other sordid matters. Ford used the word "assassination" and said he wanted to keep the Commission out of foreign affairs because such investigation would "blacken the name of every president back to Harry Truman."

Rosenthal and reporter Tom Wicker wanted to publish the story. Washington bureau chief Clifton Daniel, columnist James Reston and editorial page editor John B. Oakes felt the lunch was off the record. After some debate (and Wicker and Rosenthal's voiced misgivings), Daniel called Nessen for a decision as to whether the lunch was on the record. Nessen vociferously denied that it was, and the story was killed. Daniel Schorr broke it on March 1st on CBS and alluded to the *Times'* luncheon in the telling.

CIA & THE MEDIA

Watergate reporter Carl Bernstein examined the relationship between CIA and media in a 1977 article for *Rolling Stone* and outlined consistent co-operation as concerns spreading disinformation in foreign circles, disseminating "black propaganda" (see CIA Dictionary, p.16), introducing "Company" agents to potential foreign spies and passing money or information to spies already active.

According to Bernstein, some 400 media people held the positions indicated as of 1977 and were involved with the CIA including:

4 Key Executives

William Paley—CBS board chairman
Henry Luce—founder and president of Time, Inc.
James S. Copley—owner of the San Diego *Union* and *Tribune*
    plus numerous daily newspapers in Illinois
Hedley Donovan—editor-in-chief, *Time* magazine

3 Top-Level Liaisons

C.D. Jackson—publisher of *Life* and a Time, Inc. vice president
Ted Koop—CBS News Washington bureau chief
Sig Mickelson—president of CBS News from 1954-1961, who
    supervised the delivery of unedited film to the CIA.
    Mickelson's successor, Richard Salant, and Washington *Post*
    vice president John Hayes served on a secret CIA task
    force on beaming U.S. propaganda to Chile.

Identified as Operatives

Frank Kearns—CBS-TV reporter 1958-1971
Austin Goodrich—CBS stringer
Seymour K. Freidin—London bureau chief for Hearst
    newspapers

Valuable Assets (Not Necessarily Paid)

Jerry O'Leary—Washington *Star* reporter, who worked
    in "assessing and spotting agents."
Hal Hendrix—Miami *News* correspondent, won a Pulitzer prize
    for reporting the Cuban missile crisis. Also, he got Lee

Harvey Oswald's name one hour after John Kennedy's
assassination and was active with ITT's affairs in Chile.
C.L. Sulzberger—New York *Times* columnist
Joseph Alsop—columnist who said, "Dick Bissell (see p.15)
was my best friend from childhood."
Stewart Alsop—columnist and ex-OSS member who had "a
formal relationship."

While many of these connections were revealed in the mid-'70's,
Bernstein maintains the Church Committee and then-CIA Director George Bush made deals to avoid deep digging. Investigators
were allowed to inspect only 25 of the 400 files on journal ists with
"ties," and those were sanitized. According to an unpublished
report by the House Select Committee on Intelligence, at least 15
news organizations were still providing cover for the Agency in
1976.

In *The CIA and the Cult of Intelligence*, Victor Marchetti says the
Agency regularly debriefed three reporters after they had travelled
abroad—Joseph Alsop, Harrison Salisbury of the New York *Times*
and Drew Pearson.

Finally, there are no less than four syndicated newspaper columnists who used to toil at the Pickle Factory. The former CIA columnists are William F. Buckley (see p.38); Lewis H. Lapham, editor
of *Harper's* magazine; high-ranking former CIA official Cord Meyer;
and Tom Braden, who is also a local TV and radio personality in
Washington, D.C.

"THIS IS THE BBBS, THE BIG BROTHER BROADCASTING SYSTEM"

In *The Image Empire*, Erik Barnouw reveals that an hour before President Kennedy first addressed the nation about the Cuban missile
crisis, press secretary Pierre Salinger called ten radio stations and
told them the federal government wanted emergency use of their
facilities for an indefinite time.

They were astonished to learn that AT&T had *already* made the
arrangements. The stations were WCKR, WGBS and WMIE, Miami;
WKWF, Key West; WSB, Atlanta; WWL, New Orleans; WCKY,
Cincinnati; KAAY, Little Rock; and shortwave stations WRUL,
Scituate, Mass., and KGEI, San Carlos, Calif.

4 JOURNALIST BREAK-INS DURING THE NIXON YEARS

1. Dan Rather, CBS News White House correspondent: On April 9, 1972 at 1 a.m., Jean Rather, wife of the reporter, was awakened in their Georgetown home. Lights and the telephone were not operating. Armed with a shotgun, Rather confronted one of the burglars, who escaped. Later, police discovered fuses had been removed from the house's fuse box and two file cabinets had been opened. Removed from the cabinets were notes and scripts from interviews he had conducted in the Johnson years. The burglars left two TV sets, a hi-fi and a purse containing $100. The case has never been solved.

2. Marvin Kalb, CBS News diplomatic correspondent: Kalb's broadcast booth in the CBS studio in the State Department building was broken into twice in July, 1973. The only clue came from a colleague, who claimed two General Services Administration guards were seen in a nearby office.

3. Tad Szulc, New York *Times*: On the evening of Feb. 10, 1973, Szulc and his wife were dining with friends when his son telephoned to say "something strange" was going on in their house and that Szulc's bedroom door was locked from the inside. When he got home, Szulc broke down the bedroom door and found the room totally ransacked. Six dollars, a diamond stickpin and an old English coin were missing.

4. Thomas Kiernan, author: In early November, 1975, someone broke into Kiernan's Manhattan apartment and stole the only copy of a 382-page handwritten manuscript for a book Kiernan was writing on Nixon confidant Bebe Rebozo. The burglars also removed supporting documents and 16 tape-recorded interviews Kiernan had conducted during his research. His apartment was ransacked just one day after the author told his typist that the manuscript was ready for her; Kiernan believes the burglars tapped his telephone.

Source: *The American Police State*

***

JOURNALISTS TAPPED
ON BOBBY KENNEDY'S ORDERS

1. Mary McGrory, nationally syndicated columnist.
2. Roland Evans and Robert Novak, nationally syndicated columnists.
3. The entire New York *Times'* Washington staff.

Source: *Spooks*

5 WAYS NIXON TRIED TO GET JACK ANDERSON

1. Put him under physical surveillance
2. Tapped his suspected sources
3. Used CIA agents for round-the-clock surveillance of his house
4. Searched FBI files for blackmail material
5. Investigated Charles Colson's suggestion that Anderson be drugged so he would be incoherent on his live radio show. Colson advised rubbing the steering wheel of his car with a drug that would enter his skin. (Howard Hunt suggested killing Anderson, but this idea was not taken seriously.)

Source: *The New Muckrakers*

10 PRESS PEOPLE BEATEN BY CHICAGO POLICE DURING THE DEMOCRATIC CONVENTION (AUGUST 24-30, 1968):

August 24
1. Lawrence Green—Chicago *Daily News,* clubbed on the back.
2. John Culhane *Newsweek,* hit repeatedly on the thigh.
3. James K. Davis—*Life,* kicked in the leg, clubbed on the shoulder.
4. Frederick DeVan III—*Life,* had camera destroyed.

August 25
5. Claude Lewis—Philadelphia *Evening Bulletin,* clubbed four or five times on the head.
6. James Peipert—Associated Press, struck repeatedly on the back of the head.

August 26

7. Charles Pharris—ABC, struck on the back, had his camera broken.
8. Art Shay—*Time*, clubbed on the head.
9. Brian D. Boyer—Chicago *Sun-Times*, shoved and arrested without cause.
10. Barton Silverman—New York *Times*, billy clubbed and arrested for "interference in police actions."

The Walker Commission Report on the Chicago riots found that 49 newsmen were "hit, maced or arrested, apparently without reason, by the police" during the week of violence. In more than 40 documented cases, they were clearly indentifiable as news people. 22 reporters, 23 photographers and four members of TV crews were involved. In 10 incidents, police officers deliberately broke photographic or recording equipment.

Source: *Rights In Conflict*

TIME (INVISIBLE) INK: 9 PUBLICATIONS USING SECRET INK CODING ON QUESTIONNAIRES

According to *Privacy Journal*, these magazines and newspapers guaranteed anonymity to subscribers answering their marketing questionnaires; however, the respondents were totally unaware that the forms were imprinted with invisible ink. The overprinting allowed staff people to identify precisely everyone answering.

> *Wall Street Journal*
> *Barron's*
> *The National Observer* (defunct)
> *Fortune*
> *Reader's Digest*
> *Time*
> *Saturday Review*
> *Scientific American*
> *New York*

U.S. News & World Report uses a visible code; *Newsweek* abandoned codes in 1969 after consumer complaints. Some publications code by using the return envelope flap, the postage stamp or a telltale cut of the paper.

6 STARLETS HOWARD HUGHES PLACED UNDER SURVEILLANCE

Jean Peters—whom he subsequently married.
Elizabeth Taylor
Ava Gardner
Sophia Loren
Janet Leigh
Anne Bancroft

Source: *Spooks*

DOUBLY UNSPEAKABLE

The National Council of Teachers of English is doing its part to resist the degeneration of political discourse with its annual Doublespeak Awards.

Dr. William Lutz of Rutgers University told *The Big Brother Book of Lists* the award is ''an ironic tribute to American public figures who have perpetrated language that is grossly unfactual, deceptive, evasive, euphemistic, confusing or self-contradictory.''

Here are sample winners for the last three years:

1980

The winner was President Ronald Reagan for campaign oratory described as ''filled with inaccurate assertions and statistics and misrepresentations of his past record.'' The Los Angeles *Times* and *Time* magazine ''listed some 18 untrue or inaccurate public statements'' by Mr. Reagan. As the New York *Times* noted, Mr. Reagan ''doesn't let the truth spoil a good anecdote or effective symbol.''

President Jimmy Carter was runner-up for saying of the attempt to rescue the hostages in Iran, ''There is a deeper failure than that of incomplete success, and that is a failure to attempt a worthy effort, a failure to try.'' Lutz comments, ''He says we managed to avoid the worse failure, and, in fact, the failure we did have was a 'success.' This is a good example of doublespeak, language which pretends to communicate but doesn't. Failure equals success is the basic message we're getting here.''

Third place went to the Nuclear Regulatory Commission for listing 19 accidents at nuclear power plants as one ''abnormal occurrence'' if they stem from a common reactor design problem. Another ''abnormal occurrence'' occurred so frequently (12 times) that it was called a ''normally expected occurrence.''

1981

The winner was former Secretary of State Alexander Haig for his description of the murders of three American nuns and a religious lay worker in El Salvador: "I'd like to suggest to you that some of the investigations would lead one to believe that perhaps the vehicle that the nuns were riding in may have tried to run a road-block or may have accidentally been perceived to have been doing so and there had been an exchange of fire and then perhaps those who inflicted the casualities sought to cover it up."

Lutz comments, "Casualties are wounds or deaths inflicted by accident in a war. These women were shot in the head at close range, and at least two were raped. These 'casualties' involve the first accidental rape in history, as far as I know."

1982

The winner was a Republican National Committee commercial showing a postman delivering Social Security checks and saying "They included the 7.4 percent cost-of-living raise that President Reagan promised."

Lutz says, "In fact, the cost-of-living increases had been provided automatically by law since 1975 and President Reagan tried three times to roll them back or delay them but was overruled by congressional opposition." He added that a Republican official asked the Chicago *Tribune*, "Since when is a commercial supposed to be accurate? Do women really smile when they clean their ovens?"

The group also gives a George Orwell Award for Distinguished Contributions to Honesty and Clarity in Public Language. Recent winners include: *Hucksters in the Classroom: A Review of Industry Propaganda in the Schools* by Sheila Harty (1980), *Language-The Loaded Weapon* by Dwight Bolinger (1981) and *Nukespeak: Nuclear Language, Visions and Mindset* by Stephen Hilgartner, Richard C. Bell and Rory O'Connor (1982).

LINGUISTIC MUTATION

No discussion of doublespeak would be complete without mentioning the nuclear industry. Perhaps because nuclear realities are so horrifying to contemplate, atomic authorities have been among the world's most prolific generators of doublespeak.

The mutation of the nuclear vocabulary is well documented in *Nukespeak* (see above). In the book, Hal Stroube, PR strategist for Pacific Gas & Electric, explains that finding "palatable synonyms" for "scarewords" like "criticality," "poison curtain" and "maximum credible accident," "make[s] our job of public understanding more difficult."

"Public understanding" must have taken a back seat to "palatability" in the Energy Department's selection of names for underground nuclear tests. Since "Edam" in 1975, cheeses have been the favorite atomic appellations, ultimately culminating in a one-megaton "Muenster." Similarly, varieties of grapes and cocktails were popular in naming '60's blasts.

Energy Department policy dictates that names, besides being easy to pronounce, should not "connote or imply aggressiveness, a relation to war, weapons or explosives, the military . . . [or] reflect on weapons programs." Accordingly, the next generation of tests will be denoted by kinds of pasta. "Shells" will not be used for obvious reasons.

Always looking on the bright side, the AEC measures fallouts in S.U.'s, or, Sunshine Units, the ratio of Strontium-90 (which gathers in the bones) to calcium. Explains Gordon Dunning of the AEC's Biology and Medicine Division to a Congressional hearing on "Project Sunshine," "You have to have some unit."

MY LAI AND THE MEDIA

On March 16, 1968, U.S. soldiers murdered 109 Vietnamese civilians in a village called My Lai 4; First Lieut. William L. Calley, Jr. conducted the killings on higher orders.

Disturbed by rumors about the murders at "Pinkville" (My Lai's color on U.S. Army maps), Ronald Ridenhour, a former helicopter door-gunner, sent letters about it to President Nixon and 29 Congressmen. Only Rep. Morris Udall (D-Ariz.) responded, and, after pressure from Udall, the Army began a full-scale investigation more than a year later on April 23, 1969.

Associated Press ran a 190-word item on September 6th out of Fort Benning, Ga., but NOT A SINGLE NEWSPAPER OR BROADCASTING STATION ASKED FOR FURTHER INFORMATION. The New York *Times* ran it on the bottom of page 38 two days later.

A lawyer friend told reporter Seymour Hersh about the story on October 22nd. After some preliminary digging, Hersh approached *Life* and *Look*, who weren't interested. Knowing he was onto something and needing to travel to put the puzzle together, Hersh was given $2,000 by the Fund for Investigative Journalism to do further research.

30,000 air miles later, Hersh finally interviewed Calley in person on November 11th. Writing the story on the plane back to Washington, Hersh gave it to David Obst's *Dispatch News Service*, which sold it to 36 newspapers for $100 each. It was run on November 13th by *The Times* of London, the San Francisco *Chronicle*, Boston *Globe* and St. Louis *Post-Dispatch*. (The New York *Times* ran its own account the same day.)

Hersh won the Pulitzer Prize for his reporting and subsequently joined the New York *Times*. He was able to write "30" to the story on June 4, 1972 by reporting that the Army had charged Major General Samuel W. Koster and Brigadier General George H. Young, Jr. with 43 acts of misconduct in covering up the massacre.

***

THE 10 MOST FREQUENTLY CENSORED BOOKS IN AMERICAN HIGH SCHOOLS

The following list is based upon a 1982 survey conducted by the National Council of Teachers of English.

1. *Go Ask Alice*, anonymous diary of a teen-aged girl
2. *Catcher in the Rye*, J.D. Salinger
3. *Our Bodies, Ourselves*, Boston Women's Health Collective
4. *Forever*, Judy Blume
5. *Of Mice and Men*, John Steinbeck
6. *A Hero Ain't Nothing But A Sandwich*, Alice Childress
7. *My Darling, My Hamburger*, Paul Zindel
8. *Slaughterhouse Five*, Kurt Vonnegut
9. *Grapes of Wrath*, John Steinbeck
10. *Huckleberry Finn*, Mark Twain

Source: Los Angeles *Times*, Dec. 19, 1982

***

READY ON THE LEFT?

Censorship does not always come from the well-meaning right of the political spectrum. The New York-based Council on Interracial Books for Children regularly reviews books for questionable racist or sexist material. Some books that have failed the test include:

1. *Mary Poppins*
2. *Huckleberry Finn*
3. *Tom Sawyer*
4. *Little Black Sambo*
5. *Five Chinese Brothers*
6. Some early *Nancy Drew* mysteries

Source: Los Angeles *Times*, Oct. 7, 1980

***

WHY JOHNNY CAN'T READ, AT LEAST IN TEXAS

In 1981, Texas State Commissioner of Education Raymon L. Bynum refused to certify either the *American Heritage Dictionary* or *Webster's New Collegiate Dictionary* for use in 12th grade classes in the state. He said both dictionaries contained obscene words, and he cited the dictionaries' own definitions of seven questionable words as proof.

According to the Los Angeles *Times*, Feb. 14, 1982, Houghton-Mifflin Co., publisher of the *American Heritage Dictionary*, agreed to delete the seven words for Texas; however, G & C Merriam Co., publisher of Webster's, refused.

Under Texas law, at least two books must be adopted in any given category for use in the public schools. Since only one dictionary was acceptable to Bynum, neither could be used.

The students wound up working with a 1969 dictionary.

***

SELECTED BOOKS PEOPLE WANT BANNED

The American Booksellers Association (ABA) has compiled a list of books which people have attempted to ban. The reasons behind the attempts are given according to the following key:

1. Ethnic
2. Inappropriate for young readers, including improper grade level
3. Objectionable language
4. Obscene
5. Political
6. Pornographic
7. Religious
8. Special interest group
9. Cultural
10. Ethical
11. Literary Standards.

Standard Non-fiction

American Heritage Dictionary—2,3,4
The Bible—1. 7,9
The Gospel—7
The Koran—7
The Talmud—5
Analects by Confucius—5,9
On the Origin of Species by Charles B. Darwin—2,7
Dialogo Sopra I Due Massini Sistemi Del Mondo by Galileo Galilei—7
History of the Decline and Fall of the Roman Empire by Edward Gibbon—5,7
Declaration of Independence—5
United States Constitution—5
The State and Revolution by Lenin—5
The Prince by Niccolo Machiavelli—5
Das Kapital by Karl Marx—5
The Rights of Man by Thomas Paine—5
Pensées by Blaise Pascal—7
Confessions by Jean Jacques Rousseau—4,10

Contemporary Non-fiction

Inside the Company: CIA Diary by Philip Agee—5
Trial of the Catonsville Nine by Daniel Berrigan—2
Our Bodies, Ourselves—Boston Women's Health Book Collective—4
Manchild in the Promised Land by Claude Brown—2,3,4
Soul on Ice by Eldridge Cleaver—1,2,5,7,11

Man's Body: An Owner's Manual by Diagram Group—2
Woman's Body: An Owner's Manual by Diagram Group—2
Studies in the Psychology of Sex by Havelock Ellis—3,4
Anne Frank: The Diary of a Young Girl by Anne Frank—2,4
The Art of Loving by Erich Fromm—2
Black Like Me by John Howard Griffin—2
Mein Kampf by Adolf Hitler—5
The Valachi Papers by Peter Maas—5
The Death of a President by William Manchester—8
The CIA and the Cult of Intelligence by Victor Marchetti & John
    D. Marks—5
The Learning Tree by Gordon Parks—1,2,3,4,7
What I Believe by Bertrand Russell—7
Values Clarification by Sidney Simon—2,10
The Electric Kool-Aid Acid Test by Tom Wolfe—2

Classic Fiction and Drama

The Divine Comedy by Dante Alighieri—4,5,6
Wonder Stories by Hans Christian Andersen—2,4
Lysistrata by Aristophanes—4
Droll Stories by Honoré de Balzac—4
The Flowers of Evil by Charles Baudelaire—9,10
The Wizard of Oz by Frank L. Baum—2,11
The Decameron by Boccaccio—4,6
Alice's Adventures in Wonderland by Lewis Carroll—9,10,11
Don Quixote by Miguel de Saavedra Cervantes—7,10
The Green Pastures by Marc Connelly—7
Adventures of Robinson Crusoe by Daniel Defoe—2
The Adventures of Sherlock Holmes by Sir Arthur Conan Doyle—7
Silas Marner by George Eliot—2
Citizen Tom Paine by Howard Fast—2,5
Tom Jones by Henry Fielding—4,7
The Great Gatsby by F. Scott Fitzgerald—3,4
Madame Bovary by Gustave Flaubert—4,9,10
Faust by Johann Wolfgang von Goethe—5,7
Jude the Obscure by Thomas Hardy—7
The Scarlet Letter by Nathaniel Hawthorne—2,4,10
For Whom the Bell Tolls by Ernest Hemingway—4
The Odyssey by Homer—2,5
Brave New World by Aldous Huxley—2,5,6,7

From Here to Eternity by James Jones—4
Ulysses by James Joyce—4
Paradise Lost by John Milton—2,7
Gone with the Wind by Margaret Mitchell—2
All Quiet on the Western Front by Erich Maria Remarque—4,5
King Lear by William Shakespeare—3,5
Man and Superman by George Bernard Shaw—4
Prometheus Unbound by Percy Bysshe Shelley—5,7,10
Gulliver's Travels by Jonathan Swift—4,5
Mary Poppins by P. L. Travers—2
The Adventures of Tom Sawyer by Mark Twain—2
Candide by Voltaire—4
Charlotte's Web by E. B. White—2
Leaves of Grass by Walt Whitman—3

Contemporary Fiction and Drama

Go Ask Alice, Anonymous—2,4
Another Country by James Baldwin—4
Jaws by Peter Benchley—2,3,4
The Exorcist by William P. Blatty—2,4,11
Are You There God? It's Me, Margaret by Judy Blume—3
A Clockwork Orange by Anthony Burgess—2,4,11
Naked Lunch by William Burroughs—4
Deliverance by James Dickey—2,3
The Ginger Man by J. P. Donleavy—4
The Black Book by Lawrence Durrell—4
Invisible Man by Ralph Ellison—1
Sanctuary by William Faulkner—4
Our Lady of the Flowers by Jean Genet—4
Lord of the Flies by William Golding—2
I Claudius by Robert Graves—2
Catch-22 by Joseph Heller—2,4
One Flew Over the Cuckoo's Nest by Ken Kesey—2,11
Flowers for Algernon by Daniel Keyes—2,6
Lady Chatterley's Lover by D. H. Lawrence—4
Rosemary's Baby by Ira Levin—2,4,11
The Naked and the Dead by Norman Mailer—3,4
The Fixer by Bernard Malamud—2,3,7,10,11
The Thorn Birds by Colleen McCullough—2
Death of a Salesman by Arthur Miller—2,3

Tropic of Cancer by Henry Miller—4,6
Lolita by Vladimir Nabokov—4,9,10
1984 by George Orwell
Doctor Zhivago by Boris Pasternak—5
The Bell Jar by Sylvia Plath—2
The Godfather by Mario Puzo—2
The Carpetbaggers by Harold Robbins—4
Goodbye, Columbus by Philip Roth—6
Catcher in the Rye by J. D. Salinger—2,3,4,5,7,10
Love Story by Erich Segal—2
In the Night Kitchen by Maurice Sendak—2,4
Rage of Angels by Sidney Sheldon—6
One Day in the Life of Ivan Denisovich by Aleksandr
    Solzhenitsyn—2,3,5
Of Mice and Men by John Steinbeck—2,3,4,7,10
Cat's Cradle by Kurt Vonnegut—2
Forever Amber by Kathleen Winsor—4

Source: *Bloomsbury Review*, September-October, 1982

THE HOLLYWOOD 98

This list of movies banned since 1946 from the book, *Banned Films*, is confined to pictures whose showings were prohibited by government action for one of 10 reasons:

1. Might inspire criminal acitivity
2. Portray blacks as equal to whites or shows integrated social situations
3. Offensive to good morals
4. Religious objections
5. Not appropriate for Sunday showing
6. Obscenity, indecency
7. Presents "racial friction at a time when all groups should be united against everything that is subversive"
8. Harmful or not suitable for young persons
9. Distributor refused to submit film for examination for required permit
10. "Indecent intrusion into the most private aspects" of the filmed prisoners' lives

1946-1959

The Outlaw—6
Amok—1,3
Mom and Dad—6
Curley—2
The Miracle—4
La Ronde—3
Latuko—6
M—1,3
Miss Julie—5
Pinky—2
The Moon is Blue—6
Native Son—7

Baby Doll—6
The Game of Love—6
The Garden of Eden—6
The Man with the Golden Arm—1
Wild Weed—3
Lady Chatterley's Lover—3
Naked Amazon—6
And God Created Woman—6
The Anatomy of a Murder—6
Desire Under the Elms—8
Don Juan—9
The Lovers—6

1960-1969

Never on Sunday—3
The Connection—6
The Virgin Spring—3,6
Women of the World—6
Bachelor Tom Peeping—6
491—6
Have Figure Will Travel—6
Lorna—6
Revenge at Daybreak—9
A Stranger Knocks—6
The Twilight Girls—6
The Bedford Incident—9
Bunny Lake is Missing—9
The Dirty Girls—6
The Unsatisfied—6
Un Chant d'Amour—6
This Picture is Censored—6
Via Maria—8
A Woman's Urge—6

Body of a Female—6
I, a Woman—6
I Am Curious-Yellow—6
Mondo Freudo—6
Rent-a-Girl—6
Alimony Lovers—6
Carmen, Baby—6
The Female—6
The Fox—6
Therese and Isabelle—6
Titicut Follies—10
The Wicked Die Slow—6
Angelique in Black Leather—6
Blue Movie—6
Candy—6
The Language of Love—6
Odd Triangle—6
Pattern of Evil—6
Yellow Bird—6

1970-1981

The Collection—6
The Libertine—6
The Secret Sex Lives of Romeo
    and Juliet—6
Starlet—6
The Vixen—6
Where Eagles Dare—6
Without a Stitch—6
Woodstock—8
The Art of Marriage—6
Cindy and Donna—6
Computer Game—6
It All Comes Out in the End—6
The Killing of Sister George—3
Lysistrata—6
Magic Mirror—6
Pornography in Denmark—6
Sexual Freedom in Denmark—6
Carnal Knowledge—6

Cry Uncle—6
Deep Throat—6
Sinderella—6
Behind the Green Door—6
The Exorcist—6
The Last Picture Show—6
Last Tango in Paris—6
The Newcomers—6
Class of '74—6
School Girl—6
Stewardesses—6
The Devil in Miss Jones—6
Gun Runners—6
I Am Sandra—6
Naked Came the Stranger—6
Caligula—6
Emmanuelle—6

Source: *Banned Films*

ONE PRESSBURGER, HOLD THE FREEDOM

Freedom of the press is not one of Supreme Court Chief Justice Warren Burger's favorite causes. He once got into a shoving match with a CBS reporter trying to film a speech at a bar association meeting, and his sentiments come through in the court's decisions as chronicled by *Inquiry* magazine.

1. *Branzburg v. Hayes* (1972), holding that reporters must answer grand jury questions regarding confidential sources. This ruling struck at the very heart of investigative reporting, since sources could no longer be guaranteed effective anonymity. There's no way of telling how many journalists have said "the hell with it" rather than tackle a story that might, as a side effect, teach them firsthand about prison life.

2. *Time, Inc. v. Firestone* (1976), chipping away at the press's protection from libel suits by public figures. The court ruled that a Florida socialite involved in a notorious divorce suit was not a public figure, even though she often called press conferences during the course of the divorce proceedings.

3. *Herbert v. Lando* (1979), permitting plantiff's attorneys in a libel suit to probe the writer's "state of mind." This decision may lead to less, rather than more, careful investigation, since attorneys now advise editors not to write memos raising questions about stories, for fear that the editor's questions could be used to cast doubt on the story's credibility and the newspaper's motives.

4. *Mitchell and Doubleday v. Bindrim* (1979). This case expanded the grounds for libel, as the Court refused to hear the appeal of an author and publisher of a novel who had both been successfully sued for libel, because the book in question included "substantially inaccurate descriptions of what actually happened" in nude therapy groups. The question of how one can evaluate "substantially inaccurate descriptions" in a work of fiction, written from an author's imagination and conveying no implication of accuracy, seems not to have occurred to them.

5. *Kissinger v. Reporters Committee* (1980), ruling that Henry Kissinger—and, by extension, other government officials—could evade the Freedom of Information Act simply by spiriting away any documents they didn't care to make public. If the government no longer has the documents, Justice Rehnquist noted incisively, then it certainly can't make them public under FOIA requests.

Source: *Inquiry* magazine

PROJECT CENSORED

Project Censored, an annual nationwide media research project, was originated in 1976 by Carl Jensen, Associate Professor of Media Studies, for a seminar in mass media at Sonoma State University. Here are its findings for 1980, 1981 and 1982.

1980

1. El Salvador: characterized by most of the U.S. press as a simple morality struggle
2. Unreported automatic wiretapping of calls and cable messages in and out of the country by the National Security Agency

3. Unreported infant deaths at Three Mile Island and uranium mining in New Jersey
4. The "Benedictin coverup"—suppression of evidence that Benedictin produces serious birth defects when taken by pregnant women
5. Unreported conversion of prime agriculture land in the Third World into cash export cropland by multinational corporations, dramatically raising the starvation rate in those countries
6. Export of banned pesticides which reach our stomachs via imported foods
7. The race between the U.S. and Russia toward nuclear war in space
8. Tobacco companies withdraw ads from publications printing stories on the hazards of smoking
9. The "Seven Sister" oil companies have quietly bought up and are shelving the "alternative" solar power industry
10. The EPA's failure to monitor effectively the 78 billion pounds of toxic wastes dumped into 51,000 sites every year

1981

1. The basic cause of our economic crisis—the destruction of the free enterprise system and a competitive economy
2. Injustice at Greensboro, N.C.—members of the Ku Klux Klan and the Nazi Party were acquitted of the brutal killing of five Communist Workers Party demonstrators thanks to the support of local officials
3. Burying America in Radioactive Waste—the government's failure to monitor radioactive wastes dropped in 50 ocean dumps; atomic weapons production accounts for more than 90% of nuclear waste; the unusable $120 million nuclear waste burial chamber in New Mexico; the plan to truck thousands of tons of toxic spent atomic reactor fuel among public highways, etc.
4. A Hungry Child Died Every Two Seconds in 1981—An estimated 50 million people starve to death every year; 40,000 children died every day in 1981 and 17 million of the children born in 1982 will die before their fifth birthday
5. Our Water Is Running Out and What's Left is Being Poisoned
6. Training Terrorists in Florida—Guerilla training camps for Latin American exiles are operating openly in Florida; the government is violating its own Neutrality Act

7. The Insanity of Nuclear Weapons—Little known stories from 1981 include a fully-armed U.S. nuclear Poseidon missile accidentally dropped 17 feet at Holy Loch, Scotland; the lack of accuracy in sophisticated U.S. ICBM's; research indicating there is no "safe" level of radiation; international nuclear proliferation supported by the U.S. government and industry; missing nuclear materials due to inadequate security; Californians unknowingly live in a nuclear bunker; underground nuclear tests in Nevada leak regularly, spraying deadly radiation into California-bound air

8. Union Busting with Briefcases Not Blackjacks—a new army of union busters known as labor relations consultants are using questionable tactics

9. Defense Vulnerability and the High Cost of Whistle Blowing—The U.S. missile attack warning system is plagued by potentially catastrophic deficiencies; the engineer who tried to warn the government about them since 1973 was first criticized, then transferred and finally fired

10. Biological Weapons and Third World Targets—Race-specific weapons such as cocci (Valley Fever) and tuberculosis have been researched by the Department of Defense as biological warfare agents and Third World countries are considered to be particularly vulnerable targets for BW weapons.

1982

1. Fraudulent Safety Tests—American consumers are buying and using products which may not be safe though approved by testing laboratories and regulatory agencies. The country's largest testing lab conducted fraudulent tests on chemicals used in medication, pesticides and other products.

2. Americans Bugged by Super-Secret Court—The little-known U.S. Foreign Intelligence Surveillance Court in Washington, D.C. reviews intelligence agency requests to spy on Americans. Since 1978, through 1981, it heard 962 requests for electronic surveillance and approved all 962.

3. End of Equal Opportunity in America—Without real public input, debate, or media coverage, the federal equal opportunity machinery, from contract compliance to education to employment, was being destroyed—less than 20 years after the initiation of civil rights mandates.

4. Agent White—A powerful, but poisonous, chemical called pictoram is widely used as a pesticide from coast to coast under the trade name Tordon and may be poisoning ground-water supplies. Researchers say it kills weeds, bushes, trees—and maybe people.

5. The Real Story of Central America—Throughout 1982, Central America got widespread media coverage and yet few Americans seem to know what is really happening there. Both print and television news reports appear confusing, conflicting and less than informative.

6. Ronald Reagan: America's Chief Censor—The Reagan administration is significantly reducing information available to the public... Efforts to weaken the Freedom of Information Act and stop leaks of classified information raise the question of censorship from the Oval Office.

7. U.S. Against the World—On December 9, 1982, the United Nations General Assembly voted on a resolution to outlaw all nuclear blasts. The vote was 111 to 1 with 35 abstentions. Only the U.S. voted against.

8. U.S. Firms Traded with the Enemy—Charles Higham, in his book, *Trading With the Enemy,* charges that some of America's largest industrial and financial corporations collaborated with Nazi Germany not only before but during World War II.

9. $2 Billion Wasted on Fertilizers—Soil testing laboratories routinely over-prescribed fertilizers causing farmers to literally waste about $2 billion annually on unnecessary fertilizer.

10. Toxic Waste Firms Target Indian Reservations—Some Indian tribes are being offered more than a million dollars to open their lands to toxic waste dumps. Monitoring and enforcing federal environmental regulation of waste dumps on Indian lands is expected to be more difficult.

A MEDIA CHRONOLOGY

1933

Feb. 20—Assistant U.S. attorney Thomas E. Dewey becomes the first official to seize a book manuscript for reasons of national security. He impounds Herbert O. Yardley's *Japanese Diplomatic Secrets,* which stays classified until 1979.

1947

Nov. 24—50 movie executives meet and agree to suspend the "Hollywood 10" without pay for refusing to testify before HUAC.

1948

April 11-30—The Scripps-Howard Pittsburgh *Press* publishes the names, addresses and places of employment of 1,000 people who signed nominating petitions for Progressive Party presidential candidate Henry Wallace.

1949

July 9—After a jury can't agree on Alger Hiss's guilt or innocence, the Hearst-owned New York *Journal-American* prints the names and addresses of two minority jurors along with a report that they had been threatened.

1951

March 8—HUAC's second investigation into Hollywood Communism begins. Some 30 ex-Communists name 300 colleagues. Author David Caute later comments, "A new kind of talkie was born."

1952

March 31—An article in *American Legion* magazine prompts major movie executives to meet with the American Legion and ask for "all the information it had—large or small—that tended to connect any of their employees with Communism."

1954

Feb. 2—One day after the first hydrogen bomb explodes, an ad in the Pittsburgh *Press* reads: "The bomb's brilliant gleam reminds me of the brilliant gleam Beacon Wax gives to floors. It's a science marvel!"

March 9—CBS's "See It Now" airs a program about Senator Joseph McCarthy (R-Wisc.) After CBS refuses to advertise the show, Edward R. Murrow and producer Fred Friendly pay for an ad in the New York *Times* themselves.

April 6—Senator McCarthy rebuts the "See It Now" show with a script written by George Sokolsky. CBS pays $6,336.99 for production. CBS president Frank Stanton commissions a Roper poll after the broadcast which shows 33% of those polled consider Murrow pro-Communist or have doubts about him; however, telephone calls to CBS support Murrow over McCarthy nearly 10-1.

April 22—The Army-McCarthy hearings open. Among the networks, only ABC-TV—with the weakest daytime programming (and, therefore, the least to lose)—televised the hearings in full.

June 22—WCBS-TV newsman Don Hollenbeck commits suicide after being hounded regularly by Hearst columnist Jack O'Brian for "slanted reporting."

1956

Nov. 26—A.D.C. federal grand jury indicts New York *Times* writers Seymour Peck, Robert Shelton and Alden Whitman for contempt of Congress. All confessed past membership in the Communist Party but refused to name others in testimony before the Senate Internal Security Subcommittee. They were later reindicted by Attorney General Robert Kennedy in the mid-60s. Eleven years after they started, the cases were finally dropped after the reversal of a second conviction.

1961

April 6—Stuart Novins of CBS reports the U.S. is involved with an imminent invasion of Cuba, a story he has worked on with Tad Szulc of The New York *Times*. The *Times* tones Szulc's dispatch down, omits the fact it is "imminent" and publishes it a day later.

May 9—Shortly after the Bay of Pigs fiasco, President Kennedy proposes voluntary censorship code to representatives of seven major newspapers. They refuse to comply.

Nov. 23—"CBS Reports" deletes former Pres. Eisenhower's remarks on his regrets about the U-2 incident at insistence of his son, Lt. Col. John Eisenhower.

1967

Nov. 7—Congress passes a law establishing the Corporation for Public Broadcasting. President Johnson appoints Frank Pace, Jr., former Secretary of the Army, to head it. Pace expresses his enthusiasm for CPB and says he has already commissioned research on how public television might be used for riot control.

1968

Sept. 6—NBC acknowledges that its staff conducted illegal electronic surveillance at the recent Democratic national convention.

Nov. 25—Herbert Klein, appointed White House communications director, says, "I'm confident... truth will become the hallmark of the Nixon Administration."

1969

Feb. 1—Last Columbia Records ad appears in the Washington (D.C.) *Free Press*. The FBI had asked Columbia not to support papers "giving aid and comfort to enemies."

April 1—Seaman Roger Priest publishes an anti-war newspaper. 25 Naval intelligence officers trail him and inspect his garbage. He is eventually convicted of disloyalty and disobedience.

May 10—President Nixon orders the first of 17 illegal wiretaps on phones of journalists and government officials.

Oct. 17—White House aide Jeb Stuart Magruder suggests in a memo that the FCC officially monitor news broadcasts as soon as Dean Burch officially becomes chairman. Three days after Burch is confirmed, he telephones all three network presidents asking for verbatim transcripts of remarks made by their news commentators following a Nixon speech on Vietnam.

Dec. 25—A paramilitary Secret Army Organization, led by FBI informant Howard Godfrey, assaults offices and staff of underground San Diego paper, *Street Journal*.

1970

May 2—Former President Johnson tells Walter Cronkite his doubts about the Warren Commission's conclusion—that Lee Harvey Osward acted alone in the murder of John Kennedy. The references are deleted from the broadcast.

June 3—An FBI COINTELPRO memo proposes spraying Black Panter Party newspapers with a foul-smelling chemical to "hinder distribution."

1971

March 23—Strategic Air Command Gen. Bruce Holloway tells a House subcommittee that the U.S. needs controlled news to combat media "slanting."

June 13—The New York *Times* begins publishing articles based on a secret official history of the Vietnam War. The source material is later called "The Pentagon Papers."

June 14—Newspaper and magazine editors receive advance proofs of Lyndon Johnson's memoirs, *The Vantage Point*. Reference material for the book comes, in part, from the same secret Pentagon study being revealed in the New York *Times*.

June 15—The Justice Department moves to block the *Times* from publishing any more of the Pentagon Papers.

June 28—Daniel Ellsberg is indicted for theft of government documents—the Pentagon Papers.

Sept. 3—The New York *Times* reports that both the CIA and FBI used lie detectors on State Department personnel in an effort to plug newsleaks.

1972

Jan. 1—Congressional Quarterly reveals the TV networks have been subpoenaed 122 times in the first two and a half years of Nixon's Administration, more than a third of the time at the request of the government.

April 18—Victor Marchetti becomes the first American writer in U.S. history to suffer court-ordered censorship. Parts of his book, *The CIA and the Cult of Intelligence,* are ordered cut.

Nov. 1—Rep. William Moorhead (D-Pa.) reveals a White House plan to install government-operated FM receivers in every home, boat and auto in the country.

1973

March 9—CBS postpones telecasting David Rabe's anti-war play, *Sticks and Bones,* on the pretext that American POW's are returning home from Hanoi. Both *Time* and *Newsweek* give rave reviews to the show which doesn't air until August. Producer Joseph Papp, who had been fired by CBS 15 years earlier for taking the Fifth Amendment before HUAC, resigns his production deal writing, "I bid you all a fond farewell and leave you to your worm-eaten consciences."

May 14—Henry Kissinger tells Washington *Post* reporter Bob Woodward that he placed the national security wiretaps on reporters and government officials.

May 17—The Senate Watergate Committee begins televised hearings.

June 21—Supreme Court rules that hard-core pornography which violates local standards is not protected by the First Amendment. A Virginia prosecutor says he intends to prosecute anyone selling *Playboy* magazine.

1975
March 23—CBS-TV airs a Mike Wallace interview with former top White House aide H. R. Haldeman, having paid a reputed $25,000 for the privilege.

1976
Feb. 16—*Village Voice* publishes first half of Pike Committee report provided by Daniel Schorr. The next day, the Washington *Post* reveals him as the source, and he is forced to sign an undated resignation by CBS.

1977
Dec. 27—Former CIA director William Colby tells House investigators that Agency efforts to mold world opinion occasionally led to false news reports in the United States.

1982
Jan. 12—President Reagan's directive instructs all employees (except senior officials) employed by the State and Defense Departments and the NSA to obtain advance approval from superiors prior to any press contacts and to file written reports immediately afterward.

1983
Jan. 17—Justice Department officials notify the National Film Board of Canada that three Canadian-made documentary films are "political propaganda," under a 1938 law. The films deal with nuclear war and acid rain.

"You'd better look at what I've got on Him!"

THE FBI IN PEACE AND WAR— AND ANTI-WAR

"The Bureau of Investigation is not concerned with political or other opinions of individuals. It is concerned only with their conduct and then only with such conduct as is forbidden by the laws of the United States. When a police system passes beyond these limits, it is dangerous to the proper administration of justice and to human liberty, which it should become our first concern to cherish."

—Attorney General Harlan Fiske Stone in 1924, before J. Edgar Hoover's appointment as director of the Bureau of Investigation

DETENTION PLANS OF THE FBI

Hoover first mentioned a detention program in 1939 when telling Congress of his decision to compile "extensive indices of individuals, groups and organizations engaged in... subversive activities." On Sept. 2, 1939, the day after Poland was invaded, he asked for reports on "persons of German, Italian and Communist sympathies" for listing on a Custodial Detention Index.

On Dec. 6, 1939, criteria were expanded to include people whose presence at liberty "would be dangerous to the public peace and the safety of the United States Government." In June, 1940 Hoover asked Attorney General Robert Jackson for guidance on "a suspect list of individuals whose arrest might be considered necessary in the event [of] war." (On February 19, 1942, President Roosevelt did authorize the military to intern 112,000 Japanese Americans as well as 2,000 Japanese living in Peru.)

On April 21, 1941, assistant to the Attorney General M.F. McGuire issued a formal order requesting the FBI to transmit its "dossiers" to the Special War Policies Unit. Attorney General Francis Biddle ordered the list discontinued on July 16, 1943, because it "served no useful purpose." Not one to follow orders blindly, Hoover simply ordered the name changed to the Security Index in a confidential memo of Aug. 14, 1943 which he ordered should be mentioned *only* to the Office of Naval Intelligence and the Military Intelligence Service.

Reacting to the Red Menace, on Feb. 27, 1946, FBI Assistant Director D. Milton Ladd memoed Hoover that the FBI should "prepare security index cards on all members of the [Communist] Party," and recommended advising the Attorney General of this action. Hoover wrote Attorney General Tom Clark about Ladd's idea on March 8th, neglecting to mention the Security Index. A Clark memo of July 17th on detention of Communists concluded that martial law should be declared and *habeas corpus* suspended.

On Aug. 3, 1948, Clark (father of future Attorney General Ramsey Clark) asked Hoover to start an Emergency Detention Program pursuant to the Attorney General's Portfolio Plan. Beginning in 1948, a Communist Index was also started and contained the names of 14,000 people removed from the Security Index. Subjects transferred could redeem themselves by agreeing to inform or otherwise "indicate complete defection from subversive groups."

On Sept. 23, 1950, Congress passed the Internal Security Act over President Truman's veto. It provided for the confinement of suspected citizens in detention camps in time of emergency or insurrection. Six camps were actually established but never used.

The Reserve Index replaced the Communist Index on June 21, 1960 and was used to pinpoint special groups of individuals who "should receive priority consideration with respect to investigation." Those not considered dangerous enough for the Security Index were relegated to Section B of the new Reserve Index while Section A covered teachers, labor organizers and leaders, writers and newsmen, lawyers, doctors and scientists.

Embarrassed because Lee Harvey Oswald was not listed on any index, on Dec. 17, 1963, Hoover expanded the criteria for listing to include people "of a potential danger to the national security of the United States in time of an emergency."

The Rabble Rouser Index was begun in 1967 after the Kerner Commission on Civil Disorders asked the Bureau to identify individuals prominent in stirring up civil disorders. In 1968, the Justice Department issued revised criteria to include any person who had "revolutionary beliefs."

The emergency detention provision of the Internal Security Act was repealed by Congress on Sept. 25, 1971; however, on Oct. 22, 1971, Attorney General John Mitchell said repeal did not "limit the FBI's authority" to compile lists of dangerous subjects. On this basis, he authorized starting the Administrative Index which continued the Security Index and Reserve Index in time of national emergency.

In 1969, a new Priority Apprehension Program listed top leaders and others and amounted to 10,640 by 1970. By December, 1954, the FBI Security Index listed 26,174 Americans who might be locked up in time of war or emergency. The number kept dropping as Red Scare fears subsided, and, after Hoover's death in 1972, the number was trimmed from 15,259 to 4,786.

Although FBI Director Clarence Kelley assured Congress the Security Index had been abolished in 1971, the New York *Times* revealed on Oct. 25, 1975 that the FBI still maintained an Administrative Index of 1,200 Americans "who would merit close investigative attention" in an emergency.

In 1976, the Church Committee reported 10,000 names in the Reserve Index, mostly said to be "women's rights supporters, communists, militant blacks, Jews and tax protesters."

***

29 FAVORITE TECHNIQUES FOR DISRUPTING DISSIDENT POLITICAL GROUPS (1956-1973)

1. Sending anonymous or fictitious materials to members or groups to cause internal dissension.
2. Distributing clippings and government documents to news reporters.
3. Leaking hearsay from informers to news reporters.
4. Telling local police about violations by members of the group.
5. Using informers to disrupt meetings.
6. Writing letters to employers, credit bureaus and creditors to tell them about the political activities of activists, in order to get them fired or to adversely affect their credit.
7. Trying to prevent local merchants from doing business with political groups.
8. Interviewing activists so that they would believe "the FBI is everywhere."

9. Furnishing information to religious leaders and organizations "to persuade them to exert pressure on state and local governments, employers, and landlords to the detriment of the various groups."

10. Tipping off the press that a politician was related to a dissident group.

11. Sending anonymous letters to politicians, newspapers, television stations, and others, sometimes to create internal distrust (one of them accusing Black Panthers of being sex perverts.)

12. Making anonymous telephone calls with false information.

13. Establishing sham organizations to disrupt others.

14. Sending anonymous letters to family members alleging radical politics or immoral activities.

15. Using CB radio frequencies to spread false information.

16. Forging a group's business cards and stationery.

17. Investigating sexual relations.

18. Sending phony letters to columnists (one of them saying Jane Fonda had threatened to kill President Nixon).

19. Arranging for prostitutes to be found with dissidents.

20. Mailing phony housing forms to disrupt a group's convention.

21. Publishing fictitious newsletters.

22. Urging real estate firms to break up communal living arrangements.

23. Infiltrating a six-member black nationalist organization with two informers.

24. Subscribing to left wing periodicals.

25. Distributing leaflets before a scholar's lecture to discredit him.

26. Investigating the employees and leaders of a large church that had permitted the Communist Party to hold a rally there.

27. Arranging the arrest of key activists on drug charges.

28. In "Operation Hoodwink," publishing false leaflets purportedly from the Communist Party and circulating them to organized crime figures to prompt the underworld to retaliate against the Communists.

29. Instructing its informers to spread rumors that group leaders were informers.

Source: U.S. Department of Justice

***

MAGAZINES FOR WHICH HOOVER "WROTE" ARTICLES

Frank Donner's book, *The Age of Surveillance*, has an exhaustive bibliography of articles "written" by Hoover including the following:

> *U.S. News & World Report*—27 bylined pieces
> *American Magazine*—20 articles
> *Reader's Digest*—9 articles
> *Christianity Today*—9 stories
> *Scientific American*—"Photography in Crime Detection" May, 1940
> *Woman's Home Companion*—"Mothers Are Our Only Hope"—Jan., 1944
> *Newsweek*—"How To Fight Communism"—June 9, 1947
> *Redbook*—"God or Chaos"—Feb., 1949
> *Parade*—"Could Your Child Become A Red?"—May 11, 1952
> *American Legion*—"God and Country or Communism?"— Nov., 1957
> *Nation's Business*—"Why Reds Make Friends With Businessmen"—May, 1962
> *Harvard Business Review*—"The U.S. Businessman Faces the Soviet Spy"—Jan.-Feb., 1964
> *Popular Science*—"Now: Instant Crime Control in Your Town"—Jan., 1967
> *PTA Magazine*—"SDS and the High Schools"—Jan.-Feb., 1970
> *VFW Magazine*—"Mao's Red Shadows in America"—June, 1971

In actuality, the FBI's Crime Records Division was used as Hoover's personal propaganda machine and provided him with government-paid ghost writers. On May 11, 1971, Jack Anderson also revealed that Hoover had collected $25,000 in royalties on books written at government expense.

HOOVER'S FAVORITE COMIC STRIPS IN THE '30S

Tarzan	Secret Agent X-9
Dick Tracy	War On Crime

Source: *Investigating The FBI*

8 FILMS MADE ABOUT THE FBI OR
WITH ITS FULL COOPERATION

The House on 92nd Street, 1945
Notorious, 1946
Walk A Crooked Mile, 1948
Street With No Name, 1948
I Was a Communist for the FBI, 1951
Big Jim McClain, 1952
Walk East On Beacon, 1952
The FBI Story, 1959

The Bureau was also the subject of a popular ABC-TV series. In testimony before a Senate Subcommittee on Constitutional Rights, writer David W. Rintels said he was asked to submit a script and suggested a plot about four black girls killed when a racist bomber destroys a church in Birmingham. He was told, ''The church must be in the North, there could be no Negroes involved and the bombing could have nothing to do with civil rights.''

Hoover never allowed producer Quinn Martin to use Bureau files for material. Instead, two Bureau employees working under Hoover's guidance did research for the show while on the Bureau payroll. They furnished technical aid, offered story ideas and reviewed scripts.

5 WAYS THE FBI PLAYED MEET THE PRESS

1. When Beacon Press published *The Pentagon Papers*, its parent organization, the Unitarian Universalist Association, was investigated by the FBI, which examined donor lists and bank records.
2. When political columnists Drew Pearson and Jack Anderson investigated Sen. (and former FBI agent) Thomas Dodd (D-Conn.), FBI men photostated documents in the reporters' possession, then began snooping on their sources.
3. In 1950, lawyer Max Lowenthal published a book attacking Hoover, *The Federal Bureau of Investigation*. Friendly reporters were told, ''He is a shadowy figure who thrives on obscurity ... His name does not appear in *Who's Who*... he attended Harvard Law School like many other parlor pinks, fellow-travelers, Communists and convicted perjurers.''
4. When Fred J. Cook published *The FBI Nobody Knows*, he was discredited by Hoover backers who wanted to get at his

sources. ''We recognize that the press has an established right to protect its sources. But in this age of the anonymous smear, it does well to use this right sparingly.''

5. William W. Turner's *Hoover's FBI* caused its ex-FBI author to be investigated at every turn. Magazine editors considering material were approached by FBI agents who convinced them not to publish it. He was tailed from talk show to talk show. Tom, then host of a talk show on KYW-TV, Philadelphia, told Turner, ''We even knew what color suit you'd be wearing.''

6. Lyle Stuart, publisher of *Inside the FBI*, was placed under surveillance in 1951 after knocking Hoover's friend, Walter Winchell, in print. The Bureau referred to him as a ''known homosexual'' and a ''member of the Soviet apparatus.''

The FBI also maintained a ''No Contact'' list of reporters. Included on it were columnist Carl Rowan; Gene Miller, an investigative reporter for the Miami *Herald*; historian Henry Steele Commager; educator Robert M. Hutchins and the entire staff of the Washington *Post*.

Hoover would go to any lengths when faced with criticism. Walt Kelly, who drew *Pogo*, used a running caricature of Hoover in the comic strip; Hoover ordered cryptanalysis of the accompanying dialogue to see if its humor hid even more horrors—in code.

DEBUNKING THREE POPULAR FBI MEDIA MYTHS

Three enduring FBI myths maintain that the Bureau ''got'' gangster Johnny Dillinger, caught Bruno Richard Hauptmann, Charles Lindbergh, Jr.'s kidnapper, and nabbed master Soviet spy Rudolf Abel. According to author Robert J. Nash in *Citizen Hoover*, there are problems with all three legends.

DILLINGER

The FBI's claim that it gunned Dillinger down on July 22, 1934 outside Chicago's Biograph Theater is suspect because:

1) The man who did the shooting was not FBI man Melvin Purvis, but rather Martin Karkovich of the East Chicago Police Department.

2) An autopsy revealed the dead man was not Dillinger's height or weight; the dead man had brown eyes, and Dillinger's were blue-gray; the dead man wore prescription glasses, and Dillinger had perfect eyesight.
3) The famous Lady In Red who put the finger on Dillinger was an informant of the Hargrave Secret Service, not the FBI.

HAUPTMANN

In September, 1934, a suspicious gas station attendant jotted down the serial number of a $5 bill along with Hauptmann's license number. A few days later, a New Jersey bank teller checked the bill against the number of the Lindbergh ransom notes and told the Treasury Department in New York about it.

The Treasury agent called Lieut. James J. Finn of the New York Police Department, and Finn traced the license number of Hauptmann's car through state motor vehicle records. On Sept. 18, Finn personally arrested Hauptmann and supplied the evidence leading to his conviction.

ABEL

In 1953, a Brooklyn *Eagle* newsboy collecting for delivery at 3403 Foster Ave. was given a curious nickel; it felt too light and made a hollow ring when dropped. Discovering microfilm hidden in the nickel, he told a New York City police detective, who turned the nickel and microfilm over to the FBI. The vaunted FBI lab tried to decode columns of coded figures to no avail.

The matter would have ended there had it not been for a CIA agent in Paris, who convinced Soviet spy Reino Hayhanen to defect. Hayhanen was spirited away to the U.S. where he not only decoded the numbers on the microfilm, but also fingered Abel as director of Soviet espionage in the U.S.

GERALD FORD, WARREN REPORTER

According to William C. Sullivan, FBI assistant director, in his book, *Bureau,* ''Hoover was delighted when Gerald Ford was named to the Warren Commission. The director wrote in one of his internal memos that the bureau could expect Ford to 'look after FBI interests' and he did, keeping us fully advised of what was going on behind closed doors. He was our man, our informant on the Warren Commission.''

Hoover returned the favor by furnishing Ford with FBI file material in his abortive attempt to impeach Supreme Court Justice William O. Douglas.

HE COULDN'T CHEW GUM AND DRAFT LAWS AT THE SAME TIME EITHER

In 1976, President Gerald Ford issued Executive Order 11905 with "tough new restrictions"on domestic intelligence gathering. In *The Lawless State*, former NSC official Morton Halperin and his co-authors reveal that the restrictions sound tough until you get to the fine print. For instance:

1. Physical surveillance of Americans is prohibited unless the action is approved by an agency head and the target is or was an employee of the agency, a contractor or anyone who is in contact with such people. In fact, the Ford order grants presidential authority to tail U.S. citizens.
2. Foreign intelligence agencies (i.e. CIA) may collect information on "persons or activities that pose a clear threat to intelligence facilities or personnel," which was the very justification the CIA gave for infiltrating anti-war groups in the '60s.
3. Intelligence agencies may trail people "reasonably believed to be acting on behalf of a foreign power"—a claim made most recently by the White House in the case of the nuclear freeze proponents.
4. An intelligence agency can still claim it is considering offering someone a job—whether or not the subject would have an interest in working for the agency—as a rationale for an investigation. (The Nixon White House investigated CBS newsman Daniel Schorr on the basis of a fictitious presidential appointment.)
5. The National Security Agency's power to monitor overseas communications of any American in contact with foreigners is upheld.
6. Political assassination is banned, but the order sanctioned kidnapping, extortion, bribery, blackmail, paramilitary adventures, coups d'etat and torture by omitting any references to them.
7. All members of the executive branch and its contractors must sign an agreement not to disclose information about "intelligence sources and methods," the favorite secrecy catch-all.

THE FBI SLANG DICTIONARY

anonymous source—euphemism for an illegal investigative technique

bed to bed FISUR—physical surveillance of a subject from dawn to dusk

black bag job—breaking and entering

blue slip funds—monies used to pay confidential informants

book agent—an exceptionally zealous agent

brick agent—one who works the street ("the bricks") and hasn't been promoted

chamfering—surreptitious opening of mail

clod squad—After Hoover said of several of his supervisors, "A lot of them are clods," FBI officials formed a panel they called the "Clod Squad" to fire supervisors with traits Hoover was known to have hated.

clubs—central FBI plants where electronic surveillances are monitored

confidential source—someone overheard on an improper wiretap

electronic surveillance—a euphemism for bugging or wiretapping

graymailing—threat made by an accused lawbreaker to disclose classified information if prosecuted

green sheet—list of exhibits in FBI possession

green weenie—an FBI form which criticizes a field office for its handling of a case

informant—source (No one has ever known why "informer" won't do.)

JUNE mail—a specially coded filing system for any documents or authorization forms making reference to electronic surveillance activities and perhaps to surreptitious physical entries or "black bag jobs" as well; kept apart from main files

listening post—informant who reports on matters where he lives or works

mail cover—procedure whereby post office records names and addresses corresponding with a subject of investigation and passes them along to FBI

miketel—telephone which has been turned into an open microphone capable of intercepting all conversations within hearing range

"mission"—the job of the bureau, with an overtone of religion, diplomacy and military history

no contact list—established by Hoover, it indicated individuals who had criticized him or the FBI and were to have no contact with the Bureau

rabbi—an unofficial sponsor at FBI headquarters who gives informal help to an agent

racial calendar—established in 1968 to advise field offices of "black nationalist-type conferences and racial events and anniversaries"

"seat of government"—Hoover's grandiose name (usually capitalized) for FBI headquarters in Washington, D.C.

secure a residence—illegally break into a residence

snitch jackets—false documents planted to imply that an individual is an FBI informer, as in "Let's put a snitch jacket on him"

soft files—temporary files housing sensitive or embarrassing information

sound man—expert in electronic surveillance

surreptitious entry—break-in

terminate with extreme prejudice—assassinate

torpedo—FBI agent who spies on other agents for infractions of rules

trash cover—surveillance of a subject's garbage

vacuum cleaner—informant who reports everything he finds out

watch lists—lists of Americans whose international mail was to be opened by the CIA and international communications were to be monitored by the NSA

wildcat bug—electronic surveillance placed without FBI authorization

ORGANIZATIONS UNDER SURVEILLANCE BY THE FBI, IRS, NSA AND CIA 1940-1975

1. John Birch Society
2. U.S. Communist Party
3. The Southern Christian Leadership Conference
4. The Nation of Islam
5. International Council of Christian Churches
6. The Progressive Party
7. The National Lawyers Guild
8. Black Panther Party
9. Socialist Workers Party
10. Student Nonviolent Coordinating Committee (SNCC)

Source: *Spying on Americans*

SELECTED INDIVIDUALS UNDER SURVEILLANCE BY THE FBI, IRS, NSA AND CIA 1940-1975

1. 1948 Progressive Party candidate Henry Wallace
2. Mrs. Eleanor Roosevelt
3. U.S. Supreme Court justice William O. Douglas
4. Financier Bernard Baruch
5. 1964 Presidential candidate Barry Goldwater
4. Republican advisor Anna Chennault
5. Senator Joseph McCarthy (R-Wisc.)
6. Senator J. William Fulbright (D-Ark.)
7. Senator Wayne Morse (R-Ore.)
8. CBS correspondent Daniel Schorr
9. Morton Halperin, presidential campaign advisor to Sen. Edmund Muskie (D-Me.)
10. Anthony Lake, also a Muskie campaign advisor

Source: *Spying on Americans*

> *"I pray that we will never see the FBI sink to the depths it sank to during the final years of the Hoover Administration... People's private records were literally spread throughout the entire government of the United States with the instructions to find something on them, destroy them, discredit them... Let's assure ourselves we don't ever again leave the loopholes that can allow a man like J. Edgar Hoover to go berserk with the rights of American citizens."*
> —Congressman Stewart McKinney (R-Conn.), before a House Judiciary Subcommittee, October 18, 1979.

8 PRIVATE CITIZENS PUT ON GOVERNMENT "WATCH LISTS" IN THE '60S AND '70S

Individuals on "watch lists" had their mail checked and telegrams monitored, according to James Bamford in *The Puzzle Palace*.

1. Jane Fonda
2. Joan Baez
3. Dr. Benjamin Spock
4. Dr. Martin Luther King, Jr.
5. Rev. Ralph Abernathy
6. Eldridge Cleaver
7. Abbie Hoffman
8. David T. Dellinger

CELEBRITY SUBJECTS OF FBI DOSSIERS

Marlon Brando	Joe Louis	Robert Hutchins
Felix Frankfurter	Tony Randall	Sen. Paul Douglas
Joe Namath	Helen Keller	Paul Newman
Jesse Jackson	Dick Gregory	Martin Luther King, Jr.
Bertolt Brecht	Roy Wilkins	Jane Fonda
Garry Wills	Rock Hudson	John Kenneth Galbraith
Zero Mostel	Julian Bond	Madalyn Murray O'Hair
Harry Belafonte	Muhammad Ali	Donald Sutherland
Eartha Kitt	Lance Rentzel	Henry Steele
William Kuntsler	Jean Seberg	Commager

Sources: Department of Justice/*The Age of Surveillance*

THE 20 MOST VOLUMINOUS FILES IN THE FBI READING ROOM

In *Are You Now or Have You Ever Been in the FBI Files?*, author Ann Mari Buitrago describes the FBI's unique filing system.

Its quirks help to explain some of the apparent inconsistencies in this list. First, the Bureau files "bulky enclosures" (materials that won't fit standard files) separately (See 11). The reason for filing "John F. Kennedy assassination" (2) and "JFK assassination" (6) separately is unexplained as is the reason for maintaining separate files on "Jack Ruby" (12) and "Jack Leon Ruby, Dallas" (13).

1. Ethel and Julius Rosenberg—155,500 pages approx.
2. John F. Kennedy—assassination—120,748
3. Alger Hiss and Whittaker Chambers—54,693
4. COINTELPRO (12 Programs)—52,646
5. Martin Luther King, Jr.—assassination—44,873
6. JFK—assassination—38,638
7. Lee Harvey Oswald—36,122
8. Charles Lindbergh and Bruno Hauptmann—35,540
9. COINTELPRO (Communist Party USA)—30,779
10. National Crime Information Center—26,912
11. JFK—bulky enclosures—21,933
12. Jack Ruby—15,845
13. Jack Leon Ruby, Dallas—13,263
14. ACLU—13,180
15. Law Enforcement Assistance Administration—10,053
16. Rudolf I. Abel—8,537
17. JFK assassination—Dallas—8,500

18. Kent State Shooting—8,445
19. JFK assassination—Warren Commission—8,150
20. J. Robert Oppenheimer—security investigation—7,234

SELECTED VICTIMS OF MAIL INTERRUPTION
BY FEDERAL AGENCIES

Jane Fonda

Roy Cohn, New York attorney

Lori Paton, a New Jersey high school student who wrote to
the Socialist Workers Party as part of a school assignment

Ralph Nader

Senator Hubert Humphrey, during the Wisconsin presidential primary in 1972

William O. Douglas, Associate Justice of the Supreme Court

Congresswoman Bella Abzug, by the CIA for more than 20
years before becoming a member of Congress

A Boy Scout leader in Moscow, Idaho, writing to the Soviet
Embassy about his troop's trip to the Soviet Union

Source: *Privacy Journal*

***

9 WAYS FBI AGENTS GET INTO TROUBLE:

1. Showing disrespect to, harrassing or intimidating individuals
in the course of an investigation
2. Conducting an inadequate investigation
3. Low productivity in clerical jobs, or erroneous identification
of fingerprints
4. Failure to follow proper procedures or substandard office work
5. Personal misconduct, including drunk driving and sexual
misconduct
6. Allegations of criminal misconduct while on-duty, including
shoplifting or bribery
7. Loss of credentials, government property, or weapons, or
failure to safeguard them
8. Tardiness, abuse of leave policy
9. Embarrassing the Bureau

Source: General Accounting Office, 1977

11 CATEGORIES OF PERSONS IN FBI FINGERPRINT FILES

Criminal suspects
Convicted criminals
Persons arrested by local police
Securities dealers
Mental patients
Gun owners
Bank employees
Parents who voluntarily send their children's prints
Adults who volunteer to be on file
Current and former members of the military services
Tourists who visit FBI headquarters in Washington

Source: Federal Bureau of Investigation

***

WHO SAYS TAX DOLLARS DON'T HELP MINORITY PARTIES?

In 1962, while J. Edgar Hoover still issued alarms about the danger of the American Communist Party, membership had shrunk to a then all-time low of 8,500 (down from a high of 80,000). Ironically, 1,500 party members were FBI informers. According to *Superspies*, with one in six party members' dues and contributions covered by the bureau, the FBI was the Communist Party's chief financial supporter.

***

AND INCREASE EMPLOYMENT FOR SANITATION WORKERS?

The Baltimore *Sun* revealed that between July, 1968 and August, 1969, David O. Hale, an agent in the FBI Tucson bureau, set and exploded 18 bombs "on the theory that some selective bombing would get the Mafia fighting internally and drive it out of Tucson."

"The technology needed to realize Orwell's worst nightmares is available, poorly regulated and widely abused, but so far the United States has escaped its full potential. Elsewhere... in such totalitarian laboratories as Paraguay, Nicaragua and the Philippines, 1984 is a fait accompli.*"*

—Jim Hougan in *Spooks*

CONTROVERSIAL COUNTRIES WHICH BELONG TO INTERPOL

The International Criminal Police Organization, better known as "Interpol" after its cable address, is a *private* organization, under the jurisdiction of no country. Due to FBI and IRS membership, more than 100 countries—Soviet bloc countries, military dictatorships and "totalitarian laboratories"—have computerized access to U.S. files. Even worse, foreign police departments can *plant* damaging information on U.S. citizens—whether true or false—in FBI and IRS files.

Interpol's membership includes the following nations you might not necessarily want to invite over for dinner.

Algeria	Libya
Argentina	Pakistan
Chile	Romania
El Salvador	Saudi Arabia
Guatemala	Syria
Haiti	Turkey
Hungary	Uganda
Iran	United Arab Emirates
Iraq	Yugoslavia
Jordan	Zaire
Lebanon	

Source: Department of Justice

***

9 THINGS THE FBI CAN'T DO IN CHICAGO

1. Spy on political activists unless the conduct is forbidden by a state or federal criminal law
2. Employ any technique that impairs a law-abiding citizen's constitutional rights.

3. Defame the character or reputation of a U.S. citizen or resident alien.
4. Conduct intrusive investigations, except to the minimum extent necessary.
5. Make any unnecessary collection of information about the lawful exercise of the rights of free press, free assembly, free speech and free religion.
6. Conduct an investigation based solely on the lawful exercise of the right of free speech or any other Constitutional right.
7. Conduct "black bag jobs," warrantless, unconsented physical trespasses. (The FBI admitted to 500 black bag jobs in Chicago in the 60s and 70s.)
8. Conduct physical, photographic or electronic surveillance, except as permitted by law.
9. Conduct counterintelligence along the lines of the COINTELPRO activities of the 60s and 70s.

Source: ACLU v. City of Chicago, (Federal District Court, Northern District of Illinois, 1975)

***

MEDIA NOT SO COOL

In the wake of the break-in at FBI headquarters in Media, Pa. on March 8, 1971, FBI agents descended on nearby Powelton Village. In *Citizen Hoover,* author Robert Jay Nash reveals their efforts at disguise were a total bust. One observer said, "The FBI cars were all late-model Belair or Impala sedans with two-way radios under the dashboard and license plates beginning with '92' or '93.' The drivers all had short hair and wore white shirts."

When agents learned a Powelton resident had third-generation copies of some files, they knocked down her front door with a sledgehammer and ransacked her home while more than a hundred people watched. The agents confiscated her typewriter and stapler; neither was returned, and a $95.97 bill for damages remains unpaid.

***

7 EX-FBI AGENTS PROMINENT IN BUSINESS

1. Cartha DeLoach—executive of Pepsico
2. Harvey G. Foster—vp, American Airlines
3. John Bugas—former vp, Ford Motor Co.
4. Harold M. Perry—president, CIT Financial Corp.
5. Edwin Folz—president, international division, Campbell Soup Co.
6. George Myers—executive vp, Standard Oil Company of Indiana
7. William J. Quinn—president, Chicago, Milwaukee, St. Paul and Pacific Railroad.

Source: *Citizen Hoover*

10 CONGRESSMEN WHO WERE FORMERLY FBI AGENTS

1. Omar Burleson (D-Tex.)
2. Robert V. Denney (R-Neb.)
3. Samuel L. Devine (R-Ohio)
4. Ed Edmondson (D-Okla.)
5. Don Edwards (D-Cal.) (see below)
6. Lawrence J. Hogan (R-Md.)
7. Wiley Mayne (R-Iowa)
8. H. Allen Smith (R-Cal.)
9. Wendell Wyatt (R-Ore.)
10. William T. Cahill (R-N.J.) and later the state's governor

Don Edwards, the only one of the 10 still in Congress, has been a severe critic of intelligence agency abuses despite his FBI service. When Attorney General William French Smith announced new liberalized guidelines for the FBI on March 7, 1983, Edwards was vehemently opposed.

The new guidelines, aimed at "terrorist" groups, permit the FBI to use informants and undercover agents in the preliminary stages of political investigations and also permit the investigation of "the members of the enterprise and other persons likely to be knowingly acting in furtherance of its criminal objectives."

In the April-May, 1983 issue of *Organizing Notes*, Edwards said, "The Supreme Court has made it clear that mere advocacy is not enough to warrant prosecution, yet the FBI wants to investigate speech." Such investigations, he says, could "chill legitimate First Amendment activity."

Source: *Citizen Hoover*

HOOVER'S 8 WAYS TO SPOT
CARS CARRYING COMMUNISTS

Hoover gave the American public the following tips to catch Commies while they were out for a spin in the party flivver. He said Communists resort to:

1. Driving alternately at high and low rates of speed.
2. Entering a heavily traveled intersection on a yellow light, hoping to lose any follower or cause an accident.
3. Turning corners at high rates of speed and stopping abruptly.
4. Suddenly leaving a car and walking hurriedly down a one-way street in the direction in which vehicle traffic is prohibited.
5. Entering a dark street in a residential area at night, making a sharp U-turn, cutting into a side alley, and extinguishing the car's lights.
6. Driving in rural areas, taking a long walk in a field, then having another car meet them.
7. Waiting until the last minute, then making a sharp left turn in front of oncoming traffic.
8. Stopping at every filling station on the highway, walking around the car, always looking, then going on.

Source: *Citizen Hoover*

NO LEFT TURNS

In his book, *No Left Turns,* former FBI agent Joseph L. Schott reveals that, in 1959, he set up a 200-mile driving trip for Hoover and his trusted aide Clyde Tolson from Dallas to Austin in which the driver was forbidden from making a left turn. The bizarre directions were the result of an incident several months previously; Hoover's car had been hit from behind while his chauffeur was making a left turn.

THE FBI AND DR. MARTIN LUTHER KING, JR.

"The FBI treated the civil rights movement as if it were an alien enemy attack on the United States."
—Coretta Scott King, as quoted in *The FBI and Martin Luther King, Jr.*

MISCELLANEOUS WAYS THE FBI
TRIED TO DISCREDIT KING

Hoover's vendetta against the Rev. Martin Luther King, Jr. was the low point of the Director's public career. In addition to trying to convince King to commit suicide, insinuating that he was controlled by Communists and circulating tapes of King's sexual activities to newsmen, the Bureau:

1. Tried to block honorary degrees given to King by Marquette University and Springfield (Mass.) College. (Marquette was particularly annoying to Hoover since he had received an honorary degree from the school himself.)

2. Got the IRS to check King for tax violations. In mid-March, 1964, the IRS informed the FBI it had been unable to locate any in either King's or SCLC's tax returns. Hoover commented, "What a farce."

3. Attempted to get Francis Cardinal Spellman of New York to cancel a King audience with the Pope. The meeting took place, and Hoover said, "I am amazed that the Pope gave an audience to such a degenerate."

4. Sent damaging reports to the White House, acting Attorney General Nicholas Katzenbach, and others to try to stop King from getting the Nobel Peace Prize. Hoover commented, "King could well qualify for the 'top alley cat' prize."

5. Tried to block a Ford Foundation grant of $250,000 to King's Southern Christian Leadership Conference, but foundation president McGeorge Bundy rejected an offer to hear the case against King.

6. Tried to block a $60,000 Labor Department program to provide grocery store jobs to Atlanta blacks and attempted to cut National Science Foundation funding for the SCLC.

7. Floated a rumor that King had a secret Swiss bank account.

8. Sent allegations of King's ties to Communists to UN Ambassador Adlai Stevenson, U.N. official Ralph Bunche, Sen. Hubert H. Humphrey, Gov. Nelson Rockefeller, U.S. ambassadors in London and Oslo, Rep. John Rooney (D-N.Y.), officials of the National Council of Churches and newsmen

Mike Royko of the Chicago *Sun-Times,* Ralph McGill, Atlanta *Constitution* and political columnist Carl Rowan.

FREEDOM OF THE PRESS

David J. Garrow, who wrote *The FBI and Martin Luther King, Jr.,* was harassed repeatedly by the FBI while writing his book. FBI agents visited Garrow at the University of North Carolina, where he teaches. According to *Organizing Notes,* Nov.-Dec., 1981, at one point, an agent offered Garrow $250,000 to stop publication of the book.

More recently, a high-ranking FBI counterintelligence officer warned him that his disclosure of agents' identities would constitute a felony under the Intelligence Identities Protection Act. Knowing that the bill had not yet passed into law (it has subsequently), Garrow was not deterred.

A GRAVE IMPOSITION

Less than a month after King's assassination, the FBI renewed its request for wiretaps on SCLC headquarters which were ignored by Attorney General Ramsey Clark. Hoover also okayed a DeLoach idea to plant a newspaper story that Coretta King and Rev. Ralph Abernathy were charging that King's death was the result of a conspiracy to profit from a flow of contributions to the SCLC.

A New York wiretap on King friend and supposed Communist Stanley Levison remained in effect long after King's death. More than a year later, in fact, Nixon appointees Henry Kissinger, Egil "Bud" Krogh, Jr. and Alexander Butterfield received reports of phone conversations between Levison and King's widow, Coretta Scott King. On learning in March, 1969 that Congress was considering a proposal to make King's birthday a national holiday, Hoover approved "briefing" key Congressman *"very cautiously."*

> *"I've long been aware of the fact that my telephone is tapped...*
> *I even have agents hiding in the bushes outside of my apartment*
> *building. People come by my house and say, 'Look at Dick*
> *Gregory's bushes. They have feet.' I tell them, 'Yes, and my*
> *bushes change shifts every eight hours.'"*
> —Comedian Dick Gregory as quoted in *Superspies*

5 GOALS OF THE FBI'S "BLACK NATIONALIST HATE GROUP" COUNTER-INTELLIGENCE PROGRAM

On March 4, 1968, the FBI sent a memo to all field offices listing goals for its "black nationalist hate group" program as follows:

1. Prevent the coalition of militant black nationalist groups... An effective coalition of black nationalist hate groups might be the first step toward a real "Mau Mau" in America, the beginning of a true black revolution.

2. Prevent the rise of a "messiah" who could unify, and electrify, the militant black nationalist movement ... [Stokely] Carmichael has the necessary charisma to be a real threat this way.

3. Prevent violence on the part of black nationalist groups. This is of primary importance.

4. Prevent militant black nationalist groups and leaders from gaining respectability by discrediting them.

5. Prevent the long-range growth of militant black nationalist organizations, especially among youth.

Source: *The FBI and Martin Luther King, Jr.*

***

FBI LETTER SENT ANONYMOUSLY TO BOTH THE BLACK PANTHERS AND STUDENTS FOR A DEMOCRATIC SOCIETY

"Dear Brothers and Sisters,

Since when do us Blacks have to swallow the dictates of the honky SDS? Doing this only hinders the Party progress in gaining Black control over Black people... We say to hell with the SDS and its honky intellectual approaches which only perpetuate control of Black people by the honkies... They call themselves revolutionaries but take a look at who they are. Most of them come from well-heeled families even by honky standards... The time has come for an absolute break with any non-black group and especially those—SDS... Off the Pigs!"

Source: *Superspies*

JEAN SEBERG

Actress Jean Seberg was a highly visible supporter of the Black Panther Party in the late '60s. In 1970, the Los Angeles FBI office requested Washington's permission to float a rumor that she was pregnant via a BPP leader in an effort to discredit her, according to *Citizen Hoover*.

A "blind" item (not mentioning her by name) was published in the Los Angeles *Times*. When *Newsweek* subsequently published it, Seberg and her novelist husband Romain Gary successfully sued for libel. Seberg's baby was stillborn and she tried to kill herself every year on the anniversary of the delivery. When she committed suicide in August, 1979, Gary charged the publicity had led to the stillborn delivery, breakdown and death by her own hand.

HOOVER AND THE RNA

Hoover devoted much effort to detailing a complex plot being developed by a black group called the Republic of New Africa (RNA.) In *Citizen Hoover*, Robert Jay Nash quotes at length from a detailed Hoover memo. The Director said, in part, "RNA was established for the purpose of forming a Black nation inside the United States... Its founders proposed that efforts be made for international recognition with assistance from Fidel Castro's Cuba, Red China, Tanzania and other nations.

Steps have been taken to *buy land in Mississippi* [italics ours] where RNA proposes to build a landing strip long enough for 'Chinese jets to land.'... A training program has been formulated and a complete uniform has been designed, including leopard-skin epaulets."

STATEMENT FROM A BLACK FBI INFORMANT ON HOW HE DISRUPTED BLACK PANTHER UNITY

"Say they bust three brothers... and place them in the cell with me. We're there for three days so we get to rapping, then one day I reach in my shoe and pull out three joints and we smoke 'em. We start rapping some more and I say, 'Do you know that dirty such and such? That dirty bastard is a pig, man. I know he's a pig because he busted me.' 'Oh yeah?' they say. Then I tell them all I know about the cat... That starts it.

"Now you got three brothers believing it because their 'information' comes from a righteous brother in the jail they were smoking weed with and he told them this guy was the one who identified him to the police. Now, you see, you have planted the seeds of distrust so you start planting a little more.

"You start busting people all around him. You know they are going to kill him so you just sit and watch. When it happens, you just pick up the two or three men who killed him... you get rid of four brothers at one time plus a public outcry is raised, 'Get those crazy people off the streets.'"

Source: *Superspies*

***

KING AND THE FBI: A CHRONOLOGY

1962

Jan. 8—A report issued by the Southern Regional Council (which had close ties to the Southern Christian Leadership Conference) sharply criticizes FBI officials for standing by when local citizens and police beat up civil rights demonstrators.

May 11—Dr. King's name is added to Section A of the FBI's "Reserve Index," the number two "enemies list" behind the top-ranked "Security Index."

Oct. 24—The FBI's Crime Records Division sends stories on King's friend Jack O'Dell to five newspapers. Virtually identical stories speak inaccurately of O'Dell being "acting executive director" of the Southern Christian Leadership Conference and mentioned his past as "a concealed member of the national committee of the Communist Party."

Nov. 18—King says in a New York *Times* interview that "The FBI has not made a single arrest on behalf of Negro citizens... One of the great problems we face with the FBI in the South is that the agents are white Southerners who have been influenced by the mores of the community... If an FBI man agrees with segregation, he can't honestly and objectively investigate."

1963

Jan. 8—Hoover tells Attorney General Robert F. Kennedy that Stanley Levison, a close friend and confidant of King, is a member of the U.S. Communist Party. The FBI's allegations were based on an informant's report that, in 1954, Levison had been active in the Labor Youth League, a group described as "subversive" but not Communist.

June 22—President John F. Kennedy warns King to dissociate himself from Levison and O'Dell, both alleged to have ties to the Communist Party. "If they shoot *you* down, they'll shoot us down, too—so we're asking you to be careful."

Aug. 23—A 68-page FBI report prepared by assistant FBI director William C. Sullivan concludes the Communist Party's attempt to infiltrate the civil rights movement has been a total failure. Hoover vehemently rejects it.

Aug. 28—King delivers "I have a dream" speech at the conclusion of the March on Washington.

Aug. 30—The Bureau does an about-face. Sullivan answers Hoover's objections to his original memo and calls King's "I have a dream" speech "demagogic" and calls King "the most dangerous Negro of the future in this Nation from the standpoint of communism, the Negro and national security." He adds, "it may be unrealistic to limit ourselves as we have been doing to legalistic proofs or definitely conclusive evidence that would stand up in testimony in court or before Congressional Committees."

Oct. 10—Attorney General Robert Kennedy agrees to "technical coverage on King," approving wiretap on SCLC New York headquarters.

Oct. 15—The FBI completes a monograph called "Communism and the Negro Movement—A Current Analysis." Hoover sends copies to the White House, the Attorney General, the CIA, the military services and State and Defense departments. On Oct. 25, after approving a tap on King's home telephone, Attorney General Kennedy calls the report "very, very unfair" to King and fears it may kill the administration's civil rights bill if it is released... By the next morning, every copy is recalled.

Oct. 30—The FBI completes installation of taps on every telephone at SCLC New York headquarters. By Nov. 8th, all lines at King's home and Atlanta office were also tapped.

1964

Jan. 8—An FBI memo states that King must be taken "off his pedestal" and his influence should be vastly reduced so the FBI can select its *own* candidate "to assume the role of leadership of the Negro People."

Jan. 22—The FBI burglarizes SCLC headquarters in New York.

Nov. 18—Hoover calls King "the most notorious liar" in America before a group of women reporters. King responds two days later that Hoover "has faltered under the awesome burden, complexities and responsibilities of his office... I have nothing but sympathy for this man who has served his country so well."

Nov. 21—FBI agent Lish Whitsun flies to Miami and mails an audio tape and letter to King's Atlanta office. The letter read, "King, look into your heart. You know you are a complete fraud and a great liability to all us Negroes... You, even at an early age, have turned out not to be a leader but a dissolute, abnormal moral imbecile... King, there is only one thing left for you to do. You know what it is."

Nov. 24—Speaking in Chicago, Hoover attacks "pressure groups" headed by "Communists and moral degenerates." The next day, CORE National Director James Farmer calls for Hoover's resignation.

Nov. 9—An FBI memo terms efforts to block contributions to the SCLC "quite successful."

1967

Aug. 25—An FBI memo advocates using "any tactics" to rid the U.S. of any groups like the SCLC.

1968

April 4—Martin Luther King, Jr. is assassinated in Memphis, Tenn. touching off violence throughout the nation.

"Investigate *them*? Heck, that's mah posse."

McCARTHYISM & THE RED SCARE

> *"Joseph McCarthy was a pirate... the pirate is not amenable
> to moral laws because he recognizes none. By the very act of
> becoming a pirate, he has forced the moral code, which is
> binding on other men, to walk the plank."*

> —Author Lately Thomas in *When Even Angels Wept*

THE McCARTHY 205

On February 9, 1950, Senator Joseph McCarthy (R-Wisc.) spoke at a Lincoln Day dinner in Wheeling, West Virginia. The Republican crowd expected a hard-hitting partisan speech but were astonished to hear McCarthy say, "I have here in my hand a list of 205 that were known to the Secretary of State as being members of the Communist Party and are still working and shaping the policy of the State Department."

In *The Glory and the Dream*, William Manchester reveals that McCarthy's 205 Communists were obtained from an inquiry into the loyalty of State Department employees. It started with a letter written by Secretary of State James Byrnes to Rep. Adolph Sabath (R-Ill.) In his letter, Byrnes explained that, during a preliminary screening of some 3,000 federal employees transferred to the State Department at the end of World War II, screeners had recommended that 284 not be permanently employed.

Of those 284, 79 were dismissed and the rest hired. McCarthy subtracted 79 from 284, giving him his 205 Communists. He had no other raw data, dossiers or other evidence to back up his allegations.

DEFINITIONS OF McCARTHYISM

The Nation—Spreading unsubstantiated insinuations and making accusations, based on anonymous sources.

Random House Dictionary—public accusation of disloyalty... in many instances unsupported by proof or based on slight, doubtful or irrelevant evidence..."

American Heritage Dictionary—political practice of publicizing accusations... with insufficient regard to evidence.

Harry Truman—"the corruption of truth... the use of the big lie and unfounded accusations." In turn, McCarthy defined Trumanism as "the placing of your party above the interest of your country."

Source: *When Even Angels Wept*

SILENCING THE "VOICE"

McCarthy's first investigation as chairman of the Senate Committee on Government Operations concerned the "Voice of America." The main focus was the construction of two huge radio transmitters, built to counteract Soviet jamming, according to *Witch Hunt*.

One, Baker East, was placed near Wilmington, N.C.; the other, Baker West, near Seattle, Wash. McCarthy charged that the sites chosen were the worst possible because atmospheric conditions caused interference that disrupted radio signals. Based on the testimony of one "Voice" engineer (Lewis McKesson), he claimed the placement was deliberate sabotage by subversive "Voice" officials.

The sites were chosen by experts from MIT, the Army Signal Corps and RCA's Radio Propagation Laboratory. After "Voice" officials asked the panel to consider their decision again, the same sites were selected and MIT's Dr. Jerome B. Wiesner, later science advisor to Presidents Kennedy and Johnson, stated that McKesson's methods were "so oversimplified as to lead to erroneous conclusions."

"Voice" officials asked for yet a third study and the same conclusions were reached; McCarthy's final report said the hearings suggest "deliberate sabotage as a possible alternative to hopeless incompetence." The State Department, fearing the risks of further antagonizing McCarthy, decided to abandon the project. The transmitters, which had cost $8 million, were dismantled and placed in storage.

A great deal of the planning had been done by a "Voice" engineer named Raymond Kaplan, who felt the sabotage charges reflected on his personal loyalty. Amid the continuing suspicion, Kaplan jumped in front of a truck in Boston, and left a note saying he was taking his life because of the McCarthy investigation. He said, "Once the dogs are set on you, everything you have done from the beginning of time is suspect."

DECLARATION OF CONSCIENCE

On June 1, 1950, less than four months after McCarthy began his meteoric rise to power, seven Republican senators chastised their colleague by preparing a "Declaration of Conscience."

Margaret Chase Smith of Maine offered the resolution, which was supported by George Aiken of Vermont, Charles Tobey of New Hampshire, Irving Ives of New York, Edward Thye of Minnesota, Wayne Morse of Oregon and Robert Hendrickson of New Jersey. Smith said, "I don't want to see the Republican Party ride to political victory on the Four Horsemen of Calumny—Fear, Ignorance, Bigotry and Smear."

PUBLICATIONS McCARTHY ACCUSED OF "APING THE COMMUNIST LINE"

New York *Times*

St. Louis *Post-Dispatch*

Milwaukee *Journal*

Denver *Post*

Syracuse *Post-Standard*

Christian Science Monitor

Time

Life

Saturday Evening Post

He reserved special scorn for the Washington *Post*, Madison (Wisc.) *Capital Times* and New York *Post*, calling them "local editions of the *Daily Worker*."

Source: *When Even Angels Wept*

***

JFK AND McCARTHY

In 1952, two-time Congressman John F. Kennedy was in a close race for U.S. Senator of Massachusetts against the incumbent, Henry Cabot Lodge. McCarthy was near the height of his public support, especially among Irish Catholics in Boston, and his active support of fellow Republican Lodge would have been fatal to Kennedy's chances.

According to *Witch Hunt*, the redoubtable Joseph Kennedy turned the tide for his son. The elder Kennedy, who had contributed to McCarthy's Wisconsin race, persuaded him to stay out of Massachusetts during the campaign. With JFK's subsequent election to the Senate, Papa Joe became a financial supporter of McCarthy, and Bobby Kennedy was placed on the staff of McCarthy's Subcommittee on Government Operations.

When McCarthy's vote for censure came up in the Senate, JFK was conveniently in a Boston hospital with a back ailment. (Some wits suggested he must have been there for a backbone transplant.) Eleanor Roosevelt never forgave his neutrality and refused to support him for the presidency in 1960.

RIGHT ON JOHN

During the Watergate trials in 1974, Judge John Sirica told New York *Times* reporter Tad Szulc that, in 1950, Joe McCarthy had offered him the chief counsel post of his Senate Committee before offering it to Roy Cohn. In *Compulsive Spy*, Szulc writes that Sirica did not take the assignment because he thought McCarthy was "uncontrollable."

THE BILL OF FAR RIGHTS

In 1951, the Madison Capital *Times* of McCarthy's home state drafted a petition made up entirely of quotes from the Declaration of Independence and the Bill of Rights, according to former U.S. Army counsel John Adams in *Without Precedent*.

A reporter was sent out to solicit signatures. By the end of the day, all 111 people he had approached refused to sign it because it was "too subversive."

AND TO THINK HE LEARNED IT FROM A REDSKIN

During the Army-McCarthy brouhaha, McCarthy accused Defense Department counsel Struve Hensel of conflict of interest with evidence that had been discredited by both the IRS and McCarthy's own committee. According to then-Army counsel John Adams in his book, *Without Precedent*, McCarthy had known about the charges, yet, he had voted to confirm Hensel as assistant secretary of defense for International Security Affairs a few weeks before.

Weeks later, the charges were dropped and McCarthy admitted he was "only guessing." Hensel heard the admission and asked McCarthy why he would do such a thing. The senator responded that he had learned from an "old Indian friend" named "Indian Charlie" that "when anyone approached him in a not completely friendly fashion, (to) start kicking that person in the balls and continue to kick until there was nothing but air where the balls used to be."

***

MAY DAY, MAY DAY

On May 1, 1950, a mock Communist takeover was staged in Mosinee, Wisconsin, McCarthy's home state. Author Lately Thomas recounts in *When Even Angels Wept* that American Legionnaires in masks set up roadblocks with barbed wire, halted people for identity cards and herded those who protested into "concentration camps."

That morning, the mayor, with a pistol in his back, announced the town's complete surrender to the United Soviet States of America and commented, "God must have willed it this way, and maybe it's for the best."

The public library was "purged" and a film about Cardinal Mindszenty playing at a local theater was banned. Lunch rooms served nothing but black bread and potato soup. At the end of the day, everybody unmasked at a patriotic rally in the town square. After the phony demonstration was over, the mayor suffered a real heart attack.

THE WINDS OF WAR

According to a poll taken in August, 1950—when the Internal Security Act (McCarran Act) was under debate in the Senate—the public would have gone even farther than McCarran and his cold war colleagues.

Asked what the government should do regarding U.S. communists in the event of war with the Soviet Union:

- 28 percent settled on internment
- 18 percent favored imprisonment
- 15 percent liked the idea of exile
- 13 percent approved of deportation to the Soviet Union
- 13 percent found the idea of execution appropriate

Those who believed civil liberties applied even to Communists in wartime numbered 1 percent; the other 12 percent had no opinion.

Source: *The Rhetoric of Politics*

WORLD WAR III

On October 27, 1951, *Collier's* magazine devoted an entire issue to a *Preview of the War We Do Not Want*. Published at the height of the Red Scare, it gives chilling testimony to the reality of the Cold War mentality that prevailed at the time. The issue featured an impressive list of contributors as this selected list attests:

The Third World War—Robert E. Sherwood, prize-winning play-wright

A-Bomb Mission to Moscow—Edward R. Murrow, the renowned broadcaster

How the War Was Fought—Hanson Baldwin, New York *Times* military writer

Freedom—At Long Last—Arthur Koestler, author of *Darkness At Noon*

Women of Russia—Marguerite Higgins, famous war correspondent

Free Men At Work—Walter Reuther, labor leader

Walter Winchell in Moscow—by the archetypal gossip columnist

Moscow Olympics—Red Smith, prize-winning sportswriter

Russia's Rebirth—Sen. Margaret Chase Smith (R-Me.)

The issue also featured a "chronology" of the war:

1952

Assassination attempt on Marshal Tito's life precipitates uprising in Yugoslavia. Troops from satellite nations, backed by Red Army, cross borders... War begins when Moscow refuses to withdraw Red Army units... U.S. is joined by principal UN nations in declaration of war... Saturation A-bombing of U.S.S.R. begins... U.S. A-bombed when Red air force hits Detroit and New York.

1953

UN Air Force finally achieves air superiority... Moscow A-bombed midnight, July 22nd... Suicide task force lands behind U.S.S.R. borders, destroys remaining A-bomb stockpile... Severest rationing since beginning of war introduced in U.S.

1954

A captured Soviet general reports disappearance of Stalin. Secret police chief Beria is new Red dictator... Uprisings take place in U.S.S.R. and satellite nations... Red army gradually retreats, then disintegrates under onslaught of air and ground forces... Marines, in combined air-sea operation, capture and occupy Vladivostok.

1955

Hostilities cease as U.S.S.R. degenerates into a state of chaos... UN forces begin occupation duties in satellite nations and Ukraine.

***

THE OLD MATH

In October, 1953, President Eisenhower announced that in the first four months of his new stricter loyalty program, 1,456 employees had been sacked. Vice President Nixon later quoted the figure of 6,926.

The figures sounded good, but John Adams debunks them in *Without Precedent*. For instance, of the first 1,456, Adams says only

29 involved charges of disloyalty. The others were drinkers, "blab-bermouths," women with children born out of wedlock and homosexuals. The figure was later upped to 2,429 dismissals of which 422 were considered "subversive."

***

HUAC'S ENEMIES LIST

In 1950, *The New Republic* published a list of esteemed men and women who had been mentioned "unfavorably" in testimony before the House Un-American Activities Committee (HUAC) including the following:

Leonard Bernstein	Norman Mailer
Pearl Buck	Reinhold Niebuhr
Erskine Caldwell	Dorothy Parker
Clarence Darrow	Arthur Schlesinger
Albert Einstein	Budd Schulberg
George Gershwin	Upton Sinclair
Ernest Hemingway	Frank Lloyd Wright

Source: *When Even Angels Wept*

SPEAKERS OF THE HOUSE

In October, 1970, HUAC stirred up a furor by releasing a list of 65 "radical" campus speakers. Among those listed were John Ciardi, poetry editor of *Saturday Review,* Dr. Benjamin Spock and Reverend John C. Bennett, former president of the Union Theological Seminary in New York.

According to *Witch Hunt*, the ACLU filed a suit prohibiting publication since such publication would violate the right of free speech. U.S. District Court Judge Gerhard A. Gesell issued an injunction barring publication.

HUAC Chairman Richard Ichord (D-Mo.) had a slightly different list prepared, then asked the full House to pass a resolution prohibiting anyone from obstructing distribution of the revised report. Since Judge Gesell's injunction only applied to the original report, it could not be used to block the revised report which was printed and distributed at public expense.

A HAPPY FACULTY FOR PARODY

The Parrots of Penance

(After The Pirates of Penzance by Gilbert & Sullivan)
—Anonymous, 1952, as quoted in
A Treasury of American Political Humor

I am the very model of a member of the faculty
Because I'm simply overcome with sentiments of loyalty.
I daily think of reasons why I'm glad to be American,
And thank the Lord I've always been a registered Republican.
The thoughts I think are only thoughts approved by my community.
I pledge allegiance to the flag at every opportunity.
I haven't had a thing to do with Communist conspirators,
And neither have my relatives, descendants or progenitors.
I try to keep away from propositions controversial;
I've no opinions social, economic, or commercial.
And so you see that I must be, with sentiments of loyalty,
The perfect model of a member of the faculty.

LOYALTY, 1974

Witch Hunt reveals that in April, 1974, Ira Glasser, executive director of the ACLU's New York chapter was fired from a part-time teaching post at New York University after refusing to sign an oath swearing he would uphold the New York and U.S. Constitutions. Glasser said, "It's exacting a gesture of obeisance to the state as a requirement of teaching." The course he had been teaching before his dismissal was called "The Repressive Society."

***

"One of the tenets of democracy... is a... repugnance to
anyone who would steal from a human being that which is most
precious to him—his good name—either by imputing things to
him by innuendo or by insinuation. And it is especially an
unhappy circumstance that occasionally that is done in the name
of democracy. This I think, can tear our country apart and
destroy it if we carry it further."
—TVA director David E. Lilienthal before a
Joint Congressional Committee in 1946,
as quoted in *The Glory and the Dream*

CELEBRITIES WHO WERE REFUSED PASSPORTS
OR VISAS IN THE '40s & '50s
BECAUSE OF "COMMUNIST LEANINGS"

Novelist Graham Greene—denied a visa in 1952 because he had been a CP member for four weeks in 1923. When it was finally granted, a New York *Times* editorial decried the "...depths of puerility to which our immigration laws have been allowed to sink."

Playwright Arthur Miller—denied a passport to see his own play, *The Crucible* produced in Belgium in 1954.

Novelist Alberto Moravia—refused a visa in July, 1952 although his visit had been suggested by State Department educational-exchange officials.

Conductor Joseph Krips—not allowed to play with the Chicago Symphony Orchestra because he had conducted in Moscow and Leningrad.

Performer Maurice Chevalier—barred because he had played in pro-Communist entertainments.

Actor Edward G. Robinson—denied a passport from the late '40s until he made peace with HUAC in 1952.

Artist Rockwell Kent—refused a passport to visit Ireland in 1953; was told he would not be granted a passport "to travel anywhere for any purpose."

Poet Stephen Spender—refused a visit to lecture at Harvard in 1949.

Screenwriter Ring Lardner, Jr.—denied a passport from 1953-1958.

Screenwriter Donald Ogden Stewart—denied a passport for seven years until he got a favorable ruling from an Appeals Court in 1957.

Scientist Linus Pauling—denied a passport until he won the Nobel Prize in 1954.

Supreme Court Justice William O. Douglas—denied a passport to visit China.

Actor-Singer Paul Robeson—passport held since 1922 revoked in August, 1950. In February, 1952, U.S. officials prevented his entering Canada. With the aid of loudspeakers, he was able to give a concert across the border.

Screenwriter Carl Foreman—passport refused in 1954 but granted in 1956 after he made peace privately with HUAC chairman Francis E. Walter.

Judge William L. Clark—refused a passport to visit Germany where he had been Chief Justice of the Allied Control Commission courts.

By December 31, 1951, there was a backlog of 9,197 visa applications. In May, 1952, Secretary of State Dean Acheson explained it was his policy to withhold a passport from anyone:
1) if there was "reason to believe" he was in the Communist Party.
2) "whose conduct abroad is likely to be contrary to the best interest of the United States."
3) believed to be "going abroad to engage in activities which will advance the Communist movement."

Source: *The Great Fear*

BIG BROTHER'S PEN PALS

These are representative excerpts from letters written to federal employees during the Red Scare, according to *The Glory and the Dream*:

"Since 1943 you have been a close associate of _____, an individual who, evidence in our files indicates, has displayed an active, sympathetic interest in the principles and policies of the Communist Party..."

"Your name appeared in an article in _____ as a sponsor of a mass meeting sponsored by the National Committee to Win the Peace. (It) has been cited by the Attorney General as Communist."

"During your period of employment by _____ you made statements to the effect that you believed "the House Committee on Un-American Activities hearings in Washington, DC. are a greater threat to civil liberties than the Communist Party because they infringe on free speech."

Following any of these introductions came the punch line: "The foregoing information indicates that you have been and are a member, close affiliate or sympathetic associate of the Communist Party."

> *"I killed more people tonight than I have fingers on my hands. I shot them in cold blood and enjoyed every minute of it... They were Commies, Lee. They were Red sons-of-bitches who should have died long ago... They never thought that there were people like me in this country. They figured us all to be soft as horse manure and just as stupid."*
>
> —Mike Hammer in Mickey Spillane's *One Lonely Night*, as quoted in *The Glory and the Dream*

THE STAMP ACT

In 1954, San Antonio housewife Myrtle Glasscock Hance proposed that the public library brand with a stamp all books that had been written by authors who had been called Communists, according to *The Glory and the Dream*.

Mrs. Hance wanted a large bright red stamp put inside the book that would specify the writer's Communistic tendencies and the number of "citations" he or she had received. "The reader will then realize that in many instances he is reading Communist propaganda."

Her idea was embellished by the mayor's wife, who suggested that a list be made of the people who actually checked out the books. The list could then be either published in the San Antonio *News* or turned over to the FBI.

***

"Fascism is not defined by the number of its victims, but by the way it kills them."
—Jean Paul Sartre on the trial of the Rosenbergs,
as quoted in *The Great Fear*

BANNED AUTHORS

The following list includes "communists, fellow travelers and undesirable authors" whose books Secretary of State John Foster Dulles ordered removed from State Department libraries in the '50s. The books were removed after McCarthy pressured the State Department by investigating the International Information Administration, forerunner of the U.S. Information Agency.

Franklin P. Adams—syndicated columnist and member of the Algonquin Roundtable.

Sherwood Anderson—best known for his short stories, *Winesburg, Ohio* and *Poor White*.

Brooks Atkinson—distinguished drama critic of the New York *Times*.

W. H. Auden—his poetry dealt with social and political problems in works like *The Orators*, *The Dance of Death*, and *Age of Anxiety*.

Stephen Vincent Benet—poet best known for his Civil War epic, *John Brown's Body*, for which he received a Pulitzer Prize in 1929.

Louis Bromfield—won the Pulitzer Prize for *Autumn* and wrote *The Green Bay Tree, Possession,* and *The Rains Came.*

Van Wyck Brooks—literary critic best known for *The Flowering of New England.*

Henry Steele Commager—prize-winning historian who has written or edited literally hundreds of authoritative books.

Elmer Davis—author of *Across the Wide Missouri, The Journals of Lewis and Clark.*

John Dewey—pragmatic philosopher. Author of *How We Think, Freedom and Culture* and *The Quest For Certainty.*

Theodore Dreiser—*An American Tragedy, Sister Carrie.*

Edna Ferber—*Giant, So Big, Saratoga Trunk.*

Archibald MacLeish—twice a Pulitzer prize-winning poet (1933 and 1952) and the man who told us, "A poem should not mean but be."

Quentin Reynolds—war correspondent; biographer of the Wright Brothers, Judge Samuel Leibowitz, General Custer, Winston Churchill and Adolph Eichmann.

Arthur Schlesinger, Jr.—historian, who won the Pulitzer Prize in 1945 for *The Age of Jackson,* and wrote *Robert F. Kennedy and His Times.*

Carl Van Doren—founder and editor-in-chief of the Literary Guild and author of many books about American literature.

Mark Van Doren—poet and critic, author of critical studies of Thoreau, Dryden, and Shakespeare.

Edmund Wilson—eminent literary critic and author of *Axel's Castle, The Shock of Recognition* and *Memoirs of Hecate County.*

Source: *The Great Fear*

THE RED SCARE AND ENTERTAINMENT

"The blacklist was a time of evil, and... no one on either side who survived it came through untouched by evil... There was bad faith and good, honesty and dishonesty, courage and cowardice, selflessness and opportunism, wisdom and stupidity, good and bad on both sides... it will do no good to search for villains or heroes or saints or devils because there were none: there were only victims."

—Blacklisted screenwriter Dalton Trumbo, after receiving the Screen Writers Guild's Laurel Award in 1970, as quoted in *Naming Names*

HUACSPEAK

The House Un-American Activities Committee (HUAC) gave Hollywood a new script to learn including these three key terms:

Friendly witness: One who testified before the Committee and acted as an informer.

Unfriendly witness: One who declined to answer questions based on the First or Fifth amendment to the Bill of Rights.

Blacklisting: The unwritten understanding that show business people were not to be employed if they had:

a) been named as current or former Communists at committee hearings

b) if, when testifying, the artist refused to answer questions, claiming constitutional immunity.

The exception to blacklisting occurred when a friendly witness confessed that he or she *had* been a Communist but was *no longer* a Communist *and* offered the committee names of persons he/she suspected to be or to have been Communists.

Witnesses testifying before the House Un-American Activities Committee had basically three choices. They could:

1. Invoke the First Amendment which guarantees free speech and association—and risk going to jail. Entertainment industry witnesses who did so became known as the Hollywood 10 (see below).
2. Invoke the Fifth Amendment, with its provision against self-incrimination and lose their jobs. Howard Da Silva and actress Gale Sondergaard (''The Spider Woman'') were among the ones who did and were subsequently blacklisted.
3. Name names and hope to continue working.

SUPPORTERS OF THE COMMITTEE FOR THE FIRST AMENDMENT IN OPPOSITION TO HUAC

In the fall of 1947, the following stars signed an ad in a Hollywood trade paper denouncing HUAC for questioning actors about their political beliefs.

Lauren Bacall	Humphrey Bogart	Melvyn Douglas
Lucille Ball	Eddie Cantor	Henry Fonda
Ethel Barrymore	Kirk Douglas	Ava Gardner

John Garfield	Burt Lancaster	Robert Ryan
Paulette Goddard	Peter Lorre	Frank Sinatra
Katherine Hepburn	Groucho Marx	Orson Welles
William Holden	Gregory Peck	Robert Young
John Huston	Edward G. Robinson	

Source: *The Great Fear*

11 CATEGORIES OF PEOPLE WHO NAMED NAMES

In *Naming Names,* his chronicle of Hollywood's Red Scare, author Victor Navasky makes important, sometimes comical, distinctions among Hollywood people who "named names." People tattled on their colleagues for a variety of complex reasons, to wit:

1. The Reluctant informers: Larry Parks (*The Jolson Story*) and writer George Beck, who told the committee that not by the furthest stretch of imagination "could they be considered bomb-throwers."

2. The Willing informers: Actor Robert Taylor testified, "If I had my way they (Communists) would all be sent back to Russia or some other unpleasant place." (Screenwriter Bart Lytton closed his office on the day he was called to testify, so his staff could come and watch.)

3. The Uninformed informer: Bandleader Artie Shaw said he wasn't sure that he had been a Party member. Shaw told HUAC: "I was certainly a bad Communist. It was never my intention to be one and to the best of my knowledge I have never been one, although these people may have assumed I was." Shaw promised that in the future he would not sign anything "unless I had the advice of seven lawyers and the granting of permission or clearance by this committee."

4. Truth-telling informer: Novelist Budd Schulberg testified, in part, out of pique at the Party's interference with his literary efforts, most notably his novel, *What Makes Sammy Run.*

5. Combative informer: Playright Clifford Odets named names, but lectured HUAC on the meaning of poverty saying "When I wrote, sir, it was out of central, personal things. I did not learn my hatred of poverty, sir, out of Communism." Odets

named J. Edward Bromberg, then, years later, when delivering the eulogy at Bromberg's memorial service, said HUAC was responsible for his death.

6. Groveling informer: Nicholas Bela, Hungarian-born writer who said he was naming names out of respect to the Committee. "I want to humbly apologize for the grave error which I have committed and beg of you to forgive me."

7. Denigrating informer: Screenwriter Leopold Atlas described a Party meeting where Alvah Bessie (of the Hollywood 10) was "dripping venom" in denouncing a fellow comrade.

8. Laudatory informer: Playwright John Wexley recalled in *Naming Names* that "Leo Townsend, who named me, named me in the guise of a eulogy. He doubled the salary I was getting and praised my writing."

9. Noisy informer: Director Elia Kazan (*On the Waterfront*) who took out an ad in the New York *Times* denouncing Communism and renouncing his involvement in the Party.

10. Comic informer: Playwright Abe Burrows (*Guys and Dolls*) said although he may have looked, talked and acted like a Communist, "In my own heart I didn't believe it."

11. Miscellaneous informers: Actor Sterling Hayden (*The Asphalt Jungle*) named his former mistress; screenwriter Melvin Levy (*The Bandit of Sherwood Forest*) named his collaborator. *Song of Russia* screenwriter Richard Collins named a creditor.

***

THE HOLLYWOOD TEN

These movie people refused to testify before HUAC as to whether or not they had ever been members of the Communist Party. They were cited for contempt of Congress as a result and later served jail terms.

1. Alvah Bessie—screenwriter of *The Very Thought Of You* (1944), *Hotel Berlin* (1945) and *Objective Burma* (1945) and wrote a book based on his fighting during the Spanish Civil War entitled *Men in Battle*. He was awarded a Guggenheim Fellowship for creative writing and served as a drama critic for *New Masses*.

2. Herbert Biberman—director of *Meet Nero Wolfe* (1936) and *The Master Race* (1941). Married to blacklisted actress Gale Sondergaard.

3. Lester Cole—screenwriter on over 36 films including *Objective Burma* and *High Wall*.

4. Edward Dmytryk—directed 24 films between 1929 and 1949 including *Till the End of Time* (1946), *Crossfire* (1947), and *Hitler's Children* (1943). Some years later, much to the dismay of his co-resistors, he changed his mind and named names for the Committee.

5. Ring Lardner, Jr.—screenwriter son of the famed humorist was co-author of *Woman of the Year*, which won an Academy Award in 1942.

6. John Howard Lawson—screenwriter. First president of the Screen Writers Guild. Wrote *Action in the North Atlantic* (1943) and *Sahara (1943)*.

7. Albert Maltz—screenwriter and O. Henry winner for his short stories. Maltz worked on *This Gun for Hire*, (1942), *Pride of the Marines*, (1945) and *Destination Tokyo* (1944).

8. Samuel Ornitz—screenwriter on 25 films between 1929 and 1949, but best known for his novel, *Haunch, Paunch and Jowl*.

9. Robert Adrian Scott—writer/producer whose films included *Murder My Sweet* (1944), *Crossfire* (1947) and *Cornered* (1946).

10. Dalton Trumbo—One of the highest-paid screenwriters in Hollywood. Trumbo's credits include *Kitty Foyle* (1940), *Thirty Seconds over Tokyo* (1944), and the successful novel, *Johnny Got His Gun*.

All were convicted in U.S. District Court, and eight got the maximum sentence, a year in jail and a $1,000 fine. Biberman and Dmytryk received six-month jail terms and $1,000 fines. All ten appealed their convictions which were upheld on June 13, 1949 by the U.S. Court of Appeals for the District of Columbia. The Supreme Court declined to review the cases.

Ironically, HUAC chairman J. Parnell Thomas went to jail in 1949 after his conviction for taking kickbacks from his staff. He was locked up in a Danbury, Conn. prison where his fellow inmates included Lester Cole and Ring Lardner, Jr.

HOWARD HUGHES, BLACKLISTER

Despite the blacklist, Biberman tried to put together a movie. *Salt of the Earth* concerned a strike against New Jersey Zinc in Bayard, N.M. by the Mine, Mill and Smelter Workers Union in 1951. After the union's largely Mexican-American membership was faced with a Taft-Hartley injunction preventing picketing, the women of the union's Ladies Auxiliary took over the picket line.

Rep. Donald Jackson (R-Ca.) wrote to film industry people asking for their guidance in how to stop the film. In a teletyped message to Jackson dated Mar. 18, 1953, Howard Hughes of RKO listed five ways to stop Biberman and his fellow blacklistees:

1. Be alert to the situation
2. Investigate thoroughly each applicant for the use of services or equipment
3. Refuse to assist the Bibermans and Jarricos [blacklisted screen-writer Paul Jarrico] in the making of this picture
4. Be on guard against work submitted by dummy corporations or third parties
5. Appeal to the Congress and the State Department to act immediately to prevent the export of this film to Mexico or anywhere else.

Biberman and his associates later sued a number of film companies and unions, charging conspiracy to commit an industry-wide boycott. It was discovered that Hughes' message had been teletyped from the Hughes Tool Company in Los Angeles to its counterpart in New York and sent to Jackson from there. Since the original could not be found—although it was printed in the *Congressional Record* the day after Jackson received it—the message was ruled inadmissible evidence.

Biberman et al. lost their suit, but the film was chosen as one of the best seven films of 1955 by French film critics and subsequently won the International Grand Prize, France's "Oscar" for best picture of the year.

16 BLACKLISTED SCREENWRITERS NOMINATED FOR ACADEMY AWARDS BETWEEN 1938 & 1951

1. Edward Anhalt—*Panic in the Streets* (1950) with Edna Anhalt. Also *The Sniper* (1952) with Edna Anhalt, *Becket* (1964)
2. Alvah Bessie—*Objective Burma* (1945)

3. Sidney Buchman—*Here Comes Mr. Jordan* (1941), *Talk of the Town* (1942) with Irwin Shaw, *Jolson Sings Again* (1949). Also *Mr. Smith Goes To Washington* (1939)

4. Charles Chaplin—*The Great Dictator* (1940), *Monsieur Verdoux* (1947)

5. Guy Endore—*G.I. Joe* (1945) with Leopold Atlas, Philip Stevenson.

6. Carl Foreman—*Champion* (1949), *The Men* (1950). Also *High Noon* (1952), *The Guns of Navarone* (1961), *Young Winston* (1972)

7. Dashiell Hammett—*Watch on the Rhine* (1943)

8. Lillian Hellman—*The Little Foxes* (1941), *The North Star* (1943)

9. Ring Lardner, Jr.—*Woman of the Year* (1942) with Michael Kanin, also *M*A*S*H* (1970)

10. Albert Maltz—*Pride of the Marines* (1945). Also special award for *The House I Live In* (1945)

11. Dorothy Parker—*Smash Up—The Story of a Woman* (1947) with Frank Cavett. Also *A Star Is Born* (1937) with Alan Campbell, Robert Carson.

12. Abraham Polonsky—*Body and Soul* (1945)

13. Donald Ogden Stewart—*The Philadelphia Story* (1940). Also *Laughter* (1931) with Harry d'Abbadie of d'Arrast, Douglas Doty.

14. Dalton Trumbo—*Kitty Foyle* (1940)

15. Michael Wilson—*A Place in the Sun* (1951) with Harry Brown. Also *Five Fingers* (1952)

16. John Howard Lawson—*Blockade* (1938)

***

OSCAR'S SKELETON

From 1957 to 1959, the Academy of Motion Picture Arts and Sciences put a bylaw into effect which forbade any professed Communist—or someone who refused to say that he or she was not a Communist—from being nominated for an Academy Award.

Reel Facts reports that the Screen Writers Guild amended their agreement with the Association of Motion Picture Producers in 1953 to allow producers to deny credits to Communists or "non-cooperative" witnesses. This clause remained in SWG agreements until 1977.

According to Biberman's *Salt of the Earth*, Michael Wilson wrote the screenplay of *Friendly Persuasion* for William Wyler. When Wyler announced he was making the film at Allied Artists, Wilson asked for screen credit and was refused. Wilson appealed to the guild's arbitration committee which granted him sole screen credit.

Nevertheless, the producers exercized their right under the amended Guild contract. The Guild nominated Wilson's script for an Oscar in a secret ballot; the board of the Academy of Motion Picture Arts and Sciences eliminated his name from the final list of films from which an award could be chosen. The film subsequently represented the U.S. at the Cannes Film Festival and was chosen as best picture of the year for 1956.

***

AND ACCEPTING FOR BOB...?

In 1956, the Academy Award for Best Motion Picture Screenplay went to a Robert Rich for *The Brave One*. The Academy of Motion Picture Arts & Sciences did not know that Rich was an alias used by then-blacklisted writer Dalton Trumbo. Needless to say, Trumbo did not appear to collect his Oscar, finally taking it home in 1975.

One year later, *The Bridge on the River Kwai* won the Oscar for Best Picture; French author Pierre Boulle was credited with writing the screenplay, a difficult assignment since he didn't speak English; later, rumors confirmed that Michael Wilson wrote the screenplay with help from Carl Foreman, according to Biberman.

***

THANKS, RON

In 1947, Ronald Reagan, then president of the Screen Actors Guild publicly stated, "We will not be party to a blacklist." *Naming Names* points out that he neglected to mention that his organization refused to allow membership to Communists or un-cooperative HUAC witnesses.

YOU TOO, GEORGE

Sen. George Murphy, (R-Calif.) tap-dancing actor turned politician, commented on the blacklist era in a 1979 letter to the Los Angeles *Times* as quoted in *Naming Names:* ''The blacklisting that everyone talks about only happened in New York, it didn't happen in Hollywood.''

HUAC'S HAPPY HELPER

The American Legion was the most feared and effective of all the groups and individuals who fed HUAC information. The Legion monitored the entertainment business for communist infiltrators as late as 1960.

At its National Convention in October, 1951, the Legion ordered its officers to undertake a ''public information program'' to generate data on Communist infiltrators in the entertainment industry. The next month, its Hollywood chapter called for picketing at theaters which were screening pictures employing people who had refused to cooperate with HUAC.

American Legion Magazine also published an article that year by J. B. Matthews (who would subsequently work for Red-baiting Sen. Joseph McCarthy) which listed 66 names that HUAC missed, along with picture and political credits.

Parenthetically, the Legion named as its 1951 Man of the Year Spain's notorious fascist dictator, General Francisco Franco, and also coined the phrase ''100% Americanism'' in the 1919 preamble to its constitution.

UNDERCOVERAGE

One of the effects blacklisting had on Hollywood occurred in the area of insurance coverage. Blacklistees found they were now listed by insurance companies as ''practitioners of a hazardous vocation,'' according to *The Inquisition in Hollywood.*

Blacklisted screenwriter Guy Endore's agent told him, ''blacklisted people... are rated like steeplejacks and gangsters; they must pay an additional 50% premium (on their life insurance) because their chances of living out a normal life are that much lower than average.''

THEIR BRILLIANT CAREERS

Blacklisted screenwriters often found ways of getting around their problems, as Woody Allen's film, *The Front*, attests. They used psuedonyms, operated through agents or other writers.

For actors, it was not such a simple matter; they couldn't use anyone else's face. Therefore, a number of promising careers came to an abrupt halt and other, less glamorous, new careers had to be improvised hastily.

Actor (later acting teacher) Jeff Corey recalls he tried to make a living by digging ditches, but he quickly discovered he wasn't very good at it. Without much enthusiasm, he was about to take a job at the post office when, "to my relief, I discovered they required a loyalty oath."

Instead, he put his energies into counselling at day camps and privately running drama classes for children and at juvenile hall. He finally went back to school on the G.I. Bill and earned his credentials as a speech therapist, which helped support him through his years on the blacklist. Eventually, he earned his way back into acting on television.

Other improvised fall-back careers include:

Mary Virginia Farmer—the female lead in *Cyrano de Bergerac;* worked as a bonsai farmer.
Bob Richards—carpenter
Herbert Biberman—real estate developer (see p.211)
Bob Lees—maitre d'
Bob Karnes—carpenter
Ned Young—bartender
Lyn Moss, Dorothy Tree and Esther Sondergaard—speech therapists
Fred Rinaldo—wholesale paper salesman

SHRINK OR FINK?
THE STRANGE CASE OF PHIL COHEN

One of the enduring mysteries of the HUAC/Hollywood investigations remains the involvement of Tinsel Town psychoanalyst Phil Cohen. Given that many of Cohen's patients ended up informing on their friends when subpoenaed by HUAC, rumors circulated

11000 Chalon Road

11010 Chalon Road

11020 Chalon Road

11030 Chalon Road

Photographs by David Strick

BIBERMAN'S BLACKLISTED BUNGALOWS

When screenwriter Herbert Biberman was blacklisted, he turned to Southern California's oldest occupation to keep afloat financially: he got into the real estate business. The four houses pictured here were among many that Biberman developed. As you can see, these (as well as most of his others) were cut into the Southern California hillsides. Although the four pictured here were middle to upper-middle class houses when they were built, their location (in the newer section of exclusive Bel-Air) and the recent L.A. real estate boom means that each would today be worth over $400,000.

that Cohen was conditioning his patients to act as informers and was also reporting on them to the FBI.

In *Naming Names,* Victor Navasky says of Cohen, "He established Party contacts in Los Angeles in the '40s and soon had a thriving practice, at first members of the Party's doctors' unit and then friends recommending friends sent patients his way. He was, despite his lack of formal training, effective in his work and his reputation quickly spread in Party circles.

"...There were only a handful of acceptable therapists for Party people and, given the pressures of left-wing Hollywood life of the day, more than enough patients to go around." Navasky writes that Cohen's influence on patients remains a mystery. "At least a dozen of Cohen's patients cooperated with HUAC, but some of his patients did not."

Actor Sterling Hayden's case is typical. Before testifying, he told Cohen: "Doc, I can't go through with it. Since the subpoena two weeks back I've tried and tried to convice myself. They know I was a Party member—they don't want information, they want to put on a show, and I'm the star. They've already agreed to go over the questions with me in advance. It's a rigged show; radio and TV and the papers. I'm damned no matter what I do. Cooperate and I'm a stool pigeon. Shut my mouth and I'm a pariah."

Cohen replied, "I suggest Mr. Hayden that you try and relax—just lie down... Now then, may I remind you there's really not much difference, so far as you yourself are concerned, between talking to the FBI in private and taking the stand in Washington. You have already informed, after all. You have excellent counsel, you know, and the chances are that the public will—in time, perhaps—regard you as an exemplary man, who once made a mistake."

After informing in a meeting arranged by his lawyer, Martin Gang, Hayden recalls in his memoir, *The Wanderer,* that—after informing—he told Cohen, "Son of a bitch, Doc, I'm not sure I can take much more of this... I'll make no bones about it, I'm thinking of quitting analysis... I'll say this, too, that if it hadn't been for you I wouldn't have turned into a stoolie for J. Edgar Hoover. I don't think you have the foggiest notion of the contempt I have had for myself since the day I did that thing... Fuck it! And fuck you, too!"

"So long as the television and radio industries operate under commercial sponsorship, it is both urealistic and unfair to compel sponsors whose income position is being undermined by popular boycott of Communist or Fascist performers on their programs, to continue their sponsorship."

—Sidney Hook, professor of philosphy at New York University, as quoted in *The Great Fear.*

SELECTED COMPANIES THAT SUPPORTED THE BROADCASTING BLACKLIST IN THE '50s

Celanese Corp.
Young & Rubicam advertising agency
Borden Milk Company
Lever Brothers
American Broadcasting Company
Schlitz Brewing Company
Seabrook Farms
Hoffman Beverages
General Foods
Grand Union
Block Drug Company
American Tobacco Company
Procter & Gamble
Columbia Broadcasting System
DuMont Television
Rheingold Brewery
Libby's Frozen Foods

Source: *The Great Fear*

CBS'S BLACK EYE

During the Red Scare in December, 1950, CBS asked all 2,500 of its employees to sign loyalty oaths. Executive Vice President Joseph Ream announced that all employees would have to sign loyalty oaths based on the Attorney General's list of subversive organizations as of October 30, 1950.

CBS blacklisted Richard Rodgers, Oscar Hammerstein, Moss Hart and Jerome Robbins, among others, and dismissed floor manager Joseph Papp after he had taken the Fifth Amendment before HUAC. The company also fired John Henry Faulk after his sponsors cancelled.

Ream said later, "In retrospect, I am not proud of it," and added that he checked with two people at CBS before going ahead: president Frank Stanton—and newscaster Edward R. Murrow.

The network's timidity continued well after the Red Scare had run its course elsewhere. The Smothers Brothers, hosts of a variety show on CBS in the mid-'60s planned to show a greeting card from a Los Angeles peace group (Another Mother For Peace) as a Mother's Day tribute. The network's program practices department refused, because the group had not been cleared by the House Un-American Activities Committee.

WRITERS AND PERFORMERS
CITED IN *RED CHANNELS*

Several former FBI agents decided to turn their knowledge of the Red Menace into personal profit in the '50's. They did so by publishing *Red Channels*, which quickly became the blacklister's Bible in the broadcasting industry. The following were among those cited for Communist leanings:

Jose Ferrer	William L. Shirer
Edward G. Robinson	Howard K. Smith
Orson Welles	Lillian Hellman
Gypsy Rose Lee	Irwin Shaw
Judy Holliday	Abe Burrows
Burl Ives	Dorothy Parker
Lee J. Cobb	Arthur Miller
Pete Seeger	Leonard Bernstein
John Garfield	Aaron Copland

Source: *The Great Fear*

A RED SCARE CHRONOLOGY

1919

June 2—Two political activists place a bomb in front of the home of U.S. Attorney General A. Mitchell Palmer. That night, eight other explosives partially destroyed government buildings and the homes of business and political leaders, creating "The Red Scare" and a resultant national panic.

Nov. 7—Bureau of Investigation agents stage raids in twelve cities and arrest hundreds of members of the Union of Russian Workers, of whom only 43 were deportable aliens. On Dec. 21, this group and 200 other anarchists including Emma Goldman were deported on the ship *Buford* which was dubbed "the Soviet Ark."

1920

Jan. 2—More than 4,000 suspected radicals are arrested—mostly without warrants—in 33-city "Palmer Raids" directed by J. Edgar Hoover. The Washington *Post* comments, "There is no time to waste on hairsplitting over infringement of liberty."

1927

Aug. 23—Two avowed anarchists—29-year-old factory worker Nicola Sacco and 32-year-old fish peddler Bartolomeo Vanzetti—are executed after being found guilty of killing two men in a 1920 payroll hold-up.

1938

May 26—The House of Representatives votes 191-41 to establish the Un-American Activities Committee. It was supposed to go out of business seven months later.

1940

May 7 The American Civil Liberties Union capitulates to the House's anti-communist Dies committee by holding a heresy trial for Elizabeth Gurley Flynn, a Communist member of the ACLU board; she is subsequently purged.

June 28—Five million aliens are registered under the Smith Act, which made it illegal to "organize" or "become a member of any society, group or assembly of persons who teach, advocate or encourage the overthrow or destruction of any government in the United States by force or violence."

1941

June 28—The Justice Department Appropriations Act makes $100,000 available to the FBI to investigate federal employees who are "members of subversive organizations."

Oct. 17—Rep. Martin Dies (D-Tex.) sends Attorney General Francis Biddle the names of 1,121 government employees he regarded as "Communists or affiliates of subversive organizations." After investigation, two were dismissed.

1942

Aug. 4—Joseph McCarthy is sworn in as a first lieutenant in the Marine Corps. In 1951, he would boast of "35 bombing missions, plus liaison missions" but his record lists no combat missions at all.

1945

Jan. 3—The House of Representatives passes a resolution making the Un-American Activities Committee the first new permanent congressional committee in 150 years.

March 11—OSS agents raid the editorial headquarters of *Amerasia Journal*—a scholarly magazine of Asian affairs which often wrote critically about the governing ability of Chiang Kai-shek; they find a number of government documents.

Aug. 25—Capt. John M. Birch, a Baptist missionary and Army intelligence expert, is killed by Chinese communists in Anhwei province. Robert H. W. Welch, Jr. later formed the John Birch Society in his honor.

1946

Feb. 15—The Canadian government announces the arrest of 22 people charged with illegally passing information to representatives of the Soviet Union, following the defection of Soviet cipher clerk Igor Gouzenko.

July 26—Sec. of State James Byrnes fires 79 of 284 employees recommended for dismissal, following internal security check. Four years later—in 1950—Sen. McCarthy will fabricate the remaining 205 into being "known Communists."

Nov. 25—President Truman establishes the President's Temporary Commission on Employee Loyalty.

1947

March 22—Truman orders 2,000,000 government employees to submit to loyalty investigations in executive order 9835. In three years, only 139 were fired; none were indicted for espionage or any other crime.

Oct. 27—John Howard Lawson is the first witness called in HUAC's Hollywood hearings.

1948

March 13—Truman instructs the heads of all departments to pay no heed to any subpoena, request or demand regarding personnel information, paving the way for charges of cover-up and the subsequent rise of the Communism-in-government issue.

March 20—Attorney General Tom Clark first publishes the Attorney General's list of subversive organizations, naming 78.

April 12—The State Department—for the first time in U.S. history—refuses to grant a passport to a U.S. Congressman. Re Leo Isacson (American Labor Party-N.Y.) can't attend conference on aid for Greek guerillas in Paris because State claims the conference sponsor, the American Council for a Democratic Greece, is a Communist front group.

Aug. 3—*Time* magazine senior editor Whittaker Chambers makes his first appearance before HUAC.

Aug. 4—Ex-State Department official Alger Hiss, accused by Chambers of passing government secrets to the Russians, demands the opportunity to deny the charges under oath.

Dec. 2—Chambers produces the "Pumpkin Papers," microfilmed "evidence" of Alger Hiss' Communist activities hidden in a pumpkin on Chambers' Maryland farm.

Dec. 4—The Justice Department names 90 more U.S. groups "Communist fronts."

Dec. 15—Hiss indicted on two counts of perjury.

Dec. 20—Former State Department employee Lawrence Duggan falls or jumps to his death. Two weeks earlier, he was named as part of a 6-man spy ring—including Hiss—which passed documents to Soviet agents.

1949

May 31—Hiss's first perjury trial begins; it ended later in a hung jury.

Sept. 23—Truman announces the Soviet Union has detonated an atomic bomb.

Nov. 17—Hiss's second perjury trial begins.

1950

Jan. 7—Sen. Joseph McCarthy (R-Wisc.) dines at Washington's Colony Restaurant with Rev. Edmund A. Walsh, dean of the School of Foreign Service at Georgetown University, Charles A. Kraus, a Georgetown political science professor and William A. Roberts, a lawyer. He reminds them he is up for re-election and asks for a campaign issue; he rejects the St. Lawrence Seaway as lacking sex appeal and decides to focus on Communists in the State Department.

Jan. 21—Hiss is convicted of perjury after denying sending secret documents to Whittaker Chambers for passage to Soviet spy ring.

Feb. 3—British authorities arrest scientist Klaus Fuchs, charging him with passing atomic secrets to the Russians. Fuchs had worked at Los Alamos, New Mexico, during World War II.

Feb. 9—McCarthy delivers a speech in Wheeling, W. Va., claiming for the first time, "I have here in my hand a list of 205 that were known to the Secretary of State as being members of the Communist Party."

Feb. 10—The day after McCarthy's famous Wheeling speech, Klaus Fuchs confesses to spying for the Soviet Union and names Harry Gold as his confederate. Gold names David Greenglass, who names Morton Sobell and Julius and Ethel Rosenberg.

March 1—Fuchs is sentenced to 14 years in prison.

June 1—Margaret Chase Smith and six other Republican Senators issue a "Declaration of Conscience" accusing "certain elements" of the Republican party of trying to gain victory "through the selfish political exploitation of fear, bigotry, ignorance, and intolerance."

June 22—"Red Channels," the list of radio and TV actors suspected of being Communists, is published.

June 25—North Korean Communists, backed by the Soviet Union, launch a blitz against the Republic of Korea.

Aug. 10-11—Julius and Ethel Rosenberg are arrested on spy charges.

Sept. 23—Congress passes the Internal Security Act, which establishes "emergency" concentration camps and requires Communist groups to register with the government.

Nov. 16—The Attorney General's List grows to 197 organizations, 132 designated as Communist or Communist fronts as opposed to HUAC's 624. Many Japanese organizations were also included. In 1953, the list hits 254.

1951

Jan. 21—Hiss is found guilty on two counts of perjury.

Feb. 7—One month before the Rosenberg trial, Justice Department's James McInerney claims the judge already plans to impose death sentence "if the evidence warrants."

March 6—The trial of Julius and Ethel Rosenberg begins in Foley Square, New York City. The two are accused of selling atomic secrets to the Russians.

March 21—HUAC opens second Communism-in-Hollywood hearings.

March 22—Hiss enters Lewisburg Federal Prison in Pennsylvania and serves three years and eight months.

April 5—The Rosenbergs are sentenced to death in the electric chair.

April 28—President Truman's executive order dismisses any government employee when there is reasonable doubt as to his or her loyalty.

June 2—Attorney General Herbert Brownell offers Ethel and Julius Rosenberg clemency if they will cooperate with the government and repudiate their testimony. They refuse.

Aug. 6—Sen. William Benton (D-Conn.) asks the Senate to investigate McCarthy's role in the Maryland campaign and "other acts... to determine whether or not it should initiate action with a view toward [his] expulsion from the United States Senate..." McCarthy doctored a photograph to show Republican Sen. Joseph Tydings apparently smiling at Communist Party leader Earl Browder; the investigation reached no conclusion.

Sept. 24—Truman extends the security system to civilian departments, allowing any executive agency to classify "official information... in the interest of national security."

1952

Oct. 13—The U.S. Supreme Court declines to review the Rosenbergs' case.

Dec. 21—1,000 people come to Ossining, New York, to bring season's greetings to the Rosenbergs, but police won't let them approach Sing Sing. They sing Christmas carols at the Ossining train station instead.

1953

Feb. 11—President Eisenhower rejects Rosenbergs' petition for clemency. He says, "These two individuals have... betrayed the cause of freedom."

April 27—Eisenhower says any civilian government employee may be investigated and asks department and agency heads to dismiss disloyal employees summarily.

June 19—The Rosenbergs are executed in the electric chair at Sing Sing prison.

Oct. 13—Eisenhower orders the dismissal of any government employee who relies on the Fifth Amendment before a Congressional committee alleging disloyalty or other misconduct.

1954

Feb. 2—McCarthy's $214,000 request for his subcommittee is approved 85-1 with Sen. William Fulbright (D-Ark.) the only dissenter and Senators Kennedy, Humphrey and Kefauver, among others, voting yes.

Feb. 3—*Newsweek* reports Arthur Miller is denied a passport to Belgium to see the opening of his play, *The Crucible*, a parable of HUAC anti-communist hearings.

Feb. 24—Senator McCarthy gets Secretary of the Army Robert Stevens to sign a Memorandum of Understanding, agreeing that Army personnel will testify before his committee. The Times of London comments, "Senator McCarthy this afternoon achieved what General Burgoyne and General Cornwallis never achieved—the surrender of the American Army."

March 9—CBS's "See It Now" airs a critical profile of McCarthy, giving America its first close look at the Senator.

April 22—The televised Army-McCarthy hearings begin. Millions watch McCarthyism in action.

May 24—The Supreme Court upholds the constitutionality of the Internal Security Act, making membership in the Communist Party sufficient grounds for deportation.

July 30—Sen. Ralph Flanders (R-Vt.) introduces Senate resolution 301—"Resolved, That the conduct of the Senator from Wisconsin is unbecoming a Member of the United States Senate, is contrary to senatorial traditions, and tends to bring the Senate into disrepute, and such conduct is hereby condemned."

Aug. 2—The Senate passes a motion to refer the McCarthy censure resolution to a special committee. The charges were—contempt of the Senate and its committees; encouraging federal employees to violate the law by giving him secret information; receiving and using classified information without authorization; abuse of other Senators; abuse of General Zwicker.

Aug. 24—The Communist Control Act, Public Law 637, strips the U.S. Communist Party of "all rights, privileges and immunities attendant upon legal bodies." It was inspired in part by Sen. Hubert Humphrey's bill to make party membership a crime.

Dec. 2—The final vote on McCarthy's censure resolution shows 67 for censure, 22 (all Republicans) against.

1955

March 27—The National Academy of Sciences begins loyalty checks of persons receiving federal grants for non-secret research at private institutions.

Sept. 1—Blacklisted actor Philip Loeb of *The Goldbergs* TV series commits suicide.

1956

July 25—HUAC asks the House to cite playwright Arthur Miller, singer Pete Seeger and six others for contempt. They refused to testify on Communists in Hollywood.

1957

May 2—McCarthy dies of cirrhosis of the liver brought on by alcoholism.

1958

Sept. 5—J. Edgar Hoover writes in the New York *Times* that the Communist Party is "well on its way to achieving its current objective which is to make you believe that it is shattered, ineffective and dying."

1962

July 28—Broadcaster John Henry Faulk is awarded $3.5 million in his libel suit against right-wing Aware Inc. for helping to blacklist him during HUAC hearings on communist influence in broadcasting.

1964

June 22—U.S. Supreme Court strikes down passport restrictions on "subversives," holding that the right to travel is constitutionally protected.

1969

June—The loyalty oath for federal employees is declared unconstitutional.

1973

June 30—The Subversive Activities Control Board is closed down.

1974

June 4—Attorney General William Saxbe abolishes the Attorney General's list. Of 300 organizations, only 30 remained alive.

1975

July 31—Evidence used against convicted perjurer Alger Hiss 25 years earlier is found to contain, among other things, one blank piece of microfilm and two microfilms of Navy documents relating to fire extinguishers and life rafts.

1977

July 19—Sacco and Vanzetti are acquitted posthumously.

1981

Feb. 18—The Senate's new Security and Terrorism Subcommittee headed by Sen. Jeremiah Denton (see p.226) has its first meeting. On April 14th, the subcommittee deployed bomb-sniffing dogs to make sure the Senate chamber was "secure" and each person admitted was screened by a metal detector.

"He started a preventive war and I'm fightin' to end war."

CHAPTER 12

WARS—HOT, COLD AND SECRET

"The restrictions on legal coverage [referring to the inviolability of mail] should be removed... There is no valid argument against legal mail covers except [FBI Director] Hoover's concern that the civil liberties people may become upset. This risk is surely an acceptable one and hardly serious enough to justify denying ourselves a valuable and legal intelligence tool. Covert coverage is illegal and there are serious risks involved. However, the advantages to be derived from its use outweigh the risks."

—White House aide Tom Charles Huston's memo to President Nixon about "expanded" domestic intelligence operations of anti-war activists, as quoted in *Compulsive Spy*

THAT'LL SHOW 'EM

In the spring of 1970, FBI Director Hoover broke off relations with the CIA because the Agency would not disclose the identity of an FBI agent who gave CIA information about a vanished Russian history professor, says Frank Donner in *The Age of Surveillance*.

Eventually, revelation of the split began to "embarrass the Bureau," the number one crime on Hoover's list. He solved the PR problem with Solomonian judgment by issuing an edict abolishing liaison with the Army, Navy, Air Force and IRS as well, maintaining liaison only with the White House.

Concerned with the lack of interagency cooperation, on June 5, 1970, Nixon summoned the heads of all the U.S. intelligence agencies and scolded them for not providing sufficient information on the antiwar movement. This was the beginning of the infamous Huston Plan, which recommended illegal mail opening, "black bag jobs" (illegal entries) and illegal electronic surveillance.

SOUNDS LIKE A NATURAL FOR PARAMOUNT

In 1970, the FBI launched an effort to discredit Jane Fonda because of her growing notoriety for supporting anti-war causes, according to *The Police Threat to Political Liberty*. An anonymous letter was sent to *Daily Variety* columnist Army Archerd signed by "Morris." The writer stated that, while attending a Black Panther rally, he was shocked to see Fonda lead the audience in chanting "We will kill Richard Nixon and any other motherfucker who stands in our way."

Wesley G. Grapp, head of the L.A. FBI bureau at the time sent a memo to Hoover stating, "It is felt that knowledge of Fonda's involvement would cause her embarrassment and detract from her status with the general public." Hoover wrote back cautioning Grapp to "insure that mailing cannot be traced to the bureau."

Fonda later filed a $2.8 million lawsuit against the federal government for spying on her and maligning her. Fonda said she attended the rally but never made the statements attributed to her.

THE DENTON ENEMIES LIST

In September, 1982, Sen. Jeremiah Denton (R-Al.) objected to a Senate resolution endorsing Oct. 10, 1982 as Peace Day. He charged that Peace Links, a women's peace group organizing Peace Day, was a "sucker deal... organized in part by groups that are openly critical of, even hostile to... our country."

To support his claims, Denton entered 45 pages of documents into the Congressional Record on Oct. 29, purportedly showing that "the KGB's involvement in the so-called peace movement is well-documented."

Denton's sources include the October *Reader's Digest* and two investigative organizations,—*Western Goals Foundation* and the *Information Digest*. These last two groups were run by Rep. Larry McDonald (D-Ga.), who was killed in the Korean Air Lines 747 shot down by a Russian missile Sept. 1, 1983. The chairman of the John Birch Society, McDonald had published information that, in many cases, distorted the facts about political groups; he had also been known to share information with law enforcement agencies.

Denton noted that two of the members of Peace Links had been "publicly identified as, or linked by the Department of State with, Soviet-controlled front organizations. These are the Women Strike for Peace, an affiliate of the Soviet controlled Women's International Democratic Federation, and Women's International League for Peace and Freedom."

After describing Peace Links as a growing grassroots movement, he goes on to describe the KGB's covert means of swaying peace supporters to support the Soviet desire that American arms be cut back while theirs remain at current levels. The methods he describes are part of a Soviet "Active Measures" plan that involves forgery, disinformation and political operations.

The most successful method so far, Denton feels, is the proliferation of front organizations. "The function of front, 'friendship, and cultural groups is to support Soviet goals and to oppose policies and leaders whose activities do not serve Soviet interests... to contact people who would not participate in avowedly pro-Soviet or Communist organizations."

The following is a list of 44 disarmament organizations which Denton listed as Communist fronts in his Congressional Report to the Senate:

> American Committee on East-West Accord
> American Friends Service Committee
> Arms Control Association
> Business Executives Move for New National Priorities
> Campaign for Nuclear Disarmament
> Center for Defense Information
> Center for Development Policy
> Center for International Policy
> Christian Peace Conference
> Christic Institute
> Clergy and Laity Concerned
> Coalition for a New Foreign and Military Policy
> Committee for National Security
> Council for a Liveable World
> Council on Economic Priorities
> European Nuclear Disarmament
> Federation of American Scientists
> Fellowship of Reconciliation
> Ground Zero
> Institute of Defense and Disarmament
> Institute for Policy Studies
> Institute for World Order
> International Association of Democratic Lawyers
> International Physicians for the Prevention of Nuclear War
> International Union of Students
> June 12 Disarmament Coalition

Lawyers Committee on Nuclear Policy
Members of Congress for Peace Through Law
Mobilization for Survival
National Lawyers Guild
National Nuclear Weapons Freeze Campaign Clearinghouse
Nuclear Information and Resource Service
Physicians for Social Responsibility
Riverside Church Disarmament Program
SANE—A Citizens Committee for a Sane World
Stanley Foundation
Union of Concerned Scientists
U.S. Peace Council
War Resisters League
Women for Racial and Economic Equality
Women's International League for Peace and Freedom
Women Strike for Peace
World Federation of Democratic Youth
World Information Service on Energy

Source: *Congressional Record*, Oct. 29, 1982

"War corrupts and secret war corrupts secretly."
—Thomas Powers, *The Man Who Kept The Secrets*

"SECRET" WARS FOUGHT BY THE CIA

The Far East

Vietnam

The CIA had its most infamous hour in the '60s with the Phoenix program. Phoenix, hatched by future CIA Director William Colby, was officially dubbed the Intelligence Co-ordination and Exploitation Program and resulted in the killing of 20,587 people presumed to be Vietcong by the Agency.

Laos

In 1960, a coup headed by 26-year-old Laotian war hero, Army Captain Kong Le, overthrew the right-wing CIA and Pentagon-backed military government of General Phoumi Nosavan. U.S.

Ambassador Winthrop Brown (and the State Department) liked Le and supported him. The CIA remained convinced Le's coup was communist-inspired.

Le invited Laos' former head of state, Prince Souvanna Phouma, to establish a neutral government; Souvanna asked General Phoumi to join him as vice premier and minister of defense. Brown urged the State Department to recognize Souvanna's new government. The CIA hedged, formally recognizing Souvanna but supporting Phoumi with $3 million a month in aid.

The White House finally stepped in on the side of the State Department, deciding that Laos was not worth a major U.S. military commitment.

China

From 1951 to 1954, the CIA regularly air-dropped agents and other insurgents into mainland China including Jack Downey and Richard Fecteau, who were arrested Nov. 9, 1952. The Chinese identified the men as CIA agents; the State Department identified them as "civilian personnel employed by the Department of the Army."

The Chinese sentenced Downey to life in prison; Fecteau got 20 years but was released Dec. 12, 1971, two months before President Nixon's trip to China. Downey was freed March 12, 1973, six weeks after Nixon, at a press conference, called him a CIA agent—the first such public admission by the U.S.

Burma

After the communist takeover in China in 1949, some 12,000 Nationalist troops fled to Burma, and the Agency supported them in anticipation of using them to re-invade China. The troops became heavily involved in the local opium trade in defiance of the Burmese government, which believed the Chinese would use the troops as an excuse to invade.

U.S.-Burmese relations soured over the issue of the troops. Burma continued to press the matter in the United Nations until an agreement was reached in November, 1953 to withdraw them. In 1962, a leftest government seized power in a coup, and U.S.-Burmese relations have remained cool ever since.

Indonesia

President Sukarno offended CIA director Allen Dulles in the 50's by acting "immorally" neutral towards the U.S. Sukarno, a popular nationalist leader, exploited U.S.-Soviet hostility as a means of getting U.S. aid.

In 1958, the agency began supporting rebel guerillas trying to overthrow President Sukarno by supplying them with B-26 bombers. After U.S. pilot Allen Lawrence Pope was shot down on May 18th after accidentally bombing a church and killing most of the congregation. Dulles called off the operation; Sukarno was eventually overthrown in 1964 by the Indonesian Army, which thought he was getting too close to the Communists.

Philippines

Edward G. Lansdale, a model for characters in two novels, *The Quiet American* and *The Ugly American*, developed his reputation as the archetypal CIA overseas operative in the early '50s, when the CIA supported Ramon Magsaysay's successful campaign against the local communist Huk guerillas.

One operation involved fear of the *asuang*, a mythical vampire. A psywar squad planted rumors that an *asuang* lived near a communist base. Two nights later, they snatched the last man in a Huk patrol, punctured his neck vampire-fashion, hung his body upside down and put the corpse on the trail. The insurgents soon fled the region.

With the aid of Lansdale, who became an Air Force Major General, Magsaysay was elected president in 1953. The following year Lansdale was in South Vietnam working for President Ngo Dinh Diem, not quite as successfully.

The Middle East

Iran

Kermit "Kim" Roosevelt, Teddy Roosevelt's grandson, directed the 1953 CIA coup that overthrew Premier Mohammed Mossadegh after he had nationalized the oil industry. With Mossadegh out of the way, the CIA heavily supported Shah Mohammed Reza Pahlevi, who remained in absolute and despotic power until the Islamic Revolution in Iran in the late 1970s.

South America

Guatemala

In 1954, Jacobo Arbenz expropriated 400,000 acres of idle banana plantations belonging to the United Fruit Company and legalized the Communist party. CIA director Allen Dulles retaliated by spending $20 million planning Arbenz' overthrow.

The CIA funded and armed the Honduras-based troops of Col. Carlos Castillo-Armas, relying more on political and psychological propaganda than military power. On May 1, 1954 his army crossed the border, while B-26's and P-27's conducted strafings over Guatemala City. Each attack was accompanied by a barrage of phony battle broadcasts from the CIA-front Voice of Liberation radio station which convinced Arbenz that the entire country was under siege and panicked him into resigning.

Cuba

CIA interest in Cuba since Fidel Castro's 1959 revolution is well-known. According to some estimates, the Agency has devoted more energy to the overthrowing, killing or embarrassing of Castro than any other foreign head of state.

However, in the years leading up to Castro's takeover, there was considerable popular support in the U.S. for Castro's overthrow of Fulgencio Batista's regime. Even the Eisenhower Administration liked the idea of overthrowing Batista and secretly welcomed Castro's efforts.

It was not until Castro was in power that U.S. policy makers turned against him. The CIA never supported him, although it helped Batista. In 1956, the Agency established and supported BRAC, Batista's brutally anti-revolutionary police force. When Castro overthrew Batista, his followers broke the BRAC headquarters and tore it down as a symbol of their successful rebellion.

Africa

Congo

A European agent code name WI/ROGUE served as the principal figure in the intrigue surrounding Agency attempts to kill Patrice Lumumba, a popular leftist leader, in 1961.

The Senate Intelligence Committee found that Michael Mulroney was the ranking CIA officer directing WI/ROGUE. At the end of his testimony, he commented, "All of the people that I knew acted in good faith in the light of... their concept of patriotism... I think that we have too much of the "good German' in us, in that we do something because the boss says it's okay."

THESE GUYS THINK OF EVERYTHING

The following are plans suggested by the Reagan administration in the event of nuclear war, as chronicled by Daniel Kagan in "Stopping the Doomsday Clock" in *Penthouse*, Nov., 1982:

1. After an attack, older people should be sent to forage for food and water in order to reduce the risk of radiation exposure to the young, according to a study by the Oak Ridge National Laboratory.

2. Telephone books in some major cities now include inserts telling residents what to do in the event of a nuclear attack.

3. The Internal Revenue Service devised a plan called "Design for an Emergency Tax System" for tax collections after an attack. Included was a plan for a special general sales tax to be instituted after the outbreak of war.

4. Civil defense planners in New York, where a normal rush-hour traffic jam can tie up bridges and tunnels for hours, plan to evacuate 8 million people to rural areas.

5. In Los Angeles, where the traffic jams are constant, civil defense planners suggested a "Noah's Ark" scheme to evacuate the young and healthy and leave the rest to die.

The last words on this subject belong to T.K. Jones, Deputy Under Secretary of Defense for Strategic and Theater Nuclear Forces. Jones is quoted on the cover of Robert Scheer's *With Enough Shovels* as saying, "Dig a hole, cover it with a couple of doors and then throw three feet of dirt on top...It's the dirt that does it...if there are enough shovels to go around, everybody's going to make it."

A WAR CHRONOLOGY

1940

May 21—President Roosevelt authorizes Attorney General Robert Jackson to "secure information by listening devices of persons suspected of subversive activities."

1941

May 27—Roosevelt proclaims unlimited national emergency.

1942

Feb. 19—Roosevelt authorizes military to intern 112,000 Japanese-Americans in concentration camps throughout the West. The government rounds up 2,000 Japanese living in Peru and puts them in camps, too.

1945

July 16—United States tests first atomic bomb at Alamogordo, New Mexico.

Aug. 6—U.S. drops atomic bomb on Hiroshima.

Aug. 9—Atomic bomb dropped on Nagasaki.

Aug. 15—Japan surrenders.

1946

Feb. 27—Ho Chi Minh writes President Truman and the leaders of Russia, China and Great Britain to "stop the war in Indochina." His letters are ignored.

1950

Jan. 31—Truman authorizes production of the hydrogen bomb.

July 27—Truman orders 35 "military advisors" into South Vietnam and agrees to provide military and economic aid to anti-Communist government.

1952

May 8—President Eisenhower announces that U.S. has given France $60 million for the Indochina War.

1954

Feb. 10—Eisenhower admits 200 U.S. military advisors are in Vietnam.

May 8—The French garrison at Dien Bien Phu falls to Viet Minh forces led by Ho Chi Minh; Vice President Nixon urges direct American intervention.

May 26—Adm. Arthur Radford, Chairman of the Joint Chiefs of Staff, writes Defense Secretary Charles Wilson that "Indochina is devoid of decisive military objectives."

Aug. 3—The National Security Council calls the recent Geneva accords a "disaster" and orders immediate economic and military aid for South Vietnam.

1956

July 13—Defense Department sets up Committee on Classified Information to investigate leaks.

1958

Sept. 2—In the most violent U.S.-Soviet confrontation ever, MIG fighters down a U.S. spy plane on assignment over Soviet Armenia and 17 crewmen are lost.

1961

March 21—U.S. sends military advisors to Laos.

Dec. 11—President Kennedy sends the first American combat troops—4000 men—to South Vietnam.

1962

Feb. 14—Kennedy says all U.S. military advisors in Vietnam will fire if fired upon.

March 4—Richard Hughes writes in the London *Sunday Times* that U.S. military intervention in Vietnam "has already passed the point where aid can be distinguished from involvement."

June 11—Students for a Democratic Society (SDS) begins its first national convention in Port Huron, Mich.

Aug. 22—A Francois Sully story for *Newsweek* is headlined "Vietnam—The Unpleasant Truth" and says the war is "a losing proposition." Twelve days later, he receives an expulsion order from Ngo Dinh Diem.

Dec. 10—Official complaints about Sully's coverage of the war (and characterization of Madame Nhu) result in a *Newsweek* cover praising Diem's strategy and referring to Madame Nhu as a "strong-willed woman."

1963

June 11—A Buddhist monk commits suicide, burning himself to death, to protest the Diem regime of South Vietnam. Madame Nhu calls his act a "monk barbecue."

Aug. 30—Roger Hilsman, Assistant Secretary of State, writes Secretary of State Dean Rusk that Diem, threatened by a coup, "should be treated as the generals wish."

1964

Aug. 4—President Johnson uses "attacks" on U.S. ships in Vietnam's Gulf of Tonkin to justify the first U.S. air raid on N. Vietnam.

Aug. 7—Congress passes Tonkin Gulf resolution giving Johnson the power to send U.S. troops to South Vietnam without a formal declaration of war. Only Sen. William Fulbright (D-Ark.) and Ernest Gruening (D-Alas.) voted against.

Aug. 18—Ambassador Maxwell Taylor proposes a "carefully orchestrated" bombing of North Vietnam.

Oct. 21—While campaigning, Johnson tells voters in Akron, Ohio, "We are not about to send American boys nine or ten thousand miles away to do what Asian boys ought to be doing for themselves."

1965

Feb. 7—President Johnson orders the first bombing raids over North Vietnam.

April 1—Johnson and the National Security Council approve gradually escalating air strikes over North Vietnam and secretly sending U.S. ground troops to Vietnam.

April 6—National Security Advisor McGeorge Bundy orders 18,000-20,000-man increase of U.S. troops in S. Vietnam. He tells other ranking government officials, "The President desires (that) premature publicity be avoided by all precautions."

April 28—Without prior authorization by Congress, Johnson sends 405 Marines to Dominican Republic, where a civil war has erupted. He claims troops are being sent "to protect American citizens."

May 5—Number of U.S. Marines in the Dominican Republic hits 22,289. Johnson says troops are there "to help prevent another Communist state in this hemisphere."

1966

Jan. 19—Assistant Secretary of Defense John McNaughton writes in a memo, "We have in Vietnam the ingredients of an enormous miscalculation. The present objective in Vietnam is to avoid humiliation."

May 1—U.S. forces begin firing into Cambodia.

May 14—Student protests break out at several universities and, in some cases, students seize administration buildings.

June 29—U.S. begins bombing Hanoi and Haiphong.

Dec. 31—By year's end, 385,000 U.S. troops are stationed in Vietnam; 60,000 more are stationed offshore and 33,000 are in Thailand.

1967

April 15—Massive demonstrations in New York and San Francisco protest U.S. policy in Vietnam.

May 13—70,000 people parade in New York City in support of the war.

June 17—Defense Secretary Robert McNamara requests a study of U.S. involvement in Vietnam that will later be called the Pentagon Papers.

Sept. 7—464,000 American troops in Vietnam.

Oct. 15—Florence Beaumont, a housewife from La Puente, Calif., burns herself to death in front of the Los Angeles Federal Building to protest American policy in Vietnam.

Oct. 21-22—The March on the Pentagon protests U.S. Vietnam policy. 50,000 to 150,000 march and 647 are arrested.

1968

Jan. 30—Viet Cong's Tet Offensive shocks military leaders and the American public.

March 16—Responding to higher authority, Lieutenant William Calley orders the massacre of hundreds of South Vietnamese civilians at My Lai.

March 31—President Johnson announces he will not run for re-election.

June 23—Vietnam becomes the longest war in U.S. history.

Aug. 5—U.S. police network teletype a master plan for counter-intelligence to disrupt the New Left Coalition and press opposed to the Vietnam War.

Aug. 8—300 Chicago policemen riot, beating and tear-gassing anti-war demonstrators outside Conrad Hilton Hotel, while the Democratic convention is in session.

Nov. 14—"National Turn in Your Draft Card" Day. Many protestors do just that on campuses and in various cities.

1969

March 17—President Nixon approves a request by Gen. Creighton Abrams, Commander of U.S. forces in Vietnam, to bomb a Communist base inside Cambodia. The next day, Operation Breakfast, a B-52 strike, takes place.

July 8—Nixon announces the first U.S. troop withdrawals from Vietnam.

Sept. 24—Chicago 8 conspiracy trial begins.

Oct. 8—Four "Days of Rage" begin in Chicago with protests by the Weathermen, a splinter faction of SDS.

Oct. 15—Vietnam Moratorium Day. Vice-president Spiro Agnew calls the demonstrators "a corps of effete snobs who characterize themselves as intellectuals."

Nov. 15—250,000 people march on Washington, D.C. to protest the Vietnam war. Attorney General Mitchell's wife, Martha, comments that "it looks like the Russian Revolution."

Nov. 13—The My Lai massacre is fully reported by Seymour Hersh.

1970

Feb. 20—The Chicago 7—Abbie Hoffman, Jerry Rubin, Tom Hayden, Rennie Davis, David Dellinger, Lee Weiner and John Froines—are convicted of conspiracy to cross state lines and instigate a riot at the 1968 Democratic Convention.

April 30—U.S. and South Vietnamese forces cross the border into Cambodia to hit enemy bases as Nixon reveals the "Cambodian incursion" unauthorized by Congress.

May 3—Ohio Gov. James Rhodes calls Kent State Univ. anti-war protesters "brownshirts" and vows to "use every weapon of law enforcement to drive them out."

May 4—The Ohio National Guard kills four students and wounds 13 at an anti-war rally protesting U.S. involvement in Cambodia.

1971

March 29—Lieutenant Calley is found guilty of murdering at least 20 Vietnamese civilians at his court martial.

April 5—The "Harrisburg 7" is acquitted of conspiring to kidnap Henry Kissinger.

May 1—Nearly 13,000 people protest American involvement in Southeast Asia and 1,200 are arrested later by Washington, D.C. police, the largest illegal mass bust in American history.

Dec. 29—Daniel Ellsberg is indicted for espionage and conspiracy.

1972

May 8—Nixon announces the mining of North Vietnam ports.

June 13—New York *Times* publishes Pentagon Papers.

Oct. 26—Two weeks before the presidential election, National Security Advisor Kissinger announces "peace is at hand" in Vietnam.

1973

Jan. 27—A formal peace agreement signed in Paris ends Vietnam hostilities.

March 29—The last combat troops withdraw from Vietnam, and the last U.S. prisoners of war are released.

May 10—The House blocks funds for Cambodian military operations, its first such action since U.S. involvement in Indochina.

June 5—A judge in Detroit orders the government to report all illegal federal surveillance of the Weathermen. Rather than admit wrong-doing in public, the government moves for dismissal.

Aug. 15—Direct U.S. military intervention in Indochina ends with a halt in Cambodian bombing.

1974

Nov. 8—One present and seven former members of the Ohio National Guard are acquitted of killing four Kent State students during 1970 anti-war protest.

1975

Jan. 10—The Department of the Army admits it did not destroy files kept on political dissidents as it had promised Congress it would in 1971; in fact, the files had been increased and still existed.

Jan. 16—U.S. District Court in Washington, D.C. awards $12 million in damages to 1,200 war protestors jailed in the May Day demonstration of 1971.

April 30—Helicopters evacuate the last 1,000 Americans in South Vietnam. The war cost 56,555 lives, 303,654 wounded and $141 billion.

1981

May 3—50,000 people march on Pentagon protesting U.S. aid to El Salvador.

1983

Oct. 25—U.S. troops invade Grenada, claiming the recent revolution there has put American students in danger. The Reagan Administration bars any on-site coverage of the military operation by the media—print or electronic.

CHAPTER NOTES

Material for this book came from a wide variety of sources. In cases where lists, notes, quotes or anecdotes came from a single source, they were so credited in the text. Material utilizing two or more sources is credited below:

Chapter 1
"Your Tax Dollars At Work"—*The American Police State* and the Church Committee Report.

"The Baker's Dozen"—*The Man Who Kept the Secrets* and *The CIA Under Reagan, Bush & Casey*.

"OSS Alumni"—*The CIA File* and *Honorable Men: My Life in the CIA*.

"Highest of the High"—*The Intelligence Community, The American Police State* and *The CIA File*.

"Big Brother's Blatant Bungles"—*Superspies*, the script of "On Company Business," *Honorable Men* and *The Man Who Kept the Secrets*.

"CIA Triumph: The Khruschev Speech"—*CIA: The Inside Story, The Craft of Intelligence* and *The Man Who Kept the Secrets*.

"8 Ways the CIA Tried to Kill Fidel Castro"—*Compulsive Spy*, the Church Committee Report, *The Fish Is Red* and *The Man Who Kept the Secrets*.

"No Shortage of Excuses"—*The Image Empire* and *CIA: The Inside Story*.

"SMERSH"—*The Espionage Establishment* and *The Man Who Kept the Secrets*.

"The CIA Dictionary"—*Spooks, The Night Watch, Portrait of a Cold Warrior, CIA Diary, The Craft of Intelligence*, etc.

"The Family Jewels"—*The Lawless State* and *Honorable Men*.

"Rockefeller Commission"—Rockefeller Commission report, *Clearing the Air* and *Honorable Men*.

"Big Brother's Bookshelf"—*Portrait of a Cold Warrior, The CIA & the Cult of Intelligence, The Man Who Kept the Secrets, Publishers Weekly*, Feb. 18, 1983 and the Los Angeles *Times*, May 18, 1983.

"33 Conduits of CIA Funds"—*The Invisible Government* and *The CIA File*.

"National Security Chronology"—*The Craft of Intelligence, The Glory and the Dream, The World Almanac Book of Facts*, 1983 and nearly all of the above.

Chapter 2
"E. Howard Hunt"—*Compulsive Spy, The Night Watch* and *Portrait of a Cold Warrior*.

Chapter 3
"Congressmen Harassed By the IRS"—*How the IRS Seizes Your Tax Dollars and How to Fight Back* and the Los Angeles *Times*, Apr. 16, 1983.

"Voluntary Compliance"—*Abuses of the Intelligence Agencies* and the Los Angeles *Times*, Aug. 21, 1982.

"IRS Chronology"—*Inside IRS, The Glory and the Dream*, etc.

Chapter 4
"Wiretaps Officially Authorized by Attorney General Kennedy"—*The Final Days* and *Robert Kennedy and His Times*.

Chapter 5

"Big Brother's Medicine Chest"—*The American Police State, The Invisible Government, The Search for the "Manchurian Candidate"* and *The Book of Lists.*

Chapter 6

"CIA Mind-Control Pioneers"—*The Mind Manipulators,* ABC News Close-Up, "Mission: Mind Control," and *The Search for the "Manchurian Candidate."*

"Sons of the Pioneers"—*The American Police State, The Search for the "Manchurian Candidate"* and *Compulsive Spy.*

"Uncle Sam, Hippie"—*The Search for the "Manchurian Candidate"* and ABC News Close-Up, "Mission: Mind Control."

"Uncle Sam and the Acid Truth"—*The Search for the "Manchurian Candidate"* and ABC News Close-Up, "Mission: Mind Control."

"Great Milestones in Mindcontrol"—*The Mind Manipulators, Mindcontrol,* script of "On Company Business" and all of the above.

Chapter 9

"The Enemy Within"—*The CIA & The Cult of Intelligence, The Invisible Government, On Press, The New Muckrakers,* and *Publishers Weekly,* Feb. 18, 1983.

"CIA and the Media"—*Rolling Stone* magazine, *The CIA & the Cult of Intelligence* and *Editor & Publisher* Syndicate Directory, 1983.

"My Lai and the Media"—*The First Casualty* and *The New Muckrakers.*

"A Media Chronology"—*The Powers That Be, If You Have a Lemon, Make Lemonade, All the President's Men, Blind Ambition, The Final Days, The Image Empire, The Glory and the Dream, Clearing the Air,* etc.

Chapter 10

"Detention Plans of the FBI"—*Domestic Intelligence, Spying on Americans* and *The Age of Surveillance.*

"Films about the FBI"—*Citizen Hoover, Investigating the FBI* and *The Age of Surveillance.*

"FBI Meets the Press"—*Bureau, Citizen Hoover* and *The Age of Surveillance.*

"FBI Slang Dictionary"—*Are You Now or Have You Ever Been in the FBI Files?, Bureau, Citizen Hoover, Investigating the FBI* and *The Age of Surveillance.*

"Celebrity Subjects of FBI Dossiers"—Department of Justice and *The Age of Surveillance.*

"Discrediting Martin Luther King"—*The FBI and Martin Luther King, Jr., The Lawless State* and *The American Police State.*

"Grave Imposition"—*The FBI and Martin Luther King, Jr., Compulsive Spy* and *The American Police State.*

"FBI King Chronology"—All of the above.

Chapter 11

"Declaration of Conscience"—*Without Precedent* and *Witch Hunt.*

"HUACSpeak"—*Naming Names* and *Only Victims.*

"The Hollywood 10"—*Reel Facts, Naming Names,* and *Only Victims.*

"16 Blacklisted Screenwriters Nominated for Oscars"—*The Great Fear* and *Reel Facts.*

"HUAC's Happy Helper"—*The Committee, The Great Fear* and *Naming Names.*
"CBS's Black Eye"—*CBS: Reflections in a Bloodshot Eye* and *The Great Fear.*
"A Red Scare Chronology"—*The Atom Bomb Spies, A Journal of the Plague Years, When Even Angels Wept, The Committee* and all of the above.

Chapter 12
"A War Chronology"—*The Vantage Point, Kent State, RN: The Memoirs of Richard Nixon,* Vol. 1, *The First Casualty, The Sixties, The Glory and the Dream, The World Almanac Book of Facts,* 1983 and others.

BIBLIOGRAPHY

Adams, John. *Without Precedent*. W. W. Norton & Co., 1983

Agee, Philip. *Inside the Company: CIA Diary*. Bantam Books, 1976

American Friends Service Committee. *The Police Threat to Political Liberty*. 1979

Archer, Jules. *Superspies*. Delacorte Press, 1977

Bamford, James. *The Puzzle Palace*. Houghton Mifflin Company, 1982

Barnouw, Erik. *The Image Empire: A History of Broadcasting in the U.S.*, Vol. III. Oxford University Press, 1970

Bernstein, Carl and Bob Woodward. *All the President's Men*. Simon & Schuster, 1974

Biberman, Herbert. *Salt of the Earth: The Story of a Film*. Beacon Press, 1965

Borosage, Robert and John D. Marks, eds. *The CIA File*. Viking Press, 1976

Buitrago, Ann Mari. *Are You Now or Have You Ever Been in the FBI Files?* Grove Press, 1981

Caute, David. *The Great Fear*. Simon & Schuster, 1978

Ceplair, Larry and Steven Englund. *The Inquisition in Hollywood*. Anchor Press, 1980

Cline, Dr. Ray S. *The CIA Under Reagan, Bush & Casey*. Acropolis Books, 1981

Colby, William E. and Peter Forbath. *Honorable Men: My Life in the CIA*. Simon & Schuster, 1978

Cowan, Paul, Nick Egleson and Nat Hentoff. *State Secrets: Police Surveillance in America*. Holt, Rinehart & Winston, 1974

Crouse, Timothy. *The Boys on the Bus*. Random House, 1973

de Grazia, Edward and Roger K. Newman. *Banned Films: Movies, Censors and the First Amendment*. R. R. Bowker, 1982

Dean, John. *Blind Ambition*. Pocket Books, 1977

Dickson, Paul. *The Electronic Battlefield*. Indian University Press, 1976

Donner, Frank J. *The Age of Surveillance: The Aims and Methods of America's Political Intelligence System*. Vintage Books, 1981

Dorman, Michael. *Witch Hunt*. Dell Publishing Co., 1978

Downie, Leonard, Jr. *The New Muckrakers*. The New Republic Book Co., 1976

Dulles, Allen. *The Craft of Intelligence*. Harper & Row, 1962

Ehrlichman, John. *Witness to Power*. Pocket Books, 1982

Epstein, Edward J. *Between Fact and Fiction*. Vintage Books, 1975

Fain, Tyrus G., Katharine C. Plant and Ross Milloy, eds. *The Intelligence Community*. R. R. Bowker Company, 1977

Felt, W. Mark. *The FBI Pyramid: From the Inside*. G. P. Putnam's Sons, 1979

Garrow, David J. *The FBI and Martin Luther King, Jr.* Penguin Books, 1981

Goodman, Walter. *The Committee*. Farrar, Strauss & Giroux, 1964

Goulden, Joseph C. *The Best Years*. Atheneum, 1976

Gulley, Bill with Mary Ellen Reese. *Breaking Cover*. Warner Books, 1980

Halberstam, David. *The Powers That Be*. Alfred A. Knopf, 1979

Halperin, Morton H., Jerry J. Berman, Robert L. Borosage and Christine M. Marwick. *The Lawless State*. Penguin Books, 1976

Hansen, George V. and Larrey D. Anderson, Jr. *How the IRS Seizes Your Tax Dollars and How to Fight Back*. Fireside Books, 1981

Harper, Alan D. *The Politics of Loyalty*. Greenwood Press, 1969

Hellman, Lillian. *Scoundrel Time*. Little, Brown, & Co., 1976

Hendricks, Evan. *Former Secrets: Government Records Made Public Through the Freedom of Information Act*. Campaign for Political Rights, 1982

Hinckle, Warren. *If You Have a Lemon, Make Lemonade*. Bantam Books, 1976

Hinckle, Warren and William Turner. *The Fish Is Red*. Harper & Row, 1981

Hougan, Jim. *Spooks*. Bantam Books, 1978

Howard, Gerald, ed. *The Sixties*. Washington Square Press, 1982

Hyde, H. Montgomery. *The Atom Bomb Spies*. Ballantine Books, 1980

Johnson, Lyndon Baines. *The Vantage Point*. Holt, Rinehart & Winston, 1971

Kanfer, Stefan. *A Journal of the Plague Years*. Atheneum, 1978

Knightley, Phillip. *The First Casualty*. Harcourt Brace Jovanovich, 1975

Lewin, Leonard C., ed. *A Treasury of American Political Humor*. Delacorte Press, 1964

Lifton, David S. *Best Evidence*. Dell Publishing Co., 1982

Manchester, William. *The Glory and the Dream*. Little, Brown & Co., 1973

Marchetti, Victor and John D. Marks. *The CIA and the Cult of Intelligence*. Dell Publishing Co., 1980

Marks, John D. *The Search for the "Manchurian Candidate."* Times Books, 1979

Metz, Robert. *CBS: Reflections in a Bloodshot Eye*. Playboy Press, 1975

Michener, James A. *Kent State*. Fawcett Crest, 1971

Miller, Tom. *The Assassination Please Almanac*. Henry Regnery Company, 1977

Morgan, Richard E. *Domestic Intelligence*. University of Texas Press, 1980

Nash, Jay Robert. *Citizen Hoover*. Nelson-Hall, 1972

Navasky, Victor S. *Naming Names*. Penguin Books, 1981

Nixon, Richard. *RN: The Memoirs of Richard Nixon*. Warner Books, 1979

Pearson, John. *Alias James Bond: The Life of Ian Fleming*. Bantam Books, 1967

Phillips, David Atlee. *The Night Watch*. Atheneum, 1977

Powers, Thomas. *The Man Who Kept The Secrets*. Pocket Books, 1979

Rips, Geoffrey. *Unamerican Activities*. City Lights Books, 1981

Rovere, Richard. *Senator Joe McCarthy*. Harper & Row, 1973

Rowan, Ford. *Technospies*. G. P. Putnam's Sons, 1978

Rubenstein, Joshua. *Soviet Dissidents: Their Struggle for Human Rights*. Beacon Press, 1980

Scheflin, Alan W. *The Mind Manipulators*. Paddington Press, 1978

Sampson, Anthony. *The Sovereign State of ITT*. Stein and Day, 1973

Schlesinger, Arthur M., Jr. *Robert Kennedy and His Times*. Ballantine Books, 1978

Schnepper, Jeff A. *Inside IRS: How Internal Revenue Works (You Over)*. Stein and Day, 1978

Schorr, Daniel. *Clearing the Air*. Houghton Mifflin, 1977

Schott, Joseph L. *No Left Turns*. Praeger, 1975

Schrag, Peter. *Mindcontrol*. Pantheon, 1978

Shawcross, William. *Sideshow*. Washington Square Press, 1979

Smith, Joseph Burkholder. *Portrait of a Cold Warrior*. Ballantine Books, 1976

Smith, Robert Ellis. *Compilation of State and Federal Privacy Laws*. Privacy Journal, 1981

Smith, Robert Ellis. *Privacy: How to Protect What's Left of It*. Anchor Press, 1979

Sobel, Lester A., ed. *Post-Watergate Morality*. Facts On File, Inc., 1978

Steinberg, Cobbett. *Reel Facts*. Vintage Books, 1982

Sullivan, William C. and Bill Brown. *Bureau: My Thirty Years in Hoover's FBI*. W. W. Norton & Co., 1979

Szulc, Tad. *Compulsive Spy: The Strange Career of E. Howard Hunt*. Viking Press, 1974

Theoharis, Athan. *Spying on Americans*. Temple University Press, 1978

Thomas, Lately. *When Even Angels Wept*. William Morrow & Co., 1973

U.S. Senate Select Committee ("Church Committee"). *Alleged Assassination Plots Involving Foreign Leaders*. W. W. Norton & Co., 1976

Watters, Pat and Stephen Gillers. *Investigating the FBI*. Doubleday, 1973

Wicker, Tom. *On Press*. Berkley Publishing Corp., 1979

Wise, David. *The American Police State*. Random House, 1976

Wise, David. *The Politics of Lying: Government Deception, Secrecy and Power*. Random House, 1973

Wise, David and Thomas B. Ross. *The Espionage Establishment*. Random House, 1967

Wise, David and Thomas B. Ross. *The Invisible Government*. Vantage Books, 1974

Woodward, Bob and Carl Bernstein. *The Final Days*. Simon & Schuster, 1976

Woodward, Bob and Scott Armstrong. *The Brethren*. Simon & Schuster, 1979